Given

by the

Lincoln Christian College

Alumni Association

As Part

of a

$100,000 Gift,

1968-1971

# CHURCH AND STATE

LUIGI STURZO

*With an Introduction by*
A . Robert  Caponigri

UNIVERSITY OF NOTRE DAME PRESS • 1962

Nihil Obstat:

ARTHUR J. SCANLAN, S.T.D.

*Censor Librorum*

Imprimatur:

✠ FRANCIS J. SPELLMAN

*Archbishop, New York*

*New York, September 8,* 1939

Copyright 1962 by

UN
DP

UNIVERSITY OF NOTRE DAME PRESS
NOTRE DAME, INDIANA

*First paperback edition by arrangement with*
*The Don Sturzo Foundation*
*Rome*

TRANSLATED BY BARBARA BARCLAY CARTER

PRINTED IN THE UNITED STATES OF AMERICA

# INTRODUCTION

From prodigy to classic within a quarter century: this, in brief, is the career of the present work: *Church and State* of Don Luigi Sturzo. When first it appeared in the 1930's,[1] the book impressed the critics by its vast, inclusive plan, and its magnificent architectural order, which provided the framework of a scholarship at once inexhaustible, accurate, and as unobtrusive as art. As time passed, however, and the book took on the character of an intellectual landmark, these features, so significant in themselves, began to recede from the foreground of attention. In their place there began to appear those characteristics which mark its inner form: the intellectual principles which control, and the "ethos" which qualifies, its vast material structure. Gradually, the realization dawned that what here confronted the reader was not a work of scholarship alone, but a true work of the spirit; a work, that is, in which there abides a moment of rare insight through which there is revealed, to borrow Hopkins' word, the "inscape" of an entire domain of the spiritual life of the West since the advent of Christianity. As a consequence, it rightfully took the place which it now occupies among the classics of modern historiography, in the company of the *Cité Antique* of Fustel de Coulanges, the *Sacrum Imperium* of Alois Dampf, the second part of the *Scienza Nuova* of Giovan Battista Vico.

Every work of this stature must remain essentially alien to the reader until he can make it a personal possession and establish it as a feature of the spiritual landscape of his own mind. To this end, however, assiduous cultivation, while necessary and indispensable, is not enough. There is necessary, in addition, a vital clue which may set in motion a flow of understanding between text and intelligence. These considerations make clear what an introduction to such a work must seek to do. It must try to provide that clue. In respect of the present work, this vital clue re-

[1] French edition, *Les Editions Internationales*, Paris, 1938; English translation, Longmans, Green and Co., 1939.

V

sides in the fact that *Church and State* is not an episode in the thought and labors of Don Luigi Sturzo, but his testament.

Don Luigi Sturzo was a man of his times: This is the key to his mind and spirit. His most outstanding characteristic was that historical identity which is the sole basis of greatness. He was of his times, moreover, not only because he faithfully reflected their perplexities and problems, but also, because, to a significant degree, he mastered them. Through the laborious mastery of the historical juncture in which he lived, he rose to a majestic command of the sweep of Western European cultural and religious history, to a profound insight into the nature and agency of man as, through history, he creates both the institutions of culture and his own existential actuality; and, finally, to a sensitivity to, and an awe in, the presence of the operation in history of a power which is not man but is solicitous of man, God's Providence.

The stature of his spirit may be justly measured by the mighty times which it has mastered. Looking backwards from his deathbed, in 1959, he could review a life of eighty-seven years which had embraced the emergence of his native Italy into the world of nations, her baptism of defeat at Caporetto, the long delirium of neo-tyranny, the holocaust of Montecassino, and her rebirth as a republic with a visage not too unlike that which he had seen her wearing in the strong dreams of his youth. This, moreover, was part of the vaster drama which saw Europe and the West surrender the liberal dream, succumb anew to forms of tyranny which she had imagined forever vanquished, become locked in a deadly struggle with the colossus of power which the Soviets, taking up the mantle of Russian imperialism, had built upon the perversion of the Marxian utopia. And he could look back upon this not as a vision conjured up by the accentuated sensibility of the death-bed, but as a drama in which he had been deeply and passionately engaged.[2]

Sturzo's mastery of his times was laboriously gained. It moved outward, in an ever-widening circle, to ever more-inclusive horizons, from a center in the problems of post-Risorgimento Italy.[3] The Italy which the Risorgimento had created could at last present to the world a sem-

[2] Cf. the present writer's "Don Luigi Sturzo" in *Review of Politics*, XIV, no. 4 (April, 1952), 147–166.

[3] Cf. the present writer's "Ethical and Sociological Bases of Italian Politics" in *Ethics*, LIX (October, 1948).

blance of unity; within, however, she was tormented by a host of problems, political, cultural, economic, demographic, which might well have
brought a less resilient people to despair. The resilience which Italy had
gained through a long and tortuous historical career stood her in good
stead; she was also fortified by the realization that there was nothing in
the past to which she could turn back. Don Sturzo early became engaged in these problems both actively and reflectively. Quite early too,
he made an initial diagnosis and evaluation of them, which projected
itself on two planes. The first involved their internal configuration, and
above all the identification of the one problem upon which all others
turned. The second involved an analysis of the degree to which Italy's
problems were symptomatic of the larger and more inclusive problems
of Europe and the West.

Sturzo's analysis of the internal problems of the new Italy was both
profound and accurate; history has subsequently borne him out in
amazing detail. Indeed, so accurate was this analysis that Italian history
between the Umbertine period and the end of World War II takes on
the aspect of a vast parenthesis or hiatus, which is closed only by the
post-war resurgence of Christian democracy. His strong sociological
sense warned him, for example, that the new nation could not thrive
(he never for a moment doubted, as some did, its survival and persistence) unless the social basis of its political and governmental structure
were broadened. His economic insight supported an early advocacy of
industrialization in the area of light industry and the education of the
manpower in the requisite skills. His fiscal sense enabled him to see the
limitations for Italy of classical economic doctrines based on an actual
or potential accumulation of private capital which was from the beginning out of Italy's reach. An assiduous study of demographic problems
led to the assumption of basically unimpugnable views on internal colo-
nization. The documentation for all of these views and the steps which
he advocated and set in motion for their realization is to be found in his
own writings, in the substantial literature which has grown up about his
thought and activity and finally in the constitution and statutes of modern Italy. They are not, however, our primary concern here. This must
lie rather with that second aspect of his diagnosis of the internal problems of Italy mentioned above: the isolation of the pivotal issue.

The problem which Sturzo identified as radical to all other problems was that of which the "Roman Question" was the symptom. In this, it must be stated at once, he differed from the vast majority of his countrymen, both those who shared and those who did not share his confessional commitment to Catholicism. The contrast with the latter is best brought out by setting his thought over against that of his great and profound opposite number: Benedetto Croce. This great historian and philosopher, representative of the entire segment of the Italian population which had become emancipated from all confessional religious ties, saw the Roman Question as a pure anachronism. No one had formed a more judicious and positive evaluation of the cultural service which the Catholic Church had rendered to European civilization; the testament of this evaluation is the classical passage contrasting the Catholic Church and the Reformation in his *History of the Baroque Era in Italy*. His theory of history led inexorably, however, to the conclusion that the age of this service was past; that the most that could be looked for from confessional and institutional religion was a certain conservative power which constantly ran the danger of becoming retrogressive. For Croce, consequently, and those of whom he was representative, the Roman Question was a surface question and not a question in depth; it called merely for diplomatic solution.

Strange as it may seem, this view was shared by many Catholics who possessed both a commitment to the Holy See and the "temporality" and an appreciation of the theological basis of the latter. Only thus can be explained the gradual waning of sympathy for the "prisoner of the Vatican" and the pressure from every side that a solution at the diplomatic level be achieved. This was the point of view which found its realization in the signing of the Lateran Accords. It would not be correct to say, as some have said, that Sturzo was entirely out of sympathy with these accords, though it would be less than the truth to say that he exhibited any marked enthusiasm for them. He too recognized that as a dimension of a *de facto* situation the Roman Question had a diplomatic aspect and therefore demanded a diplomatic solution. But he was not deluded into thinking that this diplomatic aspect in any way revealed the problem in depth. His analysis sought to pierce through to this depth-dimension of the problem and his eventual conception of the political order as involving the diarchy of church and state was based on this depth-analysis. What then, to his view, was the problem in depth which was at once concealed and revealed by the Roman Question? Nothing less than this: the problem of the form of the Christian presence in history and the nature of its relationship to the power-structure which is the basis of human social institutions.

The common point of departure of this entire line of consideration is the Christian presence in history. It is correct to say that no responsible thinker of the period showed any inclination to deny this presence. The variety of interpretation as to its form and character, however, is little less than bewildering. To create the correct context for Sturzo's thought, however, it is necessary to consider only certain salient attitudes. To begin a bit remotely, a first distinction may be drawn between those who place a majorative and those who place a pejorative interpretation upon that presence. Of the latter Nietzsche may be taken as an example, as Voltaire would have been a century earlier. Among the former, a further distinction may be drawn. On the one hand there are those, of whom Croce may again be taken as representative, who place an entirely immanent interpretation upon the Christian presence; of this attitude Croce's essay entitled "Perché non possiamo non essere Cristiani"[4] may be taken as a document. Christianity is a historical product of the human spirit. Within that history it represents a certain phase of expression and achievement both of which are positive; but like all such phases of the spirit it too is subject to that "eternal form of corruption," as Hegel called it, time. This is especially true of insights and expressions of the spirit as they are realized in institutions endowed with power-structures. Such institutions are especially liable to the law of time, that is, desuetude and even death. To Croce, the passing of the institutional form of the Christian presence is as inevitable as the passing of the "polis." It is to be lamented, but with due regard to the dangers of historical nostalgia, especially when it tries to find expression in action. Those of Croce's persuasion took a passive attitude toward the Catholic Church and for that matter the Christian churches in general; they were content to await the gradual dissolution of such institutions. Others, however, who held fundamentally to the same view of Chris-

[4] Benedetto Croce, "Perché Non Possiamo Non Essere Cristiani," Bari Laterza, 1946.

tianity, took a more aggressive attitude toward the churches. Impressed above all by the enduring power of these institutions and by the high degree of social control they had developed, the forms of neo-tyranny saw in them allies and instruments of positive advantage, and they were ready, therefore, to enter into arrangements of convenience with them and even to galvanize them with a share of their own "primitive" vitality. Such would seem to have been the motivations of Fascism in the Lateran accords and of National Socialism in the concordats. On the other hand, there were those who saw the Christian presence in history as first an incursion and secondly and subsequently as an indwelling of the transcendent. Among these Sturzo must of course be counted; but again certain distinctions must be drawn to create the proper context for his thought.

To restrict ourselves to the modern context, there had been a growing tendency toward a dualism in the conception of Christian presence among those who still recognized that this presence must take an institutional form. Under the growing pressure for "separation of church and state," destroying the ideal of unity which had informed the ideal of the "Sacrum Imperium," the manner of the Church's presence in the world and her mode of operation there took on a dual form. On the one hand, under the increasing emphasis upon the internal organization of the Church and the importance of the hierarchy as the sole *official* channel of the Church's operation, the chief mode of this operation became *diplomatic*. All of the relations between separated Church and State tended to become more and more juridical; and the juridical structure of relations was formed and administered by diplomatic processes. This constituted one level of that dualism. The other level was constituted by the charitable, humanitarian and eleemosynary. This dualism could be seen in process of formation immediately after the French revolutionary period; and the humanitarian aspect of it received its first theoretical formulation in the thought and activity of men like Ozanam. By the end of the century and the period of Don Sturzo's activity this distinction had been developed to a very considerable extent. The first level of operation was represented by the theory and practice, for example, of the concordats; the second was incorporated and formalized in the concept and organization of Catholic Action. The separation between the two levels was not of course absolute. It represented a tendency and it was counteracted by another tendency, that of channeling all activity through official and hierarchical channels. Thus in the literature and documentation of Catholic Action one formula tends more and more to recur: "the laity under the leadership of the bishops."

In his efforts to find the solution to this problem of the manner of the Christian presence in history and its mode of operation, Don Sturzo found himself uneasy under dualistic tendency. Basically it seemed to him to violate in some manner the unity of that presence. Gradually, under the pressure of the exigencies both of thought and action, an alternative doctrine formed itself in his mind. It is important to point out that this formation was gradual and that it responded simultaneously to the demands both of thought and action, in order to avoid the impression that Sturzo was in any degree doctrinaire. This concept is susceptible of formulation at different levels corresponding to the diverse exigencies which gave rise to it. In the first place a purely abstract and conceptual form can be given it. As a matter of fact, such formulation is wholly posterior both in time and logic to the other more limited forms of expression; but it has the advantage of giving a certain basic orientation to all the others, at least from the historical point of view.

The second formulation is to be found in Sturzo's political activity which falls into three stages: the activity involved in the founding of the Popular Party, the opposition to fascism, and the concern for the international community. Each of these stages embraces an intellectual and theoretical moment. Finally, all of these stages and formulations receive a theoretical expression in Sturzo's sociology, of which his theory of Church and State is the central doctrine. The final documentation of the entire process, both practical and theoretical is the present volume *Church and State*, a volume which must be called necessary and inevitable within the terms of the dynamism of Sturzo's career. It is the one book he *had* to write in order, before all history, to explicate the rationale of his life, his thought and his activity. We shall attempt a brief characterization of each of the stages and formulations distinguished above.

In its most abstract formulation, Sturzo's reply to this problem of the

Christian presence in history took its inspiration from Vico. The transcendent principle of Christianity is present in history immanently. The theoretical basis for this principle is Vico's doctrine of the "ideal and eternal history" which is immanent in time.[5] More concretely it means that the presence which entered history through Christ and the Incarnation is now present in history according to the form and laws of historical existence and action. It does not introduce a new economy which is to replace that of history. At the same time, however, it does introduce a wholly new and underived element into that history. This is the root of his doctrine of the "diarchy" which underlies his theory of Church and State. It is important to see clearly that the diarchy of Church and State does not represent simply an immanent convolution of power and social form as, for example, the doctrine of the "universal Church" in Toynbee. The presence of Christianity in history under its institutional aspect is not an example of the operation of a wider and purely immanent law. It is an autonomous phenomenon. It introduces a fresh force and principle into history. It is from its presence in history that the law of the "diarchy" takes its origin. The Christian presence in the form of the Church, is not an example of that diarchy, but its reality.

The necessity created by the immanent presence of the transcendent in history, for Sturzo, is clear. It does not mean that history is to be reconstructed from the point of view of Christianity. This is the undertaking of the so-called theology of history, an undertaking which Sturzo nowhere explicitly opposes or condemns but for which he has no direct sympathy and certainly no direct dependence. It does mean the formulation of a theory of history wide enough and dynamic enough to embrace in a complex unity this duality of presence without the undue subordination of one element to the other. Had Sturzo formulated in explicit terms a theory of history (as he had in mind to do but never accomplished), these are the exigencies it would have tried to meet. He did however formulate in his *Inner Laws of Society* and in his *Sociology of the Supernatural* the social projection of this unarticulated theory of history. It can be no part of our present purpose, obviously,

[5] Cf. The present writer's *Time and Idea: The Theory of History in G. B. Vico* (London, 1953).

to explicate this sociological theory; but it is necessary to identify certain of its salient features because these will provide eventually the guiding principles of the construction of *Church and State*. Basic is the notion that the person is the existential point at which the introjection of transcendent and immanent transpires; in the first instance in the person of Christ, in the second instance in the person of every Christian whose personality is in turn the projection of that of Christ. [It is a mistake, we may remark parenthetically, to think of Sturzo as first a metaphysical personalist and only secondly a Christian personality; the order is reversed, for it is Christianity, that is Christ as a norm in history, which reveals the personal principle for him.] The person, however, is an abstraction and a form of absence short of its inevitable projection into the social form. The first principle of this projection is that of Christ into the social institution of the Church; a projection which every Christian shares in the same manner as he shares his Christian personality, that is, in and through Christ. At the same time, it is necessary to indicate that the personal dimension of human existence revealed through Christ does not lay bare merely a new dispensation for man, so to say; it reveals at the same time, a dimension of his "natural" existence; that is, his natural character as person. It is thus that the Christian presence provides us with a fresh principle for a universal understanding of social form. The person whose actuality is revealed by the Christian presence forms the basic constitutive unit and principle of all social form and not merely of the Church. Stated in another way: without the *revelation* of the notion of person as the basis of social life, the "natural" processes of social life remain obscure. The person stands thus revealed as the basis of the entire social structure which rests upon a dual projection from that center. The dimensions of this dual projection are characterized in the widest sense as Church and State. But these are not two societies, as the older *dualisms* had it. They are dual principles, a *diarchy*, for they are the projection of the social dimension of the person, representing diverse but interrelated and integral dimensions of the same reality. That is why the person is not divided between two societies but in his own nature achieves a dual social projection which terminates in a complex unity, a "synthesis," in Sturzo's terms. These abstract statements will take on greater meaning, however, when we turn to the concrete stages by which they were first projected in Sturzo's own theoretical and practical activity.

The first concrete form in which this principle of the immanent presence of the transcendent found expression was the very mundane activity of establishing the Popular Party. The myth which has been created of Sturzo as above all an activist who acted first and theorized later is not supported by the documents. What those documents do present is a man who sought the theoretical basis of every practical step he took; and whose theories, consequently, do not tend to outstrip action but rather to follow a pattern closely correlated with and, to this extent, limited by it. His project of the Popular Party was his first theoretical as well as his first practical projection of the notion of the diarchy. The circumstances were those created by the Roman Question, but this time with respect not to the Church directly, but to the Catholic population of the new Italian State. The act by which the Church forbade the Italian Catholics to take part in the political life of the new Italian State placed them in a position of self-imposed civil disability within the state. They suffered this, under the impression that in this manner the good of the Church was to be served. Meanwhile, they also submitted to that dualistic tendency noted above, that is, to submit passively to the diplomatic action of the Church toward the new state and to make themselves socially present by means of humanitarian and charitable works through Catholic Action. Sturzo saw this as a position of impossible stalemate in which the interests of the Church and of Italian Catholics as citizens must inevitably deteriorate; not for any incidental reason, but because this situation violated the basic objective laws governing the relations of the elements involved: State, Christian as citizen and as faithful, and the Church. The theory and the project of the Popular Party was a bold attempt to cut across this anomalous and threatening situation.

The essence of the theory of the Popular Party was to return autonomy to the Christian person in order to restore the proper relation and balance between Church and State and, within the person himself between Catholic and citizen. By its act forbidding the Catholic to participate in the political life of the new Italy, the Church was substituting a principle of dualism for the principle of diarchy; the State, by making the status of citizen irrelevant to the confessional status was committing the same error. Dualism, replacing the diarchical law, was creating a situation of tension which could not be reduced at the level of the institutions confronting each other: State and Church; Church and State, taken in abstraction from the person, have no power to reduce it. The purpose was to return the decisive power to its normal seat, the person, of whom both Church and State are social projections. The party was intended to provide this area of free play for the person in an effective collectivity but also in his true character as the point of concrete introjection between these institutions. It was intended to take the initiative away from the institutions with their completely administrative and diplomatic apparatus and return it to the concrete person who as Catholic and citizen already had in his possession the effective means of mediating that abstract opposition. The basis of the party is the autonomous person. Through his autonomy he achieves balanced projection into both social and institutional spheres of Church and State. Through him these institutions achieve a viable rapport where before they exhibited to each other only the unyielding façades of entrenched abstract principles.

The success of the Popular Party proved the soundness of Sturzo's analysis. Its activity and program provided a sound basis for the hope that out of this abstract dualism there would emerge an Italy in which institutional mediation would be secured through the activity of an alert and confident citizenship. Moreover, this program provided for a systematic reduction of all of the points of opposition at which friction between the institutional structures might arise. The advent of Fascism, as is well known, defeated, for the time being, this hope and program. The reaction to Fascism on the part of Populism was not as rapid as might have been hoped; but in this, Populism shared the delayed reactions of almost every other segment of the public. However, from the ground of his theory of the diarchy as clarified by the reflection on the nature and function of the party, Sturzo was able to articulate the most decisive criticism of Fascism; a criticism which at the same time placed in clearer relief certain aspects of the notion of the diarchy itself. This analysis revealed gradually that what was taking form in the Fascist system was not a party at all but a para-state, in which the monistic principle was implicit and must inevitably assert itself. For the time being this monistic party was content to act in a dualistic framework both with respect to the State which it was in process of displacing and with respect to the Church. Toward the latter it showed itself ready to enter into the older patterns of diplomatic transactions, creating in this way a certain illusion of mutuality, equality and reciprocal action; at the same time the inward working of its basic monistic tendency moved inevitably in the direction of the reduction of this dualism.

This analysis explains the principle of Sturzo's opposition while at the same time it also makes clear why he was less than enthusiastic about the readiness of the Church in its turn to enter into the older patterns of diplomatic adjustments. Most important of all, however, is what this analysis of the situation revealed about the principle of diarchy itself. Sturzo had previously conceived the dualistic pattern as the dialectical opposite of the diarchy. Now it became clear that the dualistic pattern is but the abstract opposition of a moment of distinction implicit in the principle of diarchy. The really effective opposite to the diarchical principle was revealed to be the monistic drive which is implicit and constitutive of every social institution once its power-structure has been articulated. This includes the party as well as all other forms. Once the institution has reached a certain degree of articulation, the laws of power *as such* tend to assert themselves within it; and these laws are purely monistic in tendency.

It cannot be said that Sturzo, in exile, was particularly sanguine that the principles which he had sought to enunciate in the Popular Party would inevitably triumph, though he rejoiced to see them returned to the seat of decision after the war. His attitude after the war also made clear what he had learned from the analysis of Fascism about the monistic drive of any power-endowed institution. This expressed itself in a certain diffidence toward the very party and movement he had called into existence; or, to be more precise, toward those in the Christian Democratic movement and party who exhibited an unawareness of that power tendency. This is the key to much of his line of thought and action between 1945 and 1959; for he was active to an amazing degree up to the day of his death. The fullest impact, however, of what Don

Sturzo had concluded from his analysis of Fascism was to be felt in the arena of international relations.

Italy, as is well known, came to the state of nationhood late in the history of this process in Europe. She has been, as a consequence, a highly self-conscious nation, most acutely aware of the community of nations into which, by her unification, she had entered. She has been from the beginning especially international-minded. This characteristic of the consciousness of modern Italy is also reflected in the mind of Don Sturzo. Some have said that his concern with the problems of the international community emerged only after his exile. It must be recognized, rather, that his concern for Italy was from the beginning a concern for the international community of which he felt her to be a member. The problems of Italy and of the international community were inseparable in his thought and action. Yet it is correct to say that his experience with Fascism placed this problem in a clearer light, especially as it became apparent that here too the principle of diarchy must prove of supreme importance.

Prior to his experience with Fascism Don Sturzo had placed his trust, in the matter of the international community, in the juridical principle. The mediation which would unify this community was that of law. Fascism made clear to him that this trust in the judicial dimension was exaggerated. Social laws are operative at this level also which judicial considerations do not exhaust or even accurately reflect. In a word, he saw that a sociological problem underlay the problem of the international community. This realization did not, however, actually diminish his confidence in the power and reign of international law; what it led him to see was that such law, to be in any way effective, must be solidly established in a framework of sociological considerations. Law could not operate effectively in a sociological vacuum. Consequently, it became his purpose to determine the relevant terms of sociological analysis applicable to the international order in order to provide a secure context for international law.

He discovered that the sociological structure of the international community is governed by the same principle of diarchy which he had discerned at other levels. This must be the case unless one were prepared to recognize that on entering the international arena one passed into an area in which the Christian presence was obliterated. The question then became: what is the form of the Christian presence effective at this level? Devoid of Christian presence, the arena of international relations becomes a sheer power struggle. Nations reveal themselves, when confronted by other nations, to be motivated by that sheer power monism which he had already discerned at work in the Fascist party. The most obvious consideration would suggest that the direct countervailing principle must be the Church in her universal character. Sober reflection, however, makes it clear that the case cannot be so simple. To accept this suggestion is to assume that the Church remains untouched in her universal character by the national principle. This is not the case. As a consequence, the problem is to find a mediatorial base for the diarchical system analogous to that which he had discovered in the person in the context of the Roman Question. This base, clearly, could be none other than the nation itself, but the nation, it must at once be made clear, within which the diarchical synthesis had already been achieved in its own internal terms. This was the ideal to which he clung: the Christian nation, great and pacific. For Sturzo this mediatorial status of the nation, it should be clear at once, is not an abstract logical principle. It is a concrete historical principle. Its function is to make possible the synthesis between the dimensions of the diarchy which would render them concretely effective. The necessity for such synthesis is always present and constant. The form of this synthesis is historical. In the days of the waning Roman Empire it was precisely the vestigial structure of that empire in its juridical, administrative and organizational features which offered the basis for that synthesis. In the Middle Ages it was the ideal of the *Sacrum Imperium*. In the modern age it could only be the nation as the primary seat of the synthesis which would then become effective as the basis for the larger synthesis at the international level. The Church would be the Church of the nations, not because she moved at a level above them but because she had become the basis for a unity within them upon which the unity of the world of nations could rest securely.

By these stages Don Sturzo was led to realize that he had enunciated certain principles, within a succession of limited contexts, the force of which however was not contained nor adequately revealed by those contexts. He found himself in possession of certain concepts and principles, those of the diarchy and its historical synthesis, which reached ideally far beyond the application they had in any limited context. The logical movement of his thought consequently made it necessary that these principles be projected against the entire field of their relevance, for only as projected in this way could their validity be either established once and for all or forever be disproved. This is the necessity by which he was brought to undertake the writing of the present work *Church and State*. The field of the final relevance of those principles must be the entire career of the Christian presence in history. This meant that the diarchy of Church and State must be projected, in order to be tested, against the entire Western historical experience from the moment of that introjection of Christian presence to the present. Not that the present would close the issue or that career. Sturzo is well aware that he is composing an introduction, or at most a first chapter of a work which history itself would necessarily continue.

Having thus led the reader, by this somewhat circuitous path, to the point of ideal entry into *Church and State*, the introduction necessarily leaves him. It is no part of an introduction to present in capsule form, a resumé of what the work contains. The presence of the book itself renders all further preliminaries unnecessary. The reader may now enter these pages unaided, to follow henceforward the movement, not of any commentator's, but of Sturzo's own insight and narrative.

A. ROBERT CAPONIGRI

UNIVERSITY OF NOTRE DAME

# CHURCH AND STATE

# TRANSLATOR'S PREFACE

THE purport of the present work, as the author explains in his introduction to the French edition,[1] here omitted, is neither theological nor juridical, nor has it an apologetic character. It is a study of the outcome through the ages of the interplay of the religious values of Christianity and the civil and political values of secular society. In a word, it falls under the heading of sociology, but of that new sociology of which Don Sturzo himself is the prime mover, which, refusing to content itself with analysis and tabulation, seeks to seize the realities of associated life in their living, ever-changing and hence historical expression. It may be called historical sociology, or *integral sociology*, in that it is concerned not only with the material institution but with the spiritual impulse behind it, with the realisation that man's spiritual exigencies are as intrinsic to him as his economic needs ; it is plain historical fact that he has not lived by bread alone.

The present book is the fruit of seven years of labour and of a lifetime of profound and varied preparation. Before he embarked on the social and political action that would absorb his middle life, Don Sturzo had taken his Doctorate in Divinity at the Gregorian University of Rome and an equivalent diploma in Thomism at the Academy of Thomist Philosophy; he had in addition made a special study of Canon and Civil Law and had taught as Professor of Philosophy and Sociology. The contrast between these scholarly beginnings and his public activities is only apparent; his action was throughout animated by a vital philosophy, while through his direct experience of collective life in its most varied forms, religious and secular, municipal, economic, regional, national, international, his sociological theories were tempered and tested, acquiring a penetration that no amount of aloof enquiry could have brought. It is a dictum of Don Sturzo's favourite philosopher, Vico, that man truly knows only what he does or makes.

[1] Les Editions Internationales, Paris, 1938.

In his *Essai de Sociologie*,[1] Don Sturzo expressed the quintessence of his social theories; in the present work these appear but as recurrent *leitmotifs*, orchestrated themes shaping the crude material of history into symphonic unity. In Church and State he sees not merely institutions but the spiritual and temporal poles of all human life, individual and social, expressions of a duality to be found in every sphere, reflecting the concomitance of sense life and spiritual life in man. If Church and State tend to form a *diarchy*—defined as the co-existence of two powers, each limiting the other, but with one or the other predominant through an equally universal tendency towards a *unification* that is never complete—if at the same time there is always latent conflict between them, so that their duality may turn to dualism (a word which in Don Sturzo's vocabulary bears a sense of antagonism), it is because in every form of social life and in human society as a whole two currents are invariably present, the '*organisational*' and the '*mystical*' or ideal,[2] the one tending to conservation, to practical constructions that perpetuate an established order, the other to renewal, with sharpened awareness of present deficiencies and impellent aspirations towards a better future. The distinction between them is never absolute, for they are made up of human individuals and reflect the complexity of human minds; their action is an interweaving, the one eventually consolidating something of what the other conceives, yet they come together only to part anew; the conflict they manifest is the conflict between the ideal and its always only partial realisation, between the letter that kills and the spirit that quickens, and while the Church is essentially the expression of the mystical current in the face of the State—though, as will be seen, there are moments of history when the roles are reversed, and they are always in varying measure combined—in the Church as in the State the two forces are perennially working.

[1]Bloud and Gay, Paris, 1935.
[2]'Whereas the word "ideal" generally signifies something intellectual and rational, perceived as an idea, the word "mysticism" has a sense of faith, adherence, affection, and at the same time indicates something mysterious, like a higher force with compelling power. It is thus that we may speak of a mysticism of liberty in the XIX century, as to-day of a mysticism of force' (*Essai de Sociologie*, p. 202).

It is the variance of these forces that produces the dynamism of history, making of it a continual and creative process. For Don Sturzo, everything that comes to man as an idea impelling him to action enters into human process and forms the object of history no less than the action or institution in which it finds embodiment; thus every cross-section must be taken as a whole, with its philosophy, art, literature, economy, religious and political expression, all moulding the social physiognomy of the age and moulded by it. By what he calls *resolution into synthesis* in each new phase the various elements, ideal and practical, fall into a new pattern by which they are themselves renewed. Therefore, too, it admits of no discontinuity, but each phase is as it were a natural growth, with roots stretching far into the past.

There is no determinism in this conception, and it is because he posits human freedom as the animating principle of history, that Don Sturzo speaks always of historical process rather than of evolution, which has a certain flavour of necessity. At the same time he sees history as moving, by its immanent forces, from a transcendent principle to a transcendent end. 'A mixture of free and conditioned, of individual and social, in a continuous process—so we see history,' he has written elsewhere,[1] 'but from the providential standpoint, beneath this human ant-hill, enclosed in its cycle of conditioning factors and volitions, of thoughts and acts, are hidden higher ends, whether known or not, which reveal themselves, in their objective ripeness and in our subjective ripeness to perceive them, as willed by God.' It is a passage that sums up his outlook. Humanism and Christianity, he holds, which form the two-fold basis of our civilisation, even when they are at variance integrate each other, tending always to a synthesis, or as Blondel has it—and for him too it is a fundamental thesis—a *pacification*. The two are inseparable, and whenever an attempt is made to divide them a profound crisis ensues, social and in the individual soul.

'The sociological history of the Church,' wrote Father Bruccolieri, reviewing the French edition of the book in *La Civiltà Cattolica*, published by the Jesuits of Rome, 'even with all its dark places, is always of itself an apologia of the Christian religion. Through the cold and

[1] *Politics and Morality*, p. 215.

objective researches of the sociologist, Don Sturzo's weighty volume reveals the mind and heart of a man who sees only in Jesus Christ the solution of all the problems that perturb our age.' The Redemption, indeed, brings the synthesis of grace and nature, transmuting all human values; with Christ the divine entered into human process as the history of the Word Incarnate, the very core of humanity, an impulse always working not only in the Church but in 'the whole world which has been, mystically, conquered by Christ and potentially lives in Him'.[1] Not only the illuminations of saints and sages, in whom the divine imprint in history is most manifest, or the believer's conscious fellowship with God, but the aspirations of all men of good-will, all affirmations of truth, justice, morality, love, with the inner law by which man seeks the good, draw their sustenance from this supernatural source. And thus, even in periods of cataclysmic ruin, the Christian impulse remains, perennial principle of hope and of renewal.

It is this integral vision that makes Don Sturzo's history of Church and State, of the ever fruitful tension between spirit and matter, a living whole, in which the most revolutionary changes reveal themselves as the fruit of long preparation, the embodiments of what has been ripening, it may be for centuries, in the world of thought. We see not only the woven tapestry but the weaving. The design changes before our eyes, as united Christendom rises from the ruins of the Roman Empire, as that unity dissolves with the emergence of the sovereign States and must be sought anew, on another basis, as the State tends more and more to disengage itself from religious ties, becoming the secular State of modern times. New *motifs* are continually appearing, to blend into vaster patterns (Don Sturzo calls them syntheses) to which we may give a name—the Carolingian Renaissance . . . the Age of Humanism . . . the Romantic Period . . . but the web is continuous. Events thus seen in their context, in their origins and ambience, shaped now by powerful personalities, now by anonymous multitudes, hold a richer significance, bringing new understanding not only of the past but of the present in which the past lives on. And thus Don Sturzo carries the story from the first affirmations of Christianity, as a voice proclaiming the Good News, as a com-

[1] *Church and State*, page 560.

munity withdrawn from the world yet transforming the world, to our own day, when the problems of the very hour, social, economic, political, fall into their place in the historical process and are studied not in themselves but in their relationship to the moral values which Christianity holds, represents, fosters and actuates in its unfailing influence on political society and on human thought.

The originality and importance of such a book, with its luminous interpretations and rigorous historical accuracy are self-evident. It may, however, be of interest to quote the judgment of two continental scholars, the one a philosopher, the other an historian.

'What is it that we most admire in Don Sturzo's recent monumental work: *Church and State?*' asks Professor Archambault. 'The immense and disciplined erudition that allows him to handle with ease a mass of documents and facts which for another would be overwhelming? The surety of doctrine and thought, which never hesitates and never stumbles? The experience and the political sense which even with the finest audacities maintains a firm grasp of reality? What is certain is that we are here in the presence of a masterpiece in which none can fail to find profit.'

While Professor Palanque expresses his 'wonder in seeing how twenty centuries of the Christian past have been penetrated and assimilated without inexactitude by one who is no professed historian, and claims competence only in sociology'. It is, he declares 'a fundamental work'.

B. B. C.

# CONTENTS

9

*PART I*

THE CHURCH AND CHRISTENDOM

# CHAPTER I

## CHRISTIANITY AND THE ROMAN EMPIRE

§ 1.—The novelty of Christianity from the sociological standpoint, as compared with other religions, lay in breaking down all imperative relationship between religion and the family, clan, nation or empire, giving it a personal basis in conscience. Not in the temple at Jerusalem, the symbol and centre of the Jewish religion, but in every place might the Father be invoked and worshipped. No bond of kinship, race or nation was to be respected if it drew a man away from God and infringed the rights of conscience. No interest, no political motive could compel the performance of acts not conformable to Christian faith and morals. God must be served before men. Another innovation, logically linked to the first, was the universality of the 'Good News', addressed to all peoples and all classes, Jew or Gentile, Greek or Barbarian, rich or poor, master or slave. All were called to renounce their gods and to adore the One True God in spirit and in truth. Finally, there was the constitution of the Church, a single, visible religious society, extraneous to political or domestic institutions, autonomous and independent, founded on definite beliefs reputed as truths, indeed as truth itself.

The effects of such an event in the sociological field (as well as in other fields outside the scope of the present study) could not be other than revolutionary. A first consequence was the humanisation of the other two social forms, the family and the political society. There would be no more household gods, divine expressions of the family unity, no more empires conceived as divine forms of power. Families, kingdoms, empires would be purely human forms, means and not ends for man, unfitting means often, such as to turn him away from his true end, means in that case to be renounced and abandoned, so that each man could find the true life within himself and be able to say

21

that whoever did the will of God was to him brother, husband, father and mother.

Thus, with the inversion of the social values of the pre-Christian world, human personality took the place formerly held by the social groups. Human personality, hitherto misconceived and misprized, became, in virtue of religious recognition, the centre and end of all collective activity. It was summoned to build up society anew as by a new creation. All men are brothers, there is one father, God. Here was a new social form of an ethical and mystical character, which would transform all social relationships. Slavery, a social institution that had lasted thousands of years, lost its ethical basis, even while its economic basis remained. No longer would there be ethical justification for the polygamous family founded on the slavery of woman, for a State exercising absolute dominion over its peoples, for wars of extermination, for a caste economy, or for any form of oppression or social injustice.

The universality of Christianity is inherent in its very nature as an exclusive religion: the unity of God and the brotherhood of men must allow no social or political barriers to block the way. All the local gods must give place, all the pretensions of castes or nations must vanish. Even Judaism, from which, historically, Christianity springs, is by Christianity set aside—like the morning dusk at the coming of daylight, the forerunner on the advent of the Messiah, the symbol at the manifestation of the reality.

Christianity as a positive religion demanded a concrete, visible and permanent social form, universal and hence independent of family or State as of the exigencies of races or nations. Without such social form of its own Christianity would have remained like Confucianism, a moral doctrine and not a religion. If it had rested on a political or politico-military structure, it would have been limited by it, like Mohammedanism. The idea of a single empire embracing all Christendom was an attempt to associate the universality of the Church with the like universality claimed by the political power. When this proved impossible of realisation, the idea would prevail of national Churches bound and subject to the powers of the State. But in the spirit of Christianity and throughout its manifold and millenary experience, any limitation, any subjection to other social forms, have always proved a contradiction, and have always led to prolonged and arduous reaction for the reconquest of a wider autonomy.

By contrasting the autonomy of Christianity with the position of the pre-Christian positive religions we are not asserting that these too had not a certain autonomy, at least at an initial and virtual stage. The three basic social forms—family, political society, religious society —tend always to emerge and to win a physiognomy of their own, even when their organs and ends interpenetrate and coincide. In each form there is the intrinsic tendency towards autonomy. But before Christianity the religious form never succeeded in winning autonomy under the twofold aspect of content and of organisation, for the reason— sociologically incontestable—that no pre-Christian religion, not even Judaism, was based on human personality as a spiritual value in order through personality, and by it alone, to arrive at society as a unitary whole. On the contrary, all the pre-Christian religions were based on the unitary whole represented by particular groups, without any direct resolution into human personality. Resolution, where it occurred, was always indirect and incomplete. In the sociological field Christianity brought about an inversion and re-ordering of values. Society is nothing more than the projection of the individual; all social foundations are laid by the individual. The submergence of the individual in the social form, as in pre-Christian societies, was a deviation and in many cases a perversion; the return of the individual as the basis of every social value is a conversion and a restoration.

In the Christian conception, this conversion and restoration is effected by the Word of God, who, through the hypostatic union, rehabilitated human personality in His Name and by His sacrifice. The society founded by Jesus Christ, the Church, is a society in which each member does not lose his own personality but enhances it in mystical union with the Head, through being raised to the state of grace and personal destination to the Vision of God. In social life, the influence of this conception has been decisive, albeit with the inevitable phases of affirm- ation and negation, victory and defeat, in a laborious process that is always active and always a battle. Family, State, civilisation, feel its effects as little by little men become conscious of the immense implica- tions of the value of human personality and of its religious elevation.

§ 2.—On the eve of the Edict of Milan (A.D. 313) after nearly two and a half centuries from the first Neronian persecution, Christianity had become a moral and social force which the Empire had not been able either to subdue or to suppress. The last persecution, that of Diocletian, the most refined and the most widespread, had failed in its purpose. There were Christians in nearly every Roman province, in nearly every class and walk of life, with a very wide following among the people and the slaves. The Church had her own organisation, her own ritual and social laws, authorities, tribunals, meeting-places and places of worship, cemeteries, property and economic resources, and internal discipline. All this associative growth, created and ripened either in the darkness of the catacombs or in the broad daylight of mundane life, during the persecutions or in the periods of toleration, contained the seeds of a wider social form that was coming into being both within the ambit of the Empire and on its geographical and political margins.

This might not be perceptible to the adversaries of Christianity or even to the Christians themselves, but it was slowly taking shape. The first Christians formed a world apart. The earthly society they felt neither as an end that concerned them nor as a bond. To them the profane world was alien, indeed inimical; what they looked for was the Kingdom of God. This, understood now apocalyptically, as the End of the World, now mystically, as the reign of spirituality, now organically, as the triumph of the Church, aroused a collective expectancy that overshadowed the present and projected itself into the future. The striving towards a future to be realised more or less immediately was stimulated and enhanced by the persecutions, which detached Christians still more from the profane world. The local churches became centres of more intense life, where rich and poor were united in brotherhood, where all found moral and material help in the face of the common peril. Following St. Paul's advice to submit disputes to their own judges, Christians often had recourse to their presbyters and bishops instead of to the imperial courts. The bishops soon became recognised authorities even in matters outside the religious sphere. The deacons administered funds not only for the churches but for widows, wards and the poor. The enfranchisement of slaves was going forward, the basis of the family was changing, a sense of fraternal solidarity was growing up. The Christian community could be considered as a State within the State, yet without any intention of seeking political separation, or even a remote aim of forming a distinct political unity.

The originality of the first contacts of the nascent Christian Church with the political society, represented by the Roman Empire, is shown by the fact that the persecutions aroused no violent reaction, no revolt, and indeed no effective resistance on the part of the Christians. In any other case, the persecution of a people, race or class would have aroused in those so cruelly used some sort of resistance on a collective and public plane, and this would have led to the creation of a group-personality antagonistic to the State. But the Christians allowed themselves to be seized and put to death even joyfully; the remnants scattered, went back into hiding, in order to form fresh religious centres and to continue propaganda and proselytism.

A new crime was created: that of being a Christian. For to be a Christian meant (as the facts were interpreted) to be the enemy of the Empire, undermining the foundations of the Empire. The Christians defended themselves against this charge, yet, once the Empire was conceived of as a politico-religious unit, in which the act of imperial worship was the sign of political allegiance, Christians were indeed enemies of the Empire. They could accept neither the worship of the protecting gods, nor the cult of the deified Emperor, nor the pagan rites which permeated the whole of social life, family, city, army, court, and marked the anniversaries of good or evil omen for the community.

From a distance of time, and with clearer ideas on the distinction between the political society and the religious society, we can say that the Christians were good citizens notwithstanding, good soldiers, good imperial functionaries and so on. But at the time not only were these ideas anything but clear to non-Christians, but they would have seemed the very reverse of the truth, for through Christianity the politico-religious conception of the Empire was crumbling. To be a Christian was to be guilty of an offence entailing civil disabilities and criminal penalties. The public acts of Christians were considered null and void, they were ineligible for public office, forbidden to enfranchise slaves, degraded from military rank or expelled from the army, and liable to confiscation of property, banishment, deportation, forced labour, and corporal penalties up to the most atrocious forms of death. Every means was tried to exterminate the new enemies of the Roman Empire, and yet Christians did not cease to multiply, even in the imperial palaces.

From the sociological standpoint, during the period between the preaching of the Apostles and the Edict of Milan the Christian communities scattered over the Roman Empire might be considered as autonomous nuclei for whom the sum-total of social relationships, reduced to their most simple expression, was synthesised in the religious society. Christians, within the Empire, sharing in the earthly interests of family, class, and profession, yet felt themselves as strangers and were reputed enemies, to be outlawed and persecuted. We shall find something of the same kind at the time of the Albigensians, or of the Hussites and the early Reformers, but with a fundamental difference. In the case of the Albigensians, Hussites and Reformers, revolt and war were possible and were the natural outcome of resistance; the religious problem was carried into the political field. The Christians of the first centuries, on the contrary, denied neither political power in general nor the power of the Empire as such, nor did they put up a collective resistance either in the political field or by armed revolt. They maintained their line of resistance in their own special sphere, that of religion, which had become for them the prevailing social focus of their life. Their resistance took the form either of flight or of public profession of faith and martyrdom. They took as their starting-point the words of Christ: 'Render therefore to Caesar the things that are Caesar's; and to God the things that are God's'; they followed the two-fold precepts of St. Peter: 'Be ye subject . . . whether it be to the king . . . or to governors,' but at the same time: 'we must obey God rather than men'. And thus they brought division into the society of the time, shattering its fabric, while forming active social nuclei rendered fruitful by the greatness of their sacrifices. In the face of the Empire as a politico-religious unity, they might be said to represent a kind of *social anarchism*.

The words 'social anarchism' must not be misunderstood. In all periods when a new social element has found its way into the life of peoples and is so potent as to bring a radical modification of the social structure (and never has there been anything comparable to the Christianity that made its way into the Greco-Roman world), then the passage from one structure to another can come about only through a disintegration and reintegration. The new element is at once solvent and reconstituent. The groups that deny the established order and hence the intrinsic value of the authority in which that order centres and by which it is guaranteed, if they cannot or will not replace it by another and similar authority (it is the case of early Christianity), such groups are for practical purposes anarchic. But since the early Christians represented a new associative force, which expanded from the religious to the political plane, their anarchism was not anti-social, but truly 'social'; their action was not only destructive, but also constructive. Holding closely to the new religious conception, they did not realise how revolutionary they were, nor the crisis in which the Roman world was therefore involved.

When the collapse of the Empire began the Christians were accused of being the cause. The charge could not hold good on the political plane, but it did so on the religious plane. The capture of Valerian by the Persians (A.D. 260) was attributed by the Christians to divine chastisement. It is from that date that we find the resolvent movement towards recognition of Christianity. Diocletian's persecution was the last attempt to stamp out the enemy religion, which had become general and important in all the provinces. Galen, Massentius, Constantius, Licinius, Constantine followed a system of appeasement and toleration, which had then become inevitable. Finally Constantine, sweeping away the last obstacles and Licinius's attempts at a return to persecution, consolidated this system of toleration and religious liberty.

The historical process of Christianity during the first three centuries is in outline a process of liberation, in which the Church affirms her social autonomy, founded on freedom.

§ 3.—In the Gospel teaching freedom is not so much negative and outward as, pre-eminently, positive and inward. Freedom is the achievement or gift (according to the point of view) of a higher life that brings emancipation and detachment from that which is lower. Hence freedom is conceived as characterising the individual rather than the community; in certain respects bonds are collective, freedom is personal. The Jew is under the Mosaic Law, a collective bond laid upon him by sin, which rendered it necessary; the Christian has been personally freed from it, for he has attained the freedom of the sons of God. The letter is the bond, the spirit is freedom; the passage from the letter to the spirit is an act of liberation. The flesh is a bond, the spirit is freedom; the triumph of spirit over flesh is a liberation. Sin is a bond, truth is freedom; the overcoming of sin by truth or light is liberation.

Human personality cramped by group-religions had become the slave of the laws of the collectivity. It was necessary to break the bonds of family, caste, clan, people, race, city, empire, in order to worship God in spirit and in truth. Therefore freedom was above all a personal achievement, a positive uplifting of the spirit, a complete penetration by the new life of the Gospel, a participation in the divine. Thus conceived, freedom acquires an individual value of the highest order, and an effective and very far-reaching potentiality in the moral and religious field, where the Christian personality must by right and duty assert itself. If life itself is a hindrance to such total assertion, this hindrance is overcome by martyrdom. Earthly life has then become a bond to be broken for the sake of freedom of spirit, and death is liberation.

In the early Christian movement, freedom does not affirm itself as the collective achievement of the Church as a body, but rather as the achievement of the Christian as an individual. It is founded on the vindication of his right to his religion as the light of truth for the regeneration of his soul, reborn with baptism, placed by grace in communication with God, rising again with Christ, living its own life. All this demanded liberty, that is, the breaking of the earthly bonds that would have impeded it.

The early Christians did not raise the question whether the *res publica* or Empire ought to intervene to support the Christian religion, or should abolish the pagan religion, or had in any way the right or duty of recognising the Church. All these ideas came later. In the first three centuries all they asked was that the political authorities should hinder no one, whether citizen or slave, from professing the Christian faith, that they should not adopt a hostile attitude towards the preaching of the Gospel, nor persecute those who followed it. The liberty demanded by Christians became for the political power a limit which it could not overstep on any pretext. The day it sought to do so, it could only be by force, when it found itself faced by thousands of men who preferred torments and death. Prolonged experience of the use of force against Christians showed how little it served to overcome a religious movement that was autonomous, reforming, conquering. The Empire had to fall back on a policy of toleration till it reached the public proclamation of liberty.

In the second phase, which opens with Constantine, the religious freedom of Christians assumes a new aspect, no longer solely individual but social, no longer private but political. It might seem for a while as if Constantine's toleration were more or less the same as that granted between one persecution and another in the previous centuries; instead, effectual factors had intervened to widen its scope and change its significance. Among these factors we must note the decay of polytheistic paganism among the educated classes and the increasingly marked tendency towards the worship of one supreme god, though admitting of a demiurge (Apollo-Sun) as his manifestation and without as yet excluding the secondary gods at least as symbols. Stoicism and Neoplatonism had acted as solvents of the old religious society. And, on the other hand, because of their growing numbers and force of expansion, Christians could no longer be kept in a position of social inferiority. Christianity was now no longer a minority of initial nuclei which might be tolerated or suppressed (as it was believed) by means of persecution. In the East Christianity was in full flower, not only among the lower ranks but in the cultured and active circles. In the West, too, there were large numbers of Christians among the ruling classes and in the army, forming radiating centres in every province, in Italy, in the Gauls, in Africa, in Britain.

The first idea that seems to emerge from the imperial acts themselves (the Edict of Milan and the document known as Licinius's Prayer), is the proclamation of belief in 'the Almighty Supreme God, creator of all things and dwelling in heaven', as the god of the Empire, common to pagans and Christians, while each man is left free to follow his own religion. But the Roman Empire was not like the laic and vaguely theistic modern State, nor did Constantine think of depriving it of an official religion. In a first period he was torn between the traditional religion or his favourite sun-cult and Christianity. But he tended towards an ever clearer monotheism, and in fact towards Christianity, which he ended by embracing. The collective conscience of the time was likewise in the throes of the two streams, which under the régime of toleration openly confronted each other. The problem was a tormenting one and had two facets: could paganism remain as the official religion of the Empire? Could Christianity become the official religion of the Empire?

For the first period the Empire maintained, with certain practical attenuations, the pagan cult with its public rites, festivals, calendar, titles, endowments and priesthood, while at the same time encouraging public Christian worship, the building and endowment of basilicas, and even official participation in Christian ceremonies and councils. Roman legislation of the time reveals the two-fold influence of paganism and Christianity. Bloody sacrifices are forbidden, but the prohibition is not carried into effect. Auguries are forbidden in private houses but allowed in the temples. Later the order is given to close the temples, but it is not carried out, and indeed the privileges of the Vestal Virgins and grants for pagan worship are confirmed. On the other hand, the legions are allowed to have their own Christian priests (a kind of military chaplains); pagan and Christian emblems appear together on the coinage; the law against celibacy is rescinded; Sunday is made a day of rest and festival; certain Christian festivals are recognised as imperial feast-days; the public treasury bears the expense of certain Christian councils and the imperial post-service is placed at the disposal of bishops going to attend councils. The exemptions and privileges of the pagan priests are extended to the Christian clergy; the bishops are recognised as voluntary judges in civil questions; the bishops are exempted from the criminal jurisdiction of the Empire; the enfranchisement of slaves in Christian churches is authorised; the Church is exempted from public taxes, and so on.

It was natural that the Christian Church, once placed on a footing of freedom, albeit merely as a tolerated religion, should fight with all her strength against a paganism reputed as impiety. This struggle was carried into the moral and cultural sphere. Since the general culture of the age was classical, Christians sought to make it their own, adapting it to the ideas and exigencies of their faith, both as philosophy and as art. The persecution of Christianity by Julian the Apostate was mainly carried on in the sphere of culture and education.

The struggle against paganism brought an impulse to obtain public legislation favouring Christian ideas and principles, in respect of the family, morals and religion; hence an impulse to attain high positions in the Empire itself. Once the Emperor was a Christian, he was a part of the Christian Church, subject to its laws and precepts. From that day forth, and even earlier, churchmen became the Emperor's intimate advisers and ruling factors in imperial policy, from Hosius and Eusebius of Caesarea, at the court of Constantine, to the famous ecclesiastical counsellors of East and West in the IV and V centuries. Both general legislation and the special provisions of the Emperors tend more and more (with opportunistic oscillations) towards the establishment and predominance of waxing Christianity rather than towards the waning paganism. In the course of the IV century the positions are completely reversed; paganism ceases to be the official religion and becomes a tolerated religion, though still preserving the force of its tradition, while Christianity, formerly merely tolerated, becomes the official, or better, the prevailing religion. After the parenthesis of Julian the Apostate, the pagan cult gradually fades away. It survives in the countryside, filters into Christian circles as a residuum of culture, habits, superstitions, and contributes to laxity of morals.

Freedom of conscience and of worship, which Christians had already vindicated as an individual right, with the Edict of Milan passes to the collective plane and becomes a political problem. The conscience of the age could not admit of an Empire unattached to any religion; the Empire was constrained by events and by its own legislation in favour of freedom to balance the forces of one religion by those of the other. In order to survive and to face the barbarian invasions it had to maintain a unity between the various forces and currents that were undermining it, and to restore the consciousness of imperial 'Romanity', which early Christianity had shattered. Its religion would no longer be paganism, but a Christianity that was assimilating Greco-Roman culture within the framework of the new faith, and which alone could create a new unitary consciousness. Freedom of worship was a political means to this end, for thus Christianity came to share directly in the life of the Empire. But this freedom was granted or denied by the Emperors according to whether they favoured Christians or pagans, orthodox Christians or heretics. It was used to ensure the dominance or predominance of this or that party or faction; it was made an instrument of appeasement or a title to privilege; it was suspended or abolished when the political power required, or as a measure of public order.

The Church from the beginning, even during the persecutions, was rent by heresies. Constantine's régime of liberty was favourable not only to the development of the sound forces of the Church and of her organisation and culture, but also to the spread of heresies, among them Donatism in Africa and Arianism, first in Egypt and the East, and then also in the West. It was the time when the Church, one in the spirit of the apostolic tradition, was gaining consciousness of her structural unity through direct contacts between the chief episcopal sees, in the local councils (of which the compass steadily widened, till in 325 the first Oecumenical Council met at Nicea), and in agreements on dogmatic and disciplinary questions, such as the date for keeping Easter, lapsed Christians, or the baptism of heretics. The See of Rome held its primacy, but its authority, though recognised in West and East, was not such as to leave no margin for discussion and dissent. While the increasing number of Councils were a means both for affirmation of the Roman authority and for the development of a clearer consciousness of unity.

This movement went largely from below upwards, and from circumference to centre, and implied a general popular interest. This was a source also of turbulence and strife through the intensity of passion aroused by the clash of theories, the formulation of heresies, the subtlety and vehemence of the disputes. The Empire itself was disturbed; the intervention of the political authority justified itself either as maintenance of public order or as safeguarding the rights of the different religious communities. The Emperor Aurelian, a pagan and hostile to the Christians, intervened in the conflict at Antioch in 272 on whether the basilica belonged to the deposed bishop, Paul of Samosata, accused of Adoptionism, or to the bishop elected in his place. And Aurelian decided that it belonged to the one who was in communion with the bishops of Rome and Italy.

Constantine, while yet a pagan or a catechumen, either spontaneously or on Christian request or appeal, nearly always intervened in ecclesiastical disputes, not only for the maintenance of public order or to guarantee the legal rights of communities, but as exercising an authority that often overshadowed that of the bishops. In the question of the African Donatists, after he himself had placed the decision in the hands of Pope Miltiades and a council of bishops, he set aside their verdict and brought up the matter afresh at the Council of Arles (A.D. 314). This Council, acting on his inspiration, blamed the antimilitarism of Christians as prejudicial to the Empire. Constantine, who had himself convoked it, perhaps through irritation at the turn its assemblies were taking, dissolved it—not very graciously, it would seem, from the bishops' report to Pope Sylvester: 'Then wearying of it he ordered all to return to their sees.'

Constantine felt it his mission to intervene in ecclesiastical questions. He recognised that internal decisions were the affair of the bishops, and he called himself *episcopus forensis*, or 'external bishop'. He was still not yet a Christian when he practically presided over the Oecumenical Council of Nicea, taking sides now for this party now for that, favouring those who supported him, opposing those who resisted. St. Athanasius felt the weight of his displeasure in banishment. Arius before he died obtained from the Emperor an order that he should be re-admitted into the Christian community. Constantine's policy of direct intervention in Church matters would remain the normal line of conduct of the Byzantine Emperors, and, in certain respects, also of the Emperors of the West. This policy, which had developed through the theological, disciplinary and personal controversies between Christians, became for the imperial courts at once a system for maintaining order and a means of domination.

The attitude of Christians generally and of the ecclesiastical hierarchies was on the whole favourable to this policy. Although for a while it was not possible for them to formulate clearly the practical limits to be set to imperial intervention, it was none the less well established in the Christian conscience that any dogmatic decision and any ruling on Church discipline was a matter for the bishops, that the government of the Church was entrusted to them and not to the Emperors, that the Church was a spiritual society, independent and superior in her nature and ends to any other human society. In actual fact, however, though Councils and bishops might decide to depose an heretical bishop or to excommunicate some particular Christian (and the IV century is one series of mutual excommunications, especially in the Eastern Church), if the interested parties resisted, as they not seldom did, the force for execution of such decisions was in the hands of the Emperors. These, in order to proceed legally, adopted the decisions of the Councils as part of their legislation and reinforced them with penal sanctions. Councils followed Councils, and now one faction, now another, prevailed. The enforcement of such laws and executive and penal intervention proved favourable now to the orthodox, now to the heretics. It was a result of the system. In the case of heretics, the Church resisted and fought the pretensions of the Emperors; in the case of the orthodox, she accepted their intervention. There thus came to be a duality of forces on the politico-religious plane of the Empire. The Church did not forget that she had fought in conditions of inferiority in the days of the persecutions, and had suffered renewed persecution in a period when she openly flourished. The Empire, which in the West was growing steadily weaker and needed the Church for its defence against the barbarians, here maintained a certain balance; in the East, on the contrary, it sought to master and dominate the various seething religious and political currents, and in every field of activity its centralising intervention increased.

§ 4.—When paganism had ceased to be the official religion, and had become first a tolerated and then a persecuted and vanquished religion, the heterodox currents within Christianity carried their struggle against orthodoxy into the sphere of political influence, seeking favours for their adepts and intolerance against their adversaries. Orthodox Christianity at first defended itself on a platform of freedom, then called for protective laws for itself and laws of persecution against the heretics. These laws came into being, save that they were enforced according to the interests of the Court either for or against orthodox Christianity (Catholicism). After prolonged strife it was Catholicism that prevailed in both West and East.

In the course of this process the idea of toleration and of religious liberty was lost. Instead there was an effort to attain the politico-religious unity of the Empire through the disciplinary religious unity of the Church. But the new Empire was not the same as the old pagan one. The new Empire had become dualistic. On the one hand there was a Church that had vindicated her autonomy with the blood of her martyrs, that possessed an organic life of her own and a vitality not to be confused with that of the Empire ; on the other there was an Empire which had adopted the new religion, persecuting what survived of paganism, and intervening in religious matters either by carrying them into the political sphere or by usurping religious power.

It seems strange that at a time when the Empire was threatened by the barbarians, internally lacking in administrative cohesion, growing poorer and poorer economically, when it had, therefore, urgent problems and tasks of a purely political order, it should have involved itself in extraneous, arduous and thorny questions, insoluble as far as it was concerned, such as theological disputes. Yet this was a logical position in the historical process. The causes of the crumbling of the Empire were many, chief among them the impossibility of giving a unity to so vast an agglomeration of peoples. Hence an imperative need to impose a single system of laws, culture and religion, so as to maintain what cohesion was possible among the different and often conflicting forces involved. The intervention of the imperial power in Church matters and its repression of schisms and heresies find their source in the need for a political and moral unification of the Roman world.

It was no political motive but the pressure of events that led St. Augustine to abandon the régime of freedom and, even against the views of Rome, to call for temporal intervention in the struggle against heretics. He had wavered much, for the use of force in religious matters was repugnant to him, but when his diocese fell a prey to the violence of the Circumcellions, he not only asked for political protection for the persecuted Catholics (as was only natural), but sought to justify coercion by the temporal authority in order to force the heretics back to orthodoxy. He based his new thesis on the principle (very debatable if extended to all cases) that the heretics could not in good faith persevere in their errors. Although he had preached mildness in the punishment of heretics, and though he had condemned the application of the death penalty which would deprive them of all possibility of conversion, yet he now showed a radical change in both theory and practice and provided motives for justifying intolerance.

The political objects of the Roman Emperors and the religious objects of the bishops who turned to them coincided (from the sociological standpoint) in the idea of one Christendom and one Roman world, though in practice this might be divided for administrative purposes into two Empires, of East and West. The old order was the Empire, the new order was the Church which ramified through the Empire so as to constitute in itself a new connecting nexus. The trend of resolution wavered between an Empire sustained by the Church and a Church protected by the Empire. The Church, which now stood forth openly, triumphant over paganism and the ancient world, was a Church that was asserting itself in the cultural and theological contests as the one religious society, permanent amid the flux of centuries; the Empire felt its attraction and reflected its passions. The unity that the great Emperors, Trajan, Hadrian, Antoninus Pius, Diocletian, had failed to achieve by the triumph of a reformed paganism, Constantine, Gratian, Theodosius the Great, Theodosius II and Valentinian III sought to achieve by the triumph of a one and orthodox Christianity.

But the Church was not made to serve the Empire or to be made subservient to it. Resistance to a centralising policy was by no means rare, from St. Athanasius onwards. The vehemence of Lucifer of Cagliari in defending Athanasius against Constantius bears witness to the extent and depths of the feelings of independence that had ripened in the Church during the persecutions and which she had preserved under the new régime of the Christian Empire. St. Ambrose, not much later, is more measured in his language but no less explicit. In repulsing Theodosius from the church door, bidding him first do penance for the massacre of Thessalonica, he constituted himself at once religious and political judge of the Emperor. His famous reply to Valentinian II, who ordered him to cede certain churches to the Arians, shows the normal line of conduct of the Latin Church: *tradere basilicam non possum, sed pugnare non debeo*.[1] He thus affirms his right and duty as a bishop against the imperial decree, but he does not resist force. Leo I adopted a like attitude towards Theodosius the Younger over the bad business of the pseudo-Council of Ephesus on the monophysite heresy—the 'Robber Synod' staged by Theodosius and his counsellors (A.D. 449).

Many other examples might be given, for there was never any lack of disputes between bishops, popes and emperors. After nearly two centuries of experiences, from Constantine onwards, Gelasius I in 495 had occasion to formulate his thesis of the relations between the political and spiritual powers. He clearly vindicates the independence of the Church from the political power in spiritual matters. His thesis is dualistic, without attenuations. Both powers are from God, the one in the spiritual domain, the other in the material one. The bishops are subject to the emperors in temporal matters, the emperors to the bishops in spiritual matters. Hence the responsibility of the bishops is very great, and their dignity greater still. Gelasius vindicates the ecclesiastical immunities and summons the bishops of the East to defend their rights, which the Emperor had infringed. The Gelasian formula is identical with the earlier pronouncements of St. Ambrose, St. Leo the Great and Felix II, but the respective positions of Church and Empire are more clearly and systematically defined. Gelasius wrote nineteen years after the fall of the Empire of the West, in 476. Felix II had written eight years before it. Neither, it may be, thought that the Empire of the West would be reduced to a few provinces in the dependence of Byzantium, and that Rome would gradually come to play another part in Western Christendom. They argued with the Emperors of the East, like nearly all the Bishops of Rome, since in the East the most interesting theological controversies arose, fomented by rival factions. So indeed did their successors up to and after the great medieval schisms. The position would remain unaltered, but

[1] 'I cannot surrender the church, but I must not fight.'

the dualistic thesis was the only one that could save on the one hand the independence of the Church and on the other the character of a Christian Empire. And therefore on this thesis the whole Catholic tradition rests.

The dualistic theory, in the simplicity of its lines, certainly did not solve the problem of relations between State and Church, as it had presented itself from Constantine onwards. In practice, only the sacramental and ritual authority of the Church remained perfectly distinct from the political power. In the conciliar, jurisdictional and disciplinary activity of the Church imperial intervention was constant and often decisive. On the other hand, the power, wealth, privileges and prestige of the clergy were steadily increasing; they had therefore heavy responsibilities towards the populations unassisted by the civil authorities, oppressed by taxes, tormented by wars, decimated by pestilences, and scattered in the invasions. This interweaving of function, while in some respects it blurred the boundaries between the two powers, brought out their duality all the more plainly and tangibly. The conflicts between bishops and emperors divided not only the courts but the clergy and people; one party resisted the Emperor, the other profited by its power to triumph over the adversary.

This led to a weakening of authority in itself; hence the Fathers of the Church and ecclesiastical writers took care to present it to the faithful as a principle unaffected by contingent circumstances, raising it to a higher plane and rendering it sacred. They insisted that those who governed represented God and received their authority from God, to Whom they had to render account of their actions. Obedience, they held, was the due even of bad governors; such were sent by God as punishment for the sins of the peoples. The Fathers did not pretend to create a political theory on the origin of authority. They were well aware that the juridical conception of the age was based on the Roman tradition, and that the power of the emperors was derived from the will of the people. Justinian, a century later, declared in his Codex: '*Cum enim lege antiqua, quae regia nuncupabatur, omne jus omnisque potestas populi romani in imperatoriam translata sunt potestatem.*' [1] The

---

[1] 'By ancient law, which was called the Royal Law, all right and all power of the Roman people was transferred to the imperial power.' (Cod. L. 17, I, 77.)

Fathers brought out the moral value of authority, in accordance with the teaching of the Apostles. But it was the Fathers themselves, bishops and popes, who had to resist the intrusion of the imperial authority into the life of the Church, and they did not always do so with the vigour with which St. Basil vindicated his freedom and authority against Valentius.[1]

The body of legislation that from Constantine onwards was taking shape contained, it is true, the decisions of the Councils, but also the imperial edicts and decrees. These had an enduring authority. The Theodosian Codex of 436, that of Justinian in 539, followed by the Pandects in 533, would remain as the sources not only of civil but of ecclesiastical law, till gradually an autonomous Canon Law could be brought into being; only in the late Middle Ages did this take its place side by side with the *Corpus Juris*.

In the IV and V centuries the prevailing tendency is the affirmation of imperial authority over the Church. The Emperor issues decrees touching not only disciplinary matters but also dogmatic ones. Those of Justinian against the followers of Origen and on the dispute over the Three Chapters are famous examples. In spite of this, the sacred character of the Emperor—Vicar of God, as Ambrosiaster calls him— is generally accepted and unchallenged. The dualism of Empire and Church increases, and becomes more marked in the struggles between orthodoxy and heresy, which often degenerate into persecutions now of one side, now of the other.

[1] There is a famous dialogue between Basil and the Prefect of the East, Modestius, in the works of St. Gregory Nazianzen —

'What? You do not fear my power? '
'What could happen to me? What could I suffer?'
'One of the numerous torments that are in my power.'
'Which? Tell me them.'
'Confiscation, exile, tortures, death.'
'If you have nothing else, you can threaten at your will; these do not affect me.'
'Why, what do you mean?'
And so on, in a crescendo up to the conclusion: 'Tell the Emperor that you will not make us assent to his impiety either by violence or by persuasion.' (Orat. XX.)
Various miracles are attributed to St. Basil in his encounter with Valentius, who wanted from him, as from the other bishops, a signed assent to the Arian formulas, and whom the Saint resisted.

In all this interplay of social forces there is revealed a certain persistent residuum of the pessimistic conception of society, which lies at the bottom of the Christian soul. In current opinion and in the Early Fathers the theory had crept in that the organisation of civil society and the coercive power it implied were not primal, but the outcome of sin. Often the political society is confounded with the world, which is planted in evil. It is the Christian's duty to flee the world, to hate its pomps and rites, to take refuge in the solitude of his spirit if he cannot forsake the world physically. Blessed are they who can so forsake it! The deserts are the dwelling place of thousands upon thousands of hermits.

The negation of society implied by the asceticism of the IV and V centuries sprang from a melancholy spectacle that was two-fold—on the one hand, the social and political evils that had overwhelmed the crumbling Roman Empire, on the other, the need to withdraw from the corruption that had invaded the towns, penetrating even to the sanctuary, which was often under the sway of a rich, litigious and obsequious clergy. The way of personal freedom was sought anew, understood as liberation, detachment from evil, attainment of good. Outward liberties do not exist where intolerance and persecutions prevail. Theological conflicts are settled either in religious instance, by the authority of the Councils, or in political instance, by the authority of the Emperor. Elementary rights have often to be vindicated by revolts of hungry mobs or forsaken provinces. There remains inward liberty, the one refuge of the true Christian.

St. Augustine in his *City of God*, a complex synthesis, luminous yet full of shadows, presents the various moments of this great drama, psychological, social and mystical. For him the true city is the City of God, the city of the elect, living in communication with God. For St. Augustine all social life is produced by love—the life of the celestial city by the love of God, the life of the earthly city by love of the world. Society is order and peace, in the celestial city true order and true peace, in the earthly city a false order and a false peace. Cain stands for the earthly city, he who was the first to shed human blood, Abel for the heavenly city, which on earth has but a brief journey to make that is a return towards heaven.

In Augustine's mind the Church is not the heavenly city nor the State the earthly city, but they are respectively symbols, elements, phases of the two cities, or rather of the good and evil which these express. He passes continually from one plane to the other, from historical reality to mystical significance and vice versa. On the one hand he enumerates the evils of earthly life, wars, tyrannies, slavery, lust, avarice, pride, which find their historical development in human society. To this earthly society belong those Christians and churchmen who, as he puts it, have here below the communion of the Sacraments, but will have no part in the eternal lot of the saints. The Church is a means and symbol of the City of God, though she is not the society of the elect; civil society is the plane of development of the earthly city, though it is not for this the society of the lost.

Such is the thesis that illuminates the whole course of history, which unfolds as the conflict between the two cities. Human happenings in the light of this inherent dualism lose all intrinsic value; the pessimistic view of society is enhanced in the face of worsening evils, concern for the City of God and its triumph becomes paramount. The State is driven towards co-operation with the City of God, in spite of its inner turmoil of disorder and evil. The achievement of a Christian Empire by Theodosius must have smiled upon the minds of the age, but the collapse of that Empire (which Ambrose thought would stand for ever) brought a sense of anguish, driving men either to detachment from earthly things or to spiritual coldness.

The Pelagianism that found its way into the spiritual stream of the V century, and which would persist under different guises through the centuries, on its appearance might seem a motive for a reawakening of piety, of asceticism and for the attainment of Christian virtues. But it not only involved the problem of Grace, but it distorted the Christian conception of man, of society, of the evil in the world. For Pelagianism, in the shape it assumed through theological controversy, man, created free, could attain to virtue and good by his own might, divine Grace remaining an aid extrinsic to nature. Although this conception was framed in the supernatural system of rewards and penalties and remained within the ethico-dogmatic teachings of Christianity, in substance it introduced an optimistic naturalism.

In the face of Manicheanism which, by making evil and good a duality, disintegrated spiritual forces and altered social forces, Pelagianism sought to restore consciousness of good in an optimism general for all. Augustine, who had passed through an experience of Manicheanism and who later, in the exercise of his episcopal ministry, deepened the intuitions of his genius, showed how naturalistic optimism was not only a heresy but was psychologically and historically unreal. The conflicts in which he engaged led him to accentuate the pessimistic view of nature and society, but post-Augustinian controversy cleared up certain verbal excesses and consolidated dogmatic teaching. The two currents of the mystical stream, the pessimistic and the optimistic, would continue to evolve and to influence both the life of the Church and temporal society itself.

A more serene and disciplined form of monasticism was coming into being, through the rules that were already widespread throughout the West. Rufinus had summarised that of Basil, Jerome had translated that of Pacomius, Augustine had written his famous CCXI Letter, which was taken as a rule for religious communities, and there were also the Constitutions of Honorius of Arles, and Cassian's compendium of the rules of life of the Egyptian abbeys. The new monasticism brought the spread of the greatest possible detachment from earthly life among the ruling classes. This mystical formation had an influence on the organisation of the Church, where the worldly spirit had penetrated with wealth and honours. Missionary, episcopal and organising work tempered the men of action, who were the greater in their ministry, the surer their foundations in the spiritual life.

The two streams, the mystical and the organisational, work perennially in the Church, permeating her from end to end and from bottom to top. The mystical stream may develop into active prophetism, as with Basil in the East, Augustine and Jerome in the West; the organisational stream may form a perfect balance with the mystical, as in Leo the Great. But on both sides the boundaries may be and have been overstepped, to the point of heresy on the one hand and worldliness on the other. Thus the one acts as a brake and the other as a motor; the one may even overwhelm the other, or the roles may be reversed and the one take on the other's characteristics. This occurs far more readily in a period of formation and growth, of struggles and adaptations, as in the IV and V centuries, when the Church, emerging from the catacombs and measuring herself with the power, wealth and pride of the world, with intellectual subtleties and naturalistic deviations, found in the mysticism and sacrifices of her bishops and cenobites, fathers and doctors, the same road that had first been trodden by the martyrs, for affirming and extending herself in the world.

# CHAPTER II

## CAESARO-PAPISM AND LATIN ORGANISATION

### FROM THE FALL OF THE WESTERN EMPIRE TO CHARLEMAGNE

§ 5.—The ancient Church did not seek to merge the State into herself nor did she set out to create a civilisation of her own by changing the institutions that were her Roman heritage. But in preaching the truths of faith, in the organisation of her hierarchy and of worship and in the practice of Christian ethics and spirituality, she fulfilled a social function that was in fact a civilising one. The State remained for her an earthly factor, necessary to the life of the community, yet containing elements contradictory to the spiritual life. Property, wealth, the dominion of certain classes over others, the exercise of force, war, slavery, were likewise to be considered necessary elements of social life, though they sprang from the degeneration of the human race. Such elements, since they could not be suppressed, had to be corrected by the Christian spirit of poverty, humility, abstinence and penance. There remained the innate dualism between the life of the spirit and life of the world in the inner life of the Christian, and between the religious and supernatural ends of the Church and the earthly and social ends of fallen human nature. This dualism, between Church and State in the social sphere, between inner life and political life in the moral sphere, was tending to find a unification in the conception of a natural law. This law had to permeate the State, which represented the sum-total of power and authority over all men, even over men of the Church ; it was the ethical foundation on which Christian morality had been built. The Decalogue is presupposed by the Gospel, the Decalogue for social life, the Gospel for spiritual life; the Decalogue for the State, the Gospel for the Church.

The Christian Roman Empire, though largely Catholic, included dissidents, schismatics, heretics, pagans of Greco-Roman civilisation and unconverted barbarians. The triumphant and unifying religion was Catholicism, even in Byzance, in spite of the dualism with Rome. The conflict between the various Christian factions went on, now as controversy, now as political or court intrigue, now as revolt and persecution. Outward unification nearly always found its pole in the Empire, which though pervaded by ecclesiastical organisms, harassed by religious factions and distracted by dogmatic disputes, continued to correspond to the Greco-Roman conception of a higher and all-embracing political and legislative entity. The Church did not claim any share in political power. Bishops and popes avowed themselves subject to the Emperor or to the Teutonic kings and to the imperial or royal laws. Gelasius I emphasises the division of powers : 'In so far as spiritual action is removed from carnal incursions and "the man fighting for God must not be involved in secular business," so let not the man involved in secular business be seen presiding over the things of God . . .'[1] A century later, Gregory I declared himself subject to the commands of the Emperor Maurice, and while pointing out the violation of conscience, did not fail to transmit the imperial order that monasteries should not accept officers and soldiers as monks : 'Thus on both sides have I done what was due, since I both recommended obedience to the Emperor and did not keep silence on what I felt for God.'[2]

None the less, given the nature of the Christian religion, the Church could not fail to exert an influence on the formation, workings and activities of the political society and even of the authority representing it. (This influence was no less real in the pre-Constantine period, through the withdrawal of Christians from social life, and their effective repudiation of the politico-religious system on which the Empire rested.) The principles of the Church came to inform the family (Christian marriage), justice (the free choice of judges), culture (public and private education), public assistance or benevolence (the fund for the poor), the financial system (clergy exemption),

[1] Tract IV. 'Quatenus spiritalis actio a carnalibus distaret incursibus et "Deo militans minime se negotiis saecularibus implicaret" ac vicissim non ille rebus divinis praesidere videretur, qui esset negotiis saecularibus implicatus . . .'

[2] Epistolae I, iii, 61. Utrobique ergo quae debui exolvi, qui et imperatori obedientiam praebui et pro Deo quod sensi minime tacui.

the civil and criminal system (the *privilegium fori*), court interests (the influence of episcopal and dogmatic conflicts), manners and morals (the decisions of the Councils), and legislation (from Gratian to Justinian).

To win control of all the nerve centres of public life, in an empire, moreover, that had come off its hinges, meant inevitably either to take a share in political power or to resist it. The diarchy is created by the facts.[1] Nominally there was a single power, the Emperor, whose competence extended even to ecclesiastical matters and who intervened *de jure* in the organisation of the Church, to the point of ratifying the appointment (which was still elective) of bishops and popes. The Church claimed for herself no share in political power, neither 'direct' nor 'indirect', in the sense that would later be given to the words. None the less, in the actual fact, as part of the fabric of the Empire, in her influence on the very policies of the court, in the confusion of values between religion and politics, and through the growth of her machinery of government—at certain periods stronger and more stable than the imperial machinery—we find the Church taking a real and effective share in the secular power. This was not so much through concrete situations (which came about either spontaneously, or through imperial concession, or by the consent of the peoples or by customs which might

[1]'By diarchy we mean the formation of two powers, either within each group or in the social complexus as a whole. The formation of these two powers may be more or less organic, more or less pronounced, more or less extensive, but always, though it may be only in elementary form, the two powers will assert themselves as the focal points of the two streams, the organisational and the mystical.

In speaking of a diarchy, the idea arises of the co-existence of two sovereign powers with mutual interference; such as the diarchy of France in Tunis or Andorra, and the diarchy of Great Britain in India. These are politico-legal diarchies, formed by a kind of compromise on the title and exercise of sovereignty. The diarchy of which we are speaking is of a sociological character, whether it comes about on the political plane or on other planes of society. It would be possible to question the appropriateness of the word if this were generally current as implying a purely political sovereignty, but it is only in England that people sometimes speak of a diarchy in India; it has never this sense in France or elsewhere, where a term that used to be current was that of co-sovereignty. . . . The word "diarchy" is the most apt for expressing the idea of a social duality, finding concrete manifestation in the two forms of power, whatever their sphere, whether moral, political or religious.' (Luigi Sturzo, *Essai de Sociologie*, p. 203.)

even derive from usurpations), as through the Christian spirit itself, which, pervasive and dominant, involved the Church in an effective participation not so much in the form of power as in its spiritual substance.

From the Edict of Constantine to the creation of the Carolingian Empire, for half a thousand years (A.D. 300-800), two types of politico-religious diarchy took their course—the caesaro-papist type of Byzance and the *organisational* type of the Latin world.

The term caesaro-papism is usually applied to a politico-religious system in which the authority of the State becomes an effective, normal and centralising authority in the Church, though from outside, while the authority of the Church shares directly, though in a non-auto-nomous and often subordinate form, in the exercise of secular power. The classical type is the Byzantine, which, from the period of the schisms, would prevail in the Eastern Church and in the other Ortho-dox churches derived from it. We find an incipient and partial caesaro-papism from Constantine onwards, growing more marked after the fall of the Western Empire, when only the Emperors of the East were left in the Christian world, and oriental methods dominated the byzantinised Latin world also.

With such relations between State and Church, the Church came even to lose her autonomy of organisation and to suffer political re-striction in her sacramental and liturgical functions. The political power tended on the one hand to subordinate the Church to itself and on the other to favour and make use of her, for its own consolidation, for the maintenance of the established order, for shoring up the interests of dominant classes and families and to protect the castes, races or peoples superior to others coexisting in the same State. Under these conditions the Church fufilled a function of mediation between the dominant section and the rest, transporting the issues from the political to the religious plane, but she endured the imperial domination for the sake of security for her established order, of the maintenance of religious influence in the social fabric, of preventing the introduction of hostile innovations, heresies, or schisms into the State, and of obtaining their eventual repression by law.

With these motives, objectively disinterested and of a religious nature, other and secondary ones invariably mingled—the caste spirit of the ecclesiastic, the impulse to ensure the predominance of the clergy, respect of its privileges, defence of its wealth and the positions it had established for itself. In every age the dove-tailing of religious interests and economico-political interests in the social structure is productive of elements of caesaro-papism. This tends to make the Church coincide with the boundaries of the State or nation, whether political boundaries or zones of influence. And it naturally follows that once the political head has been invested with a higher form of religious authority, even though external, the Church (in the concrete, a given church), ceases to have any real authority over peoples politically alien if not hostile to the State. Even against the will of the ecclesiastical heads, the consequence of a diarchy of this type is implicitly a practical denial of the universality of the Church or of her unity. Another consequence of caesaro-papism is the close union between State and Church, so that in the normal course a crisis in one means a crisis in the other, the fall of the one the fall of the other. We say in the normal course, because this depends on the stage at which the Church is to be found in the consciousness of the peoples, which in critical moments may develop of itself religious energies that had remained latent.

The Latin, organisational type of diarchy differed from the caesaro-papist type in that the Church, while calling upon the civil power for help and granting to sovereigns certain faculties or privileges affecting her internal organisation, yet nearly always reacted vigorously against any effective dependence, or reasserted her independence, as the case might be. This independence in the Catholic Church was rendered visible and symbolised in the Roman pontificate. While this from the beginning had asserted and developed its primacy over all the Christian churches, events enabled it so to buttress its special position as to facilitate its task of government. The struggles with the Empire, whether of West or East, involving as they did religious questions, the protection of the forsaken peoples, the vindication of orthodoxy against heretical bishops and against the imperial courts that supported them, could not fail to foster a tradition of government, command and responsibility in papal Rome. Later, when the Popes had to defend themselves, even on the material plane, now against

satellites of the Emperors, now against the barbarian hordes, defending at the same time the people of Rome, they assumed in Italy a social
function of the highest order. The offerings of the Catholic world at
the tombs of the Apostles Peter and Paul, and the type of economy of
the time, made the Roman See one of the richest. Leo the Great
raised the papacy to a great height, even from the human standpoint,
when he twice saved Rome, from Attila and from Genseric. He stood
firm against the indocility and sedition of the Eastern theologians, he
co-operated widely with the emperors, and, when necessary, as vigorously opposed them. In brief, dogmatic and disciplinary reasons, with
outward circumstances of an economic and political nature, enabled
the Roman See to attain a moral dominion and an independence that
would lay the foundations of the Latin type of diarchy soon to prevail
throughout the Christian West.

This type of diarchy evolved in the midst of difficulties, since, as we
have seen, the intermingling of the political and ecclesiastical powers
begins with Constantine, and the caesaro-papist conception crept into
the West in the following century. But at that time in East and West
the mutual influences of the Church on the State and vice versa assumed
now one aspect now the other, according to whether factors sub-
jugating the Church to the Empire prevailed or those tending to
disengage them.

The chief differences between the caesaro-papist type of diarchy and
the Latin organisational type are two. The first is that in the latter the
Church vindicated her independence of every other power, not only
theoretically and morally, but in actual fact. This actual independence,
indeed, seems to come later. Imperial intervention when it favoured
the Church did not appear as intrusion but as co-operation. If imperial
intervention favoured the non-orthodox currents, we must distinguish between various moments and various states of mind among the
faithful and churchmen. In the different Christian communities it was
often not clear, before the decisions of the Councils (and not always
then), on which side lay orthodoxy and on which heresy.

The other difference lay in a diverse conception of the organised
religious unity of the Church. In the caesaro-papist diarchy the organic
unity of the Church came to be confounded with that of the Empire; in

the Latin organisational type, organic unity was purely ecclesiastical and super-statal. In the period from Constantine to the fall of the Western Empire, the fact that the Roman Empire covered nearly all the known world gave the impression that it providentially coincided with the universality of the Church. (It was an impression only, for already apostles and missionaries had carried the Gospel beyond the imperial borders.) But this unity, within the framework of the Empire, was shaken by the dualism of West and East, a dualism that was liable to pass from the political to the ecclesiastical plane. With the fall of the Empire of the West (476) and with the series of Byzantine emperors of varying orthodoxy, the unitary coincidence of Empire and Church was less actual, for the new Germanic kingdoms of the West were already gaining consistency and casting off all subjection. In spite of this, in the West the idea still prevailed of a Christian Empire representing all Christendom in its political aspect, as the Papacy represented it in its religious aspect. Cassiodorus, minister of Theodoric the Great (A.D. 493-525), thought to restore the Western Empire through the Ostrogoths, but it was not long before Justinian with the armies of Belisarius and Narses put an end to this dream.

Actually, from the V century onwards Rome seeks to hold her own against the East, developing in consequence the organisation of the Church in the West, adapting herself step by step to the new conditions that were arising in the barbarian-Latin kingdoms of Italy, Gaul, Spain and Africa. Not only was the religious primacy of Rome no longer questioned, but it was projected on to the civil plane.

When the barbarian world was converted to Christianity and superimposed itself on the Latin world, a great part of the civil organisation remained in the hands of churchmen, who were almost the only men able to read and write. The duty of safeguarding at one and the same time the religious organism, Latin culture and the oppressed populations impelled the clergy not only to conserve the civil positions they had won under the fallen Empire, but to obtain and claim others which, under the harsh yoke of the barbarians, would give more effectual safeguards. The victors, on the other hand, whether converted to Christianity or not, could not ignore a Church that had already become a power, clearly distinct from the Empire and from time to time its opponent. Thus, through its intrinsic importance and through the course of historical events, the Roman See was not only the natural centre of the churches, but the principal nucleus assuring the religious autonomy of the West against the caesaro-papism of Byzance, and the axis of a type of organisation better articulated and more free from the political power and barbarian oppression. Now that population had become sparse and land had gone out of cultivation, the large donations to the churches and the multiplication of monasteries, all agricultural centres, were factors in a new economy which, after the barbarian conquests, grew up round ecclesiastical bodies. The wide rural domains round churches and monasteries (such as that of Monte Cassino) formed the patrimonial basis of an ever-growing authority. The Vatican most of all, through veneration for the tomb of St. Peter, had vast possessions, constituting that 'St. Peter's Patrimony' which would later provide the fundamental title of papal dominion over Rome.

On the other hand, the converted barbarians who were forming the new kingdoms—Franks, Burgundians, Visigoths, Lombards—and those who would be converted later—Angles, Alamans, Saxons, Frisians, Bavarians, were driven by their outlook and by political necessities to invade the ecclesiastical sphere. In view of the power of the bishops and their stable function in the kingdom, kings or princes intervened in their nomination, either by ratifying the proposals of the episcopal chapters, clergy or faithful, or else by direct appointment, or even by sale of episcopal offices ; thus simony, one of the worst evils of the Church, became widespread. Seeing how many men sought a career in the church, they forbade the ordination of those who by the custom of the time, could and should bear arms. Hence two consequences : on the one hand a recruiting of the clergy from among emancipated slaves, and on the other a tendency among the clergy themselves to bear arms and lead troops. Again, monasteries and bishoprics had agricultural lands; hence the necessity, in an age when security was small or non-existent, for them to have their own men-at-arms. This paved the way for the systematic contribution of men-at-arms for the wars of the kingdom. Bishops governed, bishops who were court dignitaries, royal councillors, comptrollers of accounts, governors of provinces. The local councils legislated on church organisation and on manners and customs (especially against the Roman concubinage, which was a true type of barbaric polygamy, and against divorce or repudiation and so forth), and the kings gave legal force to their decisions. In return they claimed the right to authorise and regulate the councils and the various church assemblies.

From many standpoints political and ecclesiastical government were confused even in the new kingdoms, yet never did the State become so theocratic as to abdicate its rights, then chiefly military and fiscal, and never did the Church become so tied to the State as to lose her autonomy of organisation and the character of an universal religion. In the concrete, the Latin organisational type of diarchy, which prevailed in the West, had points of contact with the caesaro-papist type prevailing in the East, and vice versa. Not always did the Church resist the claims of the royal power; indeed in certain cases she recognised it without protest, as when the Council of Orleans in 549 admitted the right of the Frankish kings to give their consent to the nomination of bishops before these were consecrated. Yet the Western Church, while recognising or enduring political interference, did not easily surrender her rights. Therefore we find everywhere latent or open conflicts between the two authorities which, because of the interlocking of the two societies and their reciprocal compenetration, took their course and resolved themselves now on the political plane, now on the religious. Hence the gradual crystallisation of a 'mixed' law, the outcome of Roman traditions, conciliar decisions, papal decrees, imperial legislation and the customs of the Germanic peoples. Little by little Canon Law came into being, to become the juridical basis of the Christian West and a sign of the predominance of the Latin Church in the ordering of what would be called Christendom.

§ 6.—The last representative of the Roman spirit and of the dualism between State and Church when the Western Empire had fallen and was still bound to the East, was Gregory the Great (590-607). He is a truly great figure, as monk, as doctor, as Pope. His asceticism detached him from the world as that of St. Benedict of Nursia, marking thus a dualism with the worldly society of the time, whether lay or ecclesiastic. His teachings adhere closely to the tradition of the Fathers, which he continues. His thought holds traces of the moderate pessimism of the Greeks, together with the organising spirit of the Latin. In relations between the State and Church he keeps to the line laid down by Gelasius (though with formal attenuations), a line that in theory would last till Gregory VII. In practice it was otherwise: Gregory the Great may be said to have set the Western Church of the early Middle Ages on the road towards that religious unity which would be a prelude to the new moral and political unity.

With the fall of the Western Empire and the barbaric invasions in the territories of the Romano-Celtic and Romano-Slavonic peoples, even the organism of the Church, established within the framework of the Empire, was severely shaken, and many parts of Europe found it hard to maintain contact with their chief centres and with Rome. With the creation of the new kingdoms of Germanic race—partly Arian, partly still pagan, to be converted later through contact with the Latin world—local churches grew up, confined within the boundaries of the occupied territories and improvised kingdoms, and often lacking in a constant and effectual bond of discipline. Rome was then in closer contact with Constantinople, across the Mediterranean and by means of the imperial communications, than with the rest of Europe. Gregory the Great gave the impulse to the Roman missionary movement ; he reknit relations with nearly the whole world. His letters show at once his care for the Church, his moral and political guardianship of Italy and of the many parts of the Empire abandoned to hostile forces, and his zeal for the conversion of the infidel. He reformed the liturgy; the Gregorian plain song became a bond of Roman universality throughout the West. His *Regula Pastoralis* would be a widespread norm of priestly activity throughout the Middle Ages. The conversion of Arian Spain to Catholicism is of his time; Leander and Isidore of Seville are its great apostles and King Ermengild its martyr. The Lombards too are converted through the work of Theodolinda. The monk Augustine and his companions come to England for the conversion of the Anglo-Saxons and to promote appeasement with the Celts who were already Christians. Franks and Burgundians were already Catholic through the labours of the Gallo-Roman clergy ;

later the Bavarians, Alamans, Moravians, Hungarians would become so likewise. Roman or romanising bishops become apostles and martyrs of the young peoples, which were forming new kingdoms and bringing with them new customs and fresh blood.

Gregory the Great may be considered, under a certain aspect, as creator of the political power of the popes. Without wish or claim on his part, he exercised in Rome a paternal power. As the head of St. Peter's Patrimony—which had grown enormously round Rome, in Tuscany, in the islands, and even in Africa, Gaul and Dalmatia—he was one who by family tradition (he came of the famous *gens Anicia*), by experience of civil and ecclesiastical life, by his mission to Byzance as *apocrisarius* (to-day we should say nuncio), combined the perspicacious activity of the man of government with the spirituality of the monk.

Rome and Italy, caught in a vice between the new conquerors, the Lombards, and the crushing fiscal system of Byzance, now hard-pressed, now forsaken, had no protection save from the pope. Gregory did not fail in his duty. In 595 he could write to the Empress Constance: 'It is now twenty-seven years that in this city the sword of the Lombards has been suspended over our heads. I do not wish to count the sums the Church has given them day after day, to allow us to live in their midst. It suffices me tell you that just as in Ravenna there is a paymaster of the treasury, entrusted with providing for the current needs of the first army of Italy, so am I who in the same conditions pay for this city.[1]

The imperial court of Byzance, while unable to defend its Italian provinces from the vexations and incursions of the Lombards, continued to harass the Church by interference in ecclesiastical affairs. Pope Martin I, in 653 (less than fifty years after the death of Gregory), was arrested by order of the Emperor Constant II for dogmatic reasons, while Rome was occupied by the Exarch of Ravenna, Calliope; the Pope, carried to Constantinople, was relegated to the Chersonese where he died. First the monothelite heresy, then that of the iconoclasts, for several centuries agitated the Greek and Latin churches, increasing mistrust and conflict. The popes, who at that period were mainly chosen from Greeks, Syrians, Sicilians or Romans

[1]*Mon. Germ. Hist.*, Vol. I, p. 328.

(lands that were part of the Eastern Empire), were unable to overcome the ever-growing difficulties raised by the court and clergy of Byzance, while the Lombard invasion was a menace that grew visibly.

To these difficulties, grave enough in themselves, was added a third still graver, though at the time it was not fully appreciated—Islam, which constituted at once an invading and an inassimilable force. The spread of Islam after the death of Mahomet in 632 was very swift. Omar had seized Persia, Palestine, then Egypt, Cyrenaica and Tripoli. In 672 Constantinople was besieged by land and sea, but resisted. In 698 Carthage fell, the Arabs and Berbers had already passed to Islam. In 711 a part of Spain was taken. In 732 Charles Martel checked the threatened invasion of France at Poitiers.

While Charles Martel was restoring the fortunes of the Franks, which had reached a low ebb, and was meeting their enemies, perhaps he did not clearly foresee what would be the future of their kingdom in the Europe of the VIII and IX centuries. It was situated at the vital and central point of the Western system of the time; to the south it set a dyke to the Saracen invasion, while it formed a compact political group confronting the barbarian peoples of the north and north-east, and a progressive centre of attraction for the Mediterranean—strong at the very time when Byzance was receding into the distance not only through the incessant and wearisome religious wrangles but because unable to defend its Mediterranean provinces against Islam and the Lombards.

When Gregory III, in 739, asked the aid of Charles Martel against the Lombard incursions, he was met by a refusal. In calling for such aid, he had no other purpose than security and independence. This problem appeared to the popes of the time in the form of an ineluctable alternative—either to submit to the Lombards or to strengthen their own authority and their own possessions, establishing them clearly as an autonomous domain, well organised and well defended. Hence the idea of a recourse to the Franks, since the path of negotiations and peace led nowhere.

When Pepin the Short in 751 supplanted the Merovingian dynasty in the Frankish kingdom, with the consent of Pope Zacharias, the trend of papal policy became easier and more decisive. Stephen II (751-7) made a forty years' peace with the Lombard King, Astolph ; Astolph broke it, preparing to invade Ravenna. Stephen asked for a Byzantine embassy to be sent to Astolph, but it was a vain endeavour, for Astolph paid no heed. The pope himself went to the Lombard camp, to induce the King to restore peace to Ravenna and to Rome, but this step failed. Then Stephen crossed the Alps and sought Pepin.

Italian writers have often criticised Stephen's act in bringing in the foreigner, making the unification of Italy impossible for over a thousand years. Mgr. Duchesne holds that to the interests of the Church it would have made small difference if the Lombards had taken the whole of Italy, since they were Catholics and no worse than the Franks. He considers that the popes, in fighting the Lombards and in defending the autonomy of the Duchy of Rome, the Exarchate of Ravenna and the Pentapolis, acted less as popes than as guardians of the Latin heritage, of Roman culture and the traditions of the city of Rome.[1]

Assuredly, human and political motives played their part in the popes' attitude, but events were decisive where a preconceived plan was lacking. Certainly a distant protector is always preferable to a neighbouring tyrant of other race and culture. But our actions are limited to their immediate and partial results; the whole often remains beyond human foresight, and when a man seeks to embrace it he spoils and falsifies those syntheses that are shaping themselves on the plane of history. No one could then foresee that a little more than thirty years later a Frankish Empire would come into being, but it was clear that at that moment, between Franks and Lombards, there could be no other choice : either subordination or a fight till one side or the other had won final victory.

This was not Pepin's idea. He wanted rather to reconcile the Pope with the Lombards, but the danger of an alliance between Byzantines and Lombards against Rome was better understood by the popes and the Romans than by the Franks. Thither events tended. Pepin in 755

[1]'But here indeed is the difficulty. The Romans did not want to be Lombards, and their moral leader, the first among them, the pope, could not want to be Lombard. After so prolonged a struggle to preserve the quality of being a Roman, a member of the holy republic, the subject of a man who, after all, was the heir of Augustus and of Constantine, this quality had become something sacred and intangible.' (L. Duchesne, *Les Premiers Temps de l'Etat Pontifical*, p. 11.)

defeated Astolph a first time and assured to the Pope, besides the Duchy of Rome, the Exarchate of Ravenna and the Pentapolis. In 756 Astolph broke his pact and besieged Rome. Pepin defeated him and added other Adriatic cities to the Roman domain. Thus St. Peter's Patrimony became a temporal State.

Like all the events that history shapes little by little, from chance beginnings, and often apart from any clear and immediate purpose, with effects that with time outstrip all that could have been foreseen, what was known as 'The Donation of Pepin' was not looked upon as something new nor considered as questionable from the religious standpoint. There is no doubt that Pepin when he stripped Astolph of provinces that nominally belonged to Byzance was able to dispose of them as he thought fit. The term 'restitution to St. Peter' was used, since in view of the absenteeism of Byzance, there was no one but the Pope to concern himself with such provinces: these were a fragment of ancient Rome which thanks to the popes and under the shadow of St. Peter's still remained Latin.

At this point of history there appears a document known as the Donation of Constantine, or *Constitutum Constantini*, which would later form the title to which popes and Curia referred to defend their temporal rights against the Germanic Emperors. The first mention of it is in a letter of Pope Adrian I in 778. The *Constitutum* appears later included in the Isidorian (or pseudo-Isidorian) Collection, which goes back to the first half of the IX century. The first pope to make a real and official use of it was Leo IX two hundred years later. The document was finally inserted in Gratian's Decretals in the XII century.

It is believed that the Donation of Constantine was compiled in Rome, from earlier, unconnected elements. The legend of Constantine's leprosy seems to be taken from a Greek MS., and combined with the other of the donation to Pope Sylvester. The assertions concerning the papal power reflect the ideas of Gelasius I, and not yet those of the popes of the XI and XII centuries. Perhaps the legend of the donation took shape, before it found final form, in the clash between the Roman and ecclesiastical world and the Lombards, and was an attempt to answer secular claims by giving the Roman polity a sacred character, in the face of the Lombards and other neighbouring peoples who might attack St. Peter's Patrimony, now enlarged and established, and the dominion of Rome. The document was confirmed by events when Charlemagne ratified Pepin's donation, widening it to include in theory Venetian territory down to the Duchy of Benevento.

§ 7.—Charlemagne is a great figure, legendary and historical, symbolic and real. In the age of Christendom he has no peer, not only because of the aureole of poetry that surrounds him but because, emerging from the dark background of barbarian times, he found events propitious and was able to weld them into a mighty synthesis in his own person.

On the death of his brother Carloman he united all the kingdoms left by Pepin. His campaigns against the Saracens took him as far as Barcelona and Tortosa, to establish there a front of resistance. His wars against the Saxons, long and bitter and indeed barbarous, brought him to the Elbe, north of Hamburg. Maybe he had no thought of seizing the kingdom of the Lombards; his mother Gisela had arranged a marriage for him with the daughter of King Desiderius, Desiderata, whom he speedily repudiated. But the position of the Pope was becoming increasingly difficult, what with internal seditions, clerical and lay, the pressure of the Lombards, and Byzantine intrigues. Moreover, Charlemagne was perturbed at the support Desiderius was giving to the widow and sons of his brother Carloman, who would not renounce their claims to their father's kingdoms. Also, the Duke of Friuli was preparing to revolt. It was thus that Charlemagne decided to make an end of the Lombards. Desiderius was defeated and consigned to the monastery of Corbia, and Charlemagne on 5 June, 774, assumed the title of *Rex Francorum et Longobardorum*.

In imitation of the Byzantine Emperors, Charlemagne concerned himself much with Church discipline and organisation, and was able to impose his will on bishops and popes. Like all legislators of genius he knew how to create about his person (without giving them undue influence) a circle of theologians, legists, poets and writers of every kind, and he gave such an impulse to culture (which was then, and could not but be, the patrimony of churchmen, monks, abbots and bishops) as to give the impression of a renaissance. It must not be thought that before his time there was nothing, and that a tradition of culture was wanting. With Boetius and Gregory the Great the Italy of the V and VI centuries had carried on the great Latin tradition, while Gregory of Tours by his History of the Franks and the Venerable Bede by that of the Britons had created the religious and civil history of the Christian epoch.

The rebirth of culture and asceticism in Charlemagne's time is linked with the influx of Irish monasticism, which created the centres of Luxeuil in Burgundy and Bobbio in Italy, both founded by St. Columba the Elder, and with the influence of monasticism in England, which had produced the great St. Boniface, Archbishop of Magonza, to evangelise the Germanic peoples, and the Venerable Bede of Wearmouth, for the intellectual formation of his age. The monk Egbert, Bishop of York and Alcuin's master, had been Bede's disciple. Egbert in his turn sent Alcuin to Rome and elsewhere to seek manuscripts, and in 766 appointed him director of the episcopal school of York. When Alcuin went to Charlemagne's court and became his trusted counsellor, theologian, canonist and poet, his mind was already formed by a native tradition of culture.

It was natural that in such a circle as surrounded Charlemagne figures of the first rank should not be lacking. From Italy he had brought Peter of Pisa, grammarian and poet, and Paul the Deacon, known also as Paul Warnefried, the monk of Monte Cassino, famous for his *Historia Longobardorum* and for the *Homiliarium* (lessons on the Divine Office and for the use of preachers), written on Charlemagne's request. Another Italian was Paolinus of Aquileja, who took the name of Timothy in the Palatine Academy. For Charlemagne thought to form an Academy, but better than his later imitators, he created it for his own instruction and that of the members of his family and his friends and counsellors. The names they took were ambitious, beginning with Charlemagne who took that of David; Alcuin called himself Horace, Eginhard was Bezekel, and Angilbert nothing less than Homer.

Thus surrounded by a throng of cultivated and zealous churchmen, rivalling those of Rome and Byzance, Charlemagne, between one campaign and another, and even during them, busied himself with the church affairs of his kingdoms, with the appointment of bishops and abbots, with the convocation of councils. His position was that rather of a ruler than of a protector of the Church. Under certain aspects he revived the attitude of Constantine, and under others outwent him. He renewed the centres of culture, reorganising parochial and diocesan schools. Through his *missi dominici* he brought the centre into touch with the periphery, within the framework of the local churches. Bishops kept watch on the counts or governors of provinces, and these kept watch on the bishops. Supervision of the clergy to see that they fulfilled their duties was an essential part of Charlemagne's policy. His control extended even to dogmatic questions, as when he wished to impose the introduction of *Filioque* into the Creed (the Holy Spirit 'proceeding from the Father *and the Son*'),[1] and when he refused Pope Adrian I to accept the decisions of the Second Council of Nicea on the cult of sacred images.

All this is not surprising. He believed it his task to protect, defend and extend the Church, which had been committed to him to uphold amid the storms of the time—*nobis in huius saeculi fluctibus ad regendum commissa.* Thus the preface to the Caroline books.[2] In the letter addressed to the newly elected Pope, Leo III, Charlemagne made a division (wholly to his own advantage) between the tasks in the Church to be allotted to himself and to the Pope—for the Pope prayer, as for Moses (he is alluding to Exodus XVII), for himself action, so as to be able 'to safeguard the knowledge of the Catholic faith within and without'.[3]

The title of Roman Patrician conferred on Pepin the Short by Pope Stephen I, and confirmed to Charlemagne by Adrian I, implied an engagement to protect the Papacy, exposed as it was to every kind of intrigue, conflict, rebellion and war, on the part of its powerful neigh-bours and of the factions that were being formed in Rome and in the

---

[1]The words had been introduced into what is known as the Nicene Creed towards the end of the VI century in Spain, as appears from the Council of Toledo in 589, and the use extended to Gaul and elsewhere. In the dispute between Charlemagne and the Emperor Irenaeus of Constantinople the Greeks were accused of omitting the words *Filioque*, but Pope Adrian I defended the Greek Patriarch, Tarasius, on the grounds that these words were not in the Nicene text. Hence a series of discussions, in which the Frankish theologians spoke of dogma and Charlemagne found a pretext for his anti-byzantine policy.

[2]*Mon. Germ. Hist. Concilia*, Vol. II, supp., p. 2.

[3] *Foris et intus catholicae fidei agnitionem munire.* (*Id.*, Epistolae, Vol. IV, p. 137.)

provinces of the papal domain. Just as temporal and spiritual power were united in the Pope, and as the churchmen in Rome shared indiscriminately in both powers while the laity contended with them for dominion, so Charlemagne as Roman patrician exercised an office of control and protection at once political and military, religious and civil. So too his legates and ecclesiastical counsellors, sharing in this control, assumed a right of intervention in the affairs of the Roman Church that must have been judged excessive by the popes, the clergy of the Curia and the Roman people. On the election of Leo III, Charlemagne sent Angilbert to receive the homage of the Romans. Among the instructions he gave him he wrote that he should 'diligently admonish the Pope to live a virtuous life, to have a jealous care for the observance of the holy canons and to govern the Church with piety'. The superior tone of the writer of the letter (perhaps Alcuin) is in no way muffled.

Leo III suffered a serious assault (in April 799) through a plot among his high officials, among them the nephew of his predecessor Adrian I, the primicerius Pascal. Escaping from the hands of his enemies, as soon as he had recovered from the serious maltreatment he had received, he hastened to Paderborn to ask help of Charlemagne. Charlemagne had him brought back to Rome to be received with solemn honours, but wished an inquiry to be made into the charges of adultery and perjury made by his enemies. The Pope could not admit a higher jurisdiction, far less that of a layman, even of a Roman patrician, King of the Franks and Lombards, nor did he wish to seem to take refuge under the mantle of pontifical authority. Therefore, before a Council that met in December of 800, and at which Charlemagne was present, Leo III spontaneously affirmed his innocence on oath, declaring, however, that he did not wish thus to establish a precedent, nor to diminish the authority of the first See '*quae a nemine judicatur*'.

A new century was opening, and Charlemagne had gathered under his sceptre nearly all the Roman West, while holding his own against Saracens, barbarians and Byzantines. Leo III after that act of humiliation performed an act of glory. On Christmas Eve in St. Peter's he placed the imperial crown on the head of Charlemagne who knelt before him, while the people thrice repeated the famous acclamation: "To Charles,

most pious Augustus, crowned by God great and pacific Emperor of
the Romans, life and victory!' When the singing was over the Pope
in his turn prostrated himself in the rite known as 'adoration'. Charles
was Emperor. The solemn ritual used for the first time by a pope in St.
Peter's was the same as that used in Byzance. But the significance of
the rebirth of the Western Empire, which was to become 'Christendom', with two supreme powers, Emperor and Pope, was implicit in
the ceremony of that Christmas night. Leo III in taking the initiative
had surely an intuition of its historic importance. Perhaps he was looking back on the past of the Roman Empire that through his doing had
returned to life, but instead a new empire had been born, with a
character of its own. The history of an international diarchy that would
last over six centuries begins from that moment.

Eginhard, Charlemagne's historian, wrote that his master was not
wholly pleased, not because he was not glad to receive the title of
Emperor, and maybe he, or others for him (probably Alcuin), had
already thought of it. The tale of Charlemagne's displeasure may have
been circulated to ward off the resentment of Byzance and turn it on
the Pope. But the idea that the Empire was a title coming from Rome,
that the Romans were its depositaries, that it was the Pope who could
sanction and consecrate the choice of Emperor, was something that
could not escape Charlemagne and his counsellors, and all this was
implied by the act of Leo III. No writer of the time or of the succeeding
centuries sees in that act simply a religious consecration, as might be
that of a Basileus of Byzance, but instead it was understood as the act
of transmission of a title and of a power. If the centre of the West had
been displaced from Rome to Aix-la-Chapelle, if 'Romania' had lost
its economico-political character, this was not owing to Charlemagne
but to the Arab invasion of the Mediterranean: Leo III had done what
he could to render Rome once more imperial.

When Leo III crowned Charlemagne, for some thirty years, perhaps
longer, centres of culture had been acquainted with the pretended
document of the Donation of Constantine, which held in germ the
temporal power of the Pope together with the theory of the two powers
as formulated by Gelasius I. The excessive interference of the new
Emperor and of his court in religious matters aroused a certain anxiety

in Rome. The first reference in ecclesiastical literature to the theory of the two swords, taken as symbols of the two powers, temporal and spiritual, is entirely in favour of the secular ruler. It is made by Alcuin who writes to Charlemagne a year before his coronation, saying: 'Your pious care to protect the churches of Christ and to purge them within of all perverse doctrine is equalled only by your solicitude to safeguard and defend them without against the devastations of the pagans. It is the Divine Power that has invested your Venerable Excellency with the two swords.'[1] A few centuries later, the symbol of the two swords would pass to the side of the Pope and indicate his twofold power, and would lead to violent controversies on the text of St. Luke (xxii, 38, *ecce duo gladii hic*) whence the symbol was taken. We do not say that when Leo III proceeded to crown Charlemagne it was with the ideas that were current later, but it is not improbable that he divined the need to raise the position of the Pope, reduced in the temporal sphere to that of a vassal of the Frankish kingdom as would appear from the Donation of Pepin, and to exalt it to that of the founder of the new Empire. And at the same time, in the ecclesiastical field, he would also resume his disciplinary function as head, against the pretensions of Charlemagne's clergy and of the metropolitans who were usurping the powers of the Holy See.

This aspect of events would be noted later in a fresh collection of ecclesiastical documents, which passes under the name of *Isidoriana*. The great canonical collections of the time were the *Dionisiana* and the *Hispana*. This third, which appears about 850, is signed by *Isidorus Mercator* (or *Peccator*). Maybe there was a wish to make St. Isidore of Seville pass as author, where it is written: '*Incipit praefatio Sancti Isidori libri hujus*'. Hence the name *Isidoriana*. But while the two earlier collections so far as was then possible contained authentic documents or documents of a traditional character and accepted as authentic, the Isidorian Collection is a hotch-potch of authentic documents marred by interpolations of a topical nature, of manipulated passages from Greek or Latin ecclesiastical writers, reduced to the form of canons and decretals and attributed to popes, of earlier collections of dubious origin, and of pieces entirely invented. The date can be fixed with a cer-

[1] *Mon. Germ. Hist.*, Ep. IV, p. 282.

tain probability at the middle of the IX century; there are some who hold that it began to circulate between 847 and 852, the year in which we find the first quotation made from it. It was the work of monks or ecclesiastics of the Frankish kingdom, probably Brittany, though some historians would pin it down to the province of Tours or the diocese of Le Mans. The collection came to form part of the documentary patrimony of the age, and after some fifty years gained credit in the Roman Curia, which found in it a stalwart support for the authoritarian theses of the Papacy, in regard both to laymen and prelates.

The dubious character of some of these documents did not pass unnoted, and the beginnings of a critical attitude towards them appear as early as the XII century, in Peter Comestor, Godfrey of Viterbo and Stephen of Tournai. In the XIV and XV centuries they were attacked by Wyclif and Nicholas of Cusa. But the falsification was proved by textual criticism in the XVI century, when first Protestants and then Febronians used it as a weapon against the Papacy, as though it constituted the title-deeds of the papal power. But it is certain that the compilation was neither directly nor indirectly influenced by the Papacy. Probably to an honest labour of editing and rearranging the earlier collections, especially the *Hispana* (which was presented to Charlemagne by Adrian I), the compilers wished to add all the documents possible, without any critical discernment, using what manuscripts they could lay hands on. With this groundwork, vanity led them to seek to fill in the gaps in the earlier periods, with the help of the *Liber Pontificalis* and of other elements that have not come down to us, but also with that of their imagination. A third motive, that of challenging the dominion of the metropolitan bishops over the suffragan bishops, of strengthening the central authority of the Holy See and of ending the abusive interference of laymen with the clergy, drove the compilers, or others who came after, to insert non-existent phrases and passages into genuine documents, to create false ones or to make use of them if they had already been created. However this may be, the *Pseudo-Isidoriana* mirrors the situation that had come into being in the Carolingian Empire and in the Frankish Church, and is an attempt at a reaction, which joined forces with that already active in bo

Rome and the provinces, growing steadily as under Charlemagne's heirs the Empire fell to pieces.

§ 8.—The Carolingian State has three prevailing features: the military mould into which it was cast through the influence of the Teutonic races on law and custom; the strongly woven fabric of the Church, mediating between the dominant military element and the people; the serfdom of the countryside, forming the only serious means of agricultural production. From these elements springs the corporative idea of a politico-religious society, very different from the classical idea of the State or *res publica*, which had passed, tinctured with Christianity, into the Justinian conception. The Greco-Roman State was the legislating State, guardian of its subjects in a natural and social inequality between freemen and slaves, centralising all powers in itself, though these were held to be delegated by the people. Christianity added to this conception a moral one, bringing a conscientious obligation of obedience to those who governed, even if they were bad. At the same time it corrected the scope of such obedience and political subjection by a higher ethic which had to prevail, especially in the case of conflict between the political order and duty of conscience. In patristic thought the State and its coercive power, effects of Original Sin, served as correction and punishment of sin. The Christian idea that authority came from God, and that therefore those in authority (Emperor or Senate) had their own moral responsibility, eliminated two factors that in paganism gave the authority of the State an absolute value, viz. that the Emperor was *solutus a lege*, above the law, and that he deserved divine worship. In the mind and expressions of the Fathers the Emperor was considered as the Vicar of God, and hence not *solutus a lege Dei*; only in certain cases *solutus a lege hominis*, that is above positive law but not above the natural law.

In the Teutonic State the constituent elements have changed. It is no longer the entity known as the *res publica* but a corporation in the widest sense of the term, a community in which various organic factors concur autonomously in the formation of the body politic. The underlying conception is no longer that of a natural and social inequality, but that of an equality of nature, even though in practice it admitted serfdom and the enslavement of those vanquished in war. The King or chief, even when his office is hereditary, is chosen or approved by the magnates or barons, by whom he can be deposed if bad or harmful to the community. Laws are the product of assemblies or councils or assizes; the royal intervention or assent serves to complete them, sanctioning and making them enforcible. The King is not *solutus a lege*, but he too is under the law. The law is not conceived as the expression of the will of the people actuated by the royal authority, but as the practical fulfilment of tradition and earlier laws, or as the enforcement of natural and religious morality. Fiscal contributions are based on the consent of the community.

The Church could easily permeate such a structure, bringing to it what she had preserved of the Roman conception, the title of Empire, the ecclesiastical framework of provinces and dioceses, the theories of authority, law, morals, with religious sanction and ritual consecration. Between the military, illiterate heads of the new kingdoms of the West and the mass of the people who were serfs, the ecclesiastical class stands intermediary, while the monastery is an intermediary between the cities and the countryside. It was through monasticism that the serfs rose to be free men; every serf who became a monk was emancipated. Monasticism provided the greater number of the bishops and abbots, that is, the ruling element in the kingdoms and in the Empire. In the monasteries were libraries, and there the manuscripts of the time were gathered together; schools came into being in the shadow of the cathedrals and the parish churches. The imperial bureaucracy, though primitive, completed the picture and made the existence of a political unification felt.

The unitary conception of the West in the IX century was not achieved at once, but developed on two fronts. The one faced Byzance, with whom the quarrel over images from the middle of the VIII century dragged on under Photius, while the question of the Trinity prepared the way for the final rupture, which would come two centuries later. The other front faced the Saracens who became daily more dangerous to the whole of Europe. Thus little by little, while even the most representative men of the time were hardly conscious of it, what would later be called *Christendom* was taking shape—no longer the

Western Roman Empire, nor that which we shall call the Franco-Roman or simply the Holy Roman Empire, but Christendom, the unitary and resolvent conception of the whole Christian West.

With the death of Charlemagne, the dismemberment of the Empire and the struggle between his heirs, it seemed that the dream of imperial unity had vanished. The title was maintained, but not its authority. To make up for the secondary and insignificant figures of the Carolingian emperors, there arose popes of the first order, such as Leo IV, Nicholas I, Adrian II, John VIII, who kept alive the imperial unification of the West, uncertain and vacillating though it still was. Through them the influence of the Papacy increased, and amid the decadence of political forces became an ever more effectual centre of all social activity. Nicholas I (858–67) had a sense of the evolution that was proceeding when, for the first time, he clearly asserted the conception of the Pope as supreme regulator of kingdoms and kings.

But the clash of social forces was still primitive, passionate and barbaric. Very little sufficed to render ineffectual the civil and religious order created by the tentative of Carolingian civilisation. The Papacy did not escape the conditions of the environment of oppression and disorder into which Rome had fallen. In the century between Pope Stephen VI and Pope Gregory VI (896-996) the Roman pontificate suffered eclipse through the fault of unworthy popes, and the intrigues of Roman lords and powerful women. During the same period the Frankish Empire dragged on its existence, corroded by senility, losing its influence till, with the effective breakaway of many kingdoms and provinces, it no longer possessed a real political basis.

In spite of this, a unitary European mind and an ecclesiastical structure, Latin, Frankish, Teutonic had come into being, and from the post-Carolingian period the feudal system was evolving. This would break up the kingdoms into localised lots, indefinite in size and often tiny, but it would create a hierarchy in which the local forces led up towards the unity of the kingdom, and the kingdoms towards the empire and towards the Papacy, within the frame of Christendom as the operative fabric of a politico-religious reality.

The wholly teutonic concept of the deposition of kings or politico-military chiefs by councils or assemblies of nobles or magnates –

aristocratic bodies in which, after the conversion of the teutonic peoples, bishops and abbots dominated—became in the Middle Ages a politico-religious sanction and a terrible weapon in the hands, first of the local bishops, then of the Pope, not only as Head of the Church and guarantor of moral order in Christendom, but also as paramount representative of the Christian people and its rights, and even as lord and feudal suzerain of many kingdoms. Here was a three-fold sanction, religious, moral and political, showing in synthesis the whole significance of the evolution that had taken place in the conception of the State and the novelty of its relations with the Church.

The medieval diarchy is founded on the conception that the two powers, ecclesiastical and secular, are both within the Church (the secular power being no longer extraneous); that hence the two powers control and complement each other, while remaining distinct; and that finally the last word in ethico-social matters is reserved to the Church, as an entity absorbing into itself all earthly values, and through her to the Pope as the summit of all religious power.

This dualistic conception of an interlocked fabric of Church and State could be reached in the Middle Ages because the State was conceived as a corporation or community and no longer as an absolute entity. This meant an end of the spiritual incompatibility we noted in the time of the Fathers, which came from the paganism exalted in the Roman Empire and made of the State a symbol of the earthly city, the synthetic and institutional expression of the world, its pomps and vanities and pride. In the Middle Ages there is simply the social community, to be renewed by faith, quickened by the Christian spirit and consecrated by religious rites. This community is at once State and Church, it is Christendom; the boundaries of the two powers are set by the conciliar or papal decisions (later, Canon Law), but their co-operation is conceived as taking place within and not outside nor alongside the Church. The religious consecration of social life is at once a symbol and a reality. The King, the Emperor, arms and later knighthood, the craft guilds, the schools, the universities, all are blessed by the sacred rite, all become means of Christian co-operation in function of a supernatural life.

The monks who with Benedict in the VI century had withdrawn

into the abandoned countryside in order to pray and labour detached from the world, in the IX century had become the lords of wide expanses of land, with armed men for their defence and serfs for the heavier labours; their abbots and abbesses sat in the assizes of the realm. Their particular communities were considered as being within and not outside the greater community of kingdom or empire. Spiritual interests were combined with earthly interests, thus forming a new social whole. The forces of this society were still elementary, rude, not harmonised but clashing, and yet were potentialised by a new spiritual unification that was evolving.

Yet the X century, known as an age of iron, accentuated the clash of these primitive, not easily tamed forces. Indeed the trend seems to be towards a period of disintegration with the triumph of a conception in its material expression base, passion-ridden, violent, simoniacal, and sanguinary. Even the organisms that seemed to excel and overtop all others are shaken—the Papacy and the Empire, which decay morally and politically. But through the confused chaos of the X century new social factors, the seeds of which were sown in the century before, appear and ripen. Cluny in France, Monte Cassino in Italy, and many other inaccessible peaks or obscure valleys contain treasures of spiritual and civilising life. Culture, asceticism, social activities come once more from the mystical stream, which becomes in its turn a vigorous force of organisation, when the organising hierarchic elements of State and Church are a prey to anarchic convulsions and party violence.

# CHAPTER III

## PAPACY AND EMPIRE

### FIRST PERIOD (962–1153)

§ 9.—The period between the X century and the end of the XIII, or more exactly, from the consecration of Otto I as Emperor in 692 to the death of Henry VII in 1313, has a specific character, that of an international diarchy superimposed on local and national diarchies. Various elements were already in existence before the period opens, and would continue working during the XIV and XV centuries, but in spite of this it must be considered apart, with its special features.

From the death of Charlemagne, the feudal system had been taking form, for though juridically its roots were set in Roman reminiscences and economically it was conditioned by the barbarian invasions, it had not till then assumed a general and political aspect. The division of lands into fiefs, held on military tenure, the need for protection to which corresponded a duty of fealty, the creation of a feudal hierarchy, the inherence of public jurisdiction in the grant and possession of land, the rights of regalia, local dues, and serfdom, constitute a whole, political, juridical, economic, which would outlast six centuries and prolong its effects for two centuries more.

The wealth and the politico-social basis of the period was land. Land formed the greater part of Church property, and the economico-political feudalisation of the ecclesiastical system was at once effect and cause. Bishops and dignitaries of the Church, abbots and abbesses, became in turn vassals and feudal overlords, for they too needed support against their enemies or against their own subjects, and they too turned their civil possession into political and military tenure.

The fundamental fact of feudalism was the fusion of a paramount ownership of the land with sovereignty or suzerainty, and the grant of land to vassals in return for a tribute or symbol of subjection, with a bond of fealty that chiefly expressed itself as military service. The *comitatus* (a company or military band), the *commendam* (the dependence of the weaker on the stronger), the *beneficium* (a grant of land on a military tenure), were various characteristic phases of feudalism, based as it was on personal loyalty and the military mould in which society was cast. Knighthood was its typical product, which, originally individualistic, became corporational at the time of the first Crusade, with the orders of chivalry.

The infeudation of lands, as a kind of political insurance against all risks, extended so widely from lordship to lordship, from kingdom to kingdom, from lordships and kingdoms to Empire and Papacy, that the whole of the West became a network of fiefs. Thus the Pope became feudal overlord of the kingdoms of Scotland, England, Aragon, the principalities of Southern Italy, of Sicily, of Hungary. So too ecclesiastical magnates who were vassals of the Empire or of the Pope or of the kings were in their turn sovereign lords of other princes, dukes or marquises, or of vassal municipalities.

On the margins of this general infeudation stood the free cities which had kept their independence and their civic organisation. Aristocratic or merchant, such cities acted as sovereigns; such indeed were Venice, Amalfi, Salerno, Pisa and Genoa.

The feudal system had created or strengthened the subordination of the upper clergy to lay princes, in the same way as it widened the economic and political power of the clergy over their vassals and subjects. Hence the upper clergy and the lay princes came to have similar civil and military duties as inherent in the possession of land. It is not astonishing that on the one hand many bishops and feudal abbots became worldly, resembling the lay princes in everything, and that on the other the sovereign princes sought to have ecclesiastical vassals whom they could trust, men at home in camp or court, or that, worse still, in a period of scarcity of currency and poor economy, they should sell ecclesiastical benefices for a price.

A result was the intrusion into the ecclesiastical order of ignorant and gross men, laymen and men-at-arms improvised as bishops. Concubinage, simony and ignorance were its most common symptoms. A symbol of the feudal transformation of the higher, beneficed clergy was their investiture by emperor, king or overlord, with the ring and staff. The local elections and consecrations of bishops and abbots in practice were not valid without the assent of the sovereign and the investiture he conferred. The political element overlaid that which was strictly ecclesiastical.

Although the type of feudalism differed much in France, Germany, England and Italy, yet from the point of view of relations between Church and State the problem everywhere reduced itself to this: the Church, through her highest authorities, had acquired a co-share in the political, economic and military order, at the expense of her religious and disciplinary autonomy, while the State, though of feudal character, dovetailed into the fabric of the Church. The two formed a single community, feudal, military and religious.

The continuous chain stretching from small vassal units up to the universal sovereignty of Empire and Papacy corresponded to the spirit of the feudal community and its structural requirements. And though towards the end of the IX century and at the beginning of the X the Papacy had reached a low ebb through the strife of factions and the intrigues of powerful men and women, yet it never abandoned the imperial idea, not even when the Carolingian kingdom was definitely reduced to pieces (888). Benedict IV consecrated Louis of Provence as Emperor in 901 and John X chose Berengarius of Friuli in 915. These were emperors without real authority, as indeed were most of the Carolingians, till the coronation in 962 of Otto I of Saxony, who had already won power over nearly all Germany and Northern Italy.

The nomination of Otto, by an unworthy pope for personal political reasons (John XII), had not for contemporaries the solemn significance of the crowning of Charlemagne by a great pope like Leo III. It seemed merely the choice of the most powerful king of the time, certainly a happy choice. But times had changed, nearly two centuries had not passed in vain. The spread of feudalism, the formation of the weak and warring local kingdoms, the decay of the authority of Rome, the nominal consistency of the empire, the continual menace of the Saracens, the break-away of the East were historical circumstances that made the election of Otto I a turning point in the history of the

Middle Ages and a significant date in the creation of the Holy Romano-Germanic Empire.

Otto I had the same view of his function as Constantine and Charlemagne; he too considered himself a 'bishop of bishops' with the task of restoring the Papacy. The latter had to be raised to the moral height of its office, disentangled from Roman factions and made capable of undertaking the reform of the Church. If this enterprise was to succeed it was necessary for the emperors to reach an understanding with the Roman people and clergy over papal elections. And although Otto's endeavours had ambiguous results, such as the elections of Benedict V and of Leo VIII, whose legitimacy is questioned (Leo VIII does not figure in the list of popes of the Pontifical Annual), the system would later produce good results, beginning with Benedict VII (974–83) who made timely laws against simony. The two popes who, nominated by the Emperor and ratified by the Romans, stood for the new policy of reform in the Church and union of Papacy and Empire, were Gregory V, the first German pope (996–9) and Sylvester II, the first French pope (999–1003). These collaborated with Otto III in the reorganisation of Christendom. This now extended to Hungary, recognised as a new kingdom under Stephen I, which would mark for centuries the bulwark against both the Greek schism and the Crescent. Under the three Ottos (962–1003), then under St. Henry II (1014–24), and again under Henry III of Swabia (1037–56), the diarchy of State and Church in the West seemed to reach its fullest unification in the diarchy of Empire and Papacy.

It is true that the Empire, in the political sense of the word, embraced only Germany, Northern Italy (with the exception of Venice), Burgundy and the various principalities of Central Europe, and, for a limited period, Southern Italy and Sicily also. It was juridically rather than politically that it stood for the unification of all Christendom. The Empire never ceased to advance certain rights over France, the Aragonese, England, and other regions looked upon as independent, and even over the Byzantine Empire itself. Even leaving aside certain formal acts on the part of autonomous States such as England and Aragon, recognising the Empire as a term of politico-legal unification, the fact remains that in the prevailing conception of the time—from the X century up to the great controversies and the formation of the national monarchies—Empire and Papacy were the symbol of the Christian and feudal unification of Europe, and religious subjection to the Papacy was reflected in a kind of recognition of the moral (if not political) preeminence of the Empire. This was enhanced by the fact that on the one hand the emperor was approved and consecrated by the Pope, and the Pope was chosen with the consent or on the proposal of the emperor. There was a link between this system and England, Scotland, Aragon, Hungary, Sardinia, Corsica and Southern Italy, in as much as they were or would become feudal vassals of the Holy See.

To appreciate the moral and unifying value of such various and, at bottom, dissimilar elements, as converged in Papacy and Empire, we must remember that in those days the idea of a political State was lacking, and instead the idea of community or corporation had grown up, in which the diverse autonomous and heterogeneous elements were welded together by moral factors such as religious faith, feudal loyalty or allegiance, the solidarity between men of a trade, and the freedom entailed by privilege or immunity. All this would lead, between the XI and XIII centuries, to the titanic struggles between Papacy, Empire and free municipalities and would open the way to the renewal, moral and artistic, cultural and political, of the West.

§ 10.—At the beginning of the XI century the reform of the Church was urgent, and, given the structure of the society of the time, reform of the Church carried with it the reform, or rather the transformation, of political society itself. The need for a reform of the Church was felt in all circles, ecclesiastical and political, monastic and secular. The activity of the Ottos and the Henries, as that of the more enlightened pontiffs and bishops of the X century and early XI century had been directed to abolishing marriage of the clergy, repressing simony in the grant of ecclesiastical benefices, and raising the standard of religious morals and culture.

The growth of monasticism, in a great ascetic and mystical renaissance, did much for the formation of churchmen, among whom two stand out above all the rest, Peter Damiani and later Bernard of Clairvaux. St. Bruno of Cologne and St. John Gualbert of Florence revived the spirit of pure detachment and withdrawal from the world (even from the ecclesiastical world), as Benedict of Nursia had done in the VI century and St. Romuald of Ravenna in the X century.

This purely spiritual reform affected individuals, and only indirectly influenced the institutions of social life. To hear Peter Damiani, the Emperor Henry III made ecclesiastical morals flower anew; to hear Hildebrand, Henry IV had plunged the Church into the mire. Actually it was not a case of so rapid a transition in a few years, from the death of Henry III to the maturity of Henry IV. The evil existed and had filtered into the very fabric of the Church, bound as it was, economically and politically, to the feudal constitution of kingdoms and Empire. Henry III had fought the evil (in his own way) and Henry IV (in his own way) encouraged it, but under Henry III as under Henry IV, throughout Europe the ferments of degeneration were working, such as the simony, secularisation and ignorance of the clergy.

To deal with this situation there were two methods, which we find in course at the beginning of the XI century. There was that of accentuating the duality of the powers then known as *Sacerdotium* and *Regnum*, the spheres of Priest and King, so as to bring about the detachment of the clergy from all worldly, economic and political cares. And there was the other which, while affirming the moral need for detachment, would rather accentuate the political intervention of the Church, under a prevalently religious aspect, with the open aim of unifying all public powers in the Papacy. In substance, they are the familiar streams, the mystical and the organisational, perennially operative in human society, each of which gives its own aspect to individual activities and to the historical phases of events, according to the special characteristics of the different ages.

Peter Damiani and Hildebrand can be taken as symbols of the two streams, the mystical and the organisational. But it is well not to insist too much on such formulas, for both men, and their followers, imitators and defenders in their turn, acted now on the plane of political and religious organisation, now on the strictly spiritual plane of detachment and individual purification, while both engaged in the radical fight against the evils that afflicted the Church and the whole of medieval society.

We may distinguish two questions that develop and intersect in the first period of the conflict, which stretches from the death of Henry III (1036) to the Peace of Worms (1122). The first is the question of investitures, the second that of the papal power to depose a king or emperor. Gregory VII decided to make an end of the lay investitures, which for over a century had troubled the whole Western Church, and he went straight to his goal. There was no other means but to enforce the decrees prohibiting such investitures, by excommunicating and deposing both those who conferred and those who received them. And since the former were princes, kings and emperors, the latter bishops and abbots, it was at these he would have to strike, with authority and resolution. He would face the consequences—rebellions, double nominations in the case of contested benefices, schisms and wars. Only a radical cure could save the Church.

To do this, to face a truly decisive struggle, Gregory VII had to have not only a part of the clergy and people with him, but also the means for enforcing his will, and this reduced itself, in plain terms, to maintaining the excommunication of the guilty and causing it to be observed. In respect of the clergy it would be enough to persuade the faithful or monks to separate themselves from excommunicated bishops or abbots; otherwise the community, city or region that rebelled would be put under interdict. Zealous emissaries, such as Peter Damiani and many others like him, went all over Europe depriving simoniac and concubinary bishops, ensuring the canonical election of pastors better fitted to the sacred ministry, pacifying insurgent peoples, appeasing angry princes, arguing on the rights of *Regnum* and *Sacerdotium* with nimble-witted legists or pedantic canonists. Their task was no easy one; passions were heated, and the outcome was now happy, now the reverse.

Where the lay rulers were concerned, it was equally necessary to strike at the roots, even though such a policy was in itself revolutionary. Gregory VII was not a man to be checked by the first obstacles. In the beginning he was patient though firm. The first with whom he had to deal over the investitures was Philip I of France. Thereupon, the dis-

patch of nuncios and of letters, threats of excommunication and deposition, letters to the bishops of France ordering them to resist. Then the
question was laid before the Lateran Council (1075) which declared
that Philip would be considered as excommunicate if he gave no
surety of amendment—'si nunciis papae ad Gallias ituris de satisfactione
sua et emendatione securitatem ne fecerit'.[1]

Not long before had come the conquest of Sicily, Apulia and England by the Normans. After their conversion to Christianity early in
the X century they had become its champions, propagators and protectors, ready, none the less, to enter into conflict with the popes.
Gregory VII found in them allies and collaborators. The famous
Lanfranc of the school of Pavia, (who went to Avranches to teach law,
and then became a monk at Bec), followed William the Conqueror to
England. He was appointed Archbishop of Canterbury and, helped by
William (who at the same time believed in keeping the clergy more
subject to himself than to the Pope), introduced the Gregorian reform
with certain mitigations, against the married and simoniac clergy.
William II renounced the investiture of bishops by staff and ring,
almost at the same time as Koloman, King of Hungary, in the Synod
of Guastalla (1106).

The most prolonged and resounding conflict on this question was
that which Gregory sustained against Henry IV of Germany, whom
he excommunicated and deposed. Pardoned at Canossa, Henry renewed the struggle, but the Pope would not yield, deposing him a
second time and releasing his subjects from their oath of allegiance.
The Investiture Conflict between popes and emperors would continue
after Gregory VII, not only with Henry IV, who died in 1108, but
with his successor, till the Concordat of Worms (1122), when the
Pope, Calixtus II, and the Emperor Henry V would reach a compromise on their respective rights. Between the full claims of Gregory
and the agreement reached by Calixtus, came a radical essay, that of
Paschal II, which merits attention because of the light it throws on that
turbulent period. Paschal, after having several times confirmed the
decrees of prohibition, at the end of a series of negotiations won from
Henry V a pledge to renounce the investitures in return for a pledge

[1]Greg. VII, Registrum 11, p. 52.

on the Pope's part to renounce and make all bishops, abbots and beneficed clergy renounce their rights to feudal 'regalia', since it was these rights that gave a justification to the system of royal or imperial investiture. By Paschal's plan the Church did not lose the actual property involved, but this, by the fact of such renunciation, was freed from any feudal service with the loss at the same time of such rights (we should say political rights) as this entailed.

By this initiative Paschal II represented the spiritual movement of the period at its highest point. He put the axe to the roots. The text of his *Privilegium Primae Conventionis* makes it crystal clear. 'In parts of your realms bishops or abbots are so much occupied in secular concerns, that they are obliged to take assiduous part in the companies and to give military service. These things, alas! rarely if ever are accomplished without rapine, sacrilege, burning or homicide. . . . It is necessary that the bishops, freed from temporal cares, should occupy themselves with their people and should no longer absent themselves from their churches. For they, as the Apostle Paul says, keep watch knowing that they will have to give account for the souls of these.'[1]

Henry had undertaken in writing to renounce the investitures on the day of his coronation as emperor, but when he reached Rome he consulted with the German and Lombard bishops, who opposed the project. It was to his own interest to show them that it was not of his seeking and that he had no desire to deprive them of such rights. The bishops and prelates rose against the Pope, and went so far as to accuse him of heresy—as was easy enough when it was a case of material interests bound up with an ecclesiastical system of authority and dominion. Finally Henry took Pope and Cardinals prisoner, and left Rome, dragging them after him. By threatening to promote a schism and to lay waste the territory of Rome, he forced the imprisoned Pope to recognise his right of investiture. It was only for a

---

[1]'In regni autem vestri partibus episcopi vel abbates adeo curis saecularibus occupantur, ut comitatum assidue frequentare et militiam exercere cogantur. Quae nimirum aut vix aut nullomodo sine rapinis sacrilegiis incendiis aut homicidiis exhibentur . . . oportet enim episcopos curis saecularibus expeditos curam suorum agere populorum nec ecclesiis suis abesse diutius. Ipsi enim juxta apostolum Paulum "pervigilant tanquam rationem pro animabus eorum reddituri." '(*M. H. G.*, Lec. IV, Const., Vol. 1, p. 90.)

little while. The bishops themselves reacted, and Paschal repudiated the concession torn from him by violence, reconfirming the previous decrees of prohibition.

This episode did not, as might have been expected, have any wide repercussions either at the time or subsequently. Paschal's solution was not appreciated by the spiritual and mystical streams, nor did they later turn it to account; it was not seen in its true light by the organizational streams, which never had recourse to it. For the former, the retention of church properties and of the wealth of the clergy must have seemed too timid an advance in the path of reform; for the latter, the Church, in renouncing the regalia, would have abandoned her positions of direction and influence over Christendom.

The heated opposition of the clergy of Germany and Northern Italy, and perhaps of other countries also, might at first sight be attributed to the fact that many had received royal investiture and were bound to court life and the interests it created. But in many there was also the dread of a leap in the dark, a horror of drastic solutions. They must have perceived, albeit vaguely, that to accept the decision of Paschal II would have meant a revolution, upsetting the balance of the social structure by withdrawing a large part of feudal lands from their political function. Even if Paschal's measures had been put into effect, perhaps it would not have been long before matters returned to what they were before, through the difficulty of improvising another régime that would meet the needs of the turbulent and insecure situation of society of the time. Moreover, neither the popes nor the reformers had adequately worked out such a solution, which, though logical, found the historical climate unprepared for it.

Hildebrand's programme, both before and during his papacy, meant abolishing the effect, namely lay investiture, without abolishing its chief cause, the feudal power of ecclesiastical rulers. Therefore he had to carry to its widest conclusions the political conception of the age, permeated as it was by ecclesiastical elements. What he sought was to divert the course of unification from Empire to Papacy. Whereas from Otto I to Henry III, for over a century, the Emperor had been the unifying centre, from Pope Leo IX, and still more vigorously from Gregory VII, the centre of unification was coming to be the Papacy.

The latter was asserting itself in decisive fashion, facing kings and emperors, ready to excommunicate and depose them, appealing to princes and peoples, promoting alliances and military leagues. Moral and material force combined would defend the rights of the Holy See and at the same time the conception of the Papacy as centre of Christendom, or rather of the whole world.

This conception ripens little by little through the Middle Ages, and is favoured by events, so that, despite the opposition of imperial or royal courts—made for the most part by eminent ecclesiastics and subsequently also by lay legists—it comes to prevail in the general consciousness, by which it is sustained as at once an historical and logical exigency of Christian society. It is true that men like Peter Damiani grieved to see the Church mixed up with earthly interests and methods. He blamed the war of Leo IX against the Normans, which, proclaimed in the name of the Holy See, seemed to him less religious than political, and in which the Pope fell a prisoner to his enemies. Peter Damiani did not admit the use of arms on the part of the ecclesiastical authorities. But this thesis found little support in those days, when most of the bishops were invested with the rights of regalia and were obliged to give feudal service, often following the kings and emperors on the field of battle. The feudal, military character of society was such that not even Gregory VII could escape its influence. On the contrary, he was constrained by his own policy to confront the adversaries of the Papacy by armed force. In this he was aided by the Countess Mathilda of Canossa, who fought in his defence and in defence of the popes who succeeded him, and who, by the donation of her lands to the Holy See, helped to enlarge its territory. Other motives of war sprang from the Norman conquest of Southern Italy. Gregory VII, like his predecessors, as occasion demanded, now favoured, now combated the policy of the new conquerors. These had obtained from the popes a feudal title and Roger of Sicily—who sought to latinise the island, till then mainly greco-byzantine in its rites and in its relations with the ecclesiastical hierarchy, in so far as was allowed by the Saracens who dominated there—had obtained the title of Legate Apostolic. Gregory, who feared that the power of the Normans might become a menace to the Holy See, wished to limit it in Southern Italy to Apulia.

The struggles were very bitter, and he himself was defeated and put to flight. He died in exile at Salerno (1085), the champion of a vast programme of reform rather than of the method imposed on him by the conditions of the age.

His successors carried on both programme and method, with the adaptations and developments necessary. The plan of Paschal II, which had found the reforming currents unprepared for it, had no sequel. But what could not be obtained by a formidable renunciation, would come about little by little with the course of time, like a worn-out garment that is laid aside as no longer corresponding to social requirements. Dimly and confusedly, the idea remained. Half a century later (1159) when Adrian IV requested Frederick Barbarossa not to exact feudal tribute from the bishops of Northern Italy, the Emperor replied that he was ready to agree if the bishops spontaneously renounced their regalia. Earlier than that Innocent II, on the occasion of the coronation of Lothair II (1133), had forbidden the German bishops and abbots 'to seize or usurp the regalia of their offices except from the Emperor's grant'. The legal positions were unchanged, but the spirit behind them was somewhat different. As political power became more and more centralised, public administration would assume an impersonal legal character, the lawyers would be laymen, fortresses would be transformed into towns, and a rich burgess class would come into being. But the Church as a whole was so bound up with the feudal system that she was constrained to make this the basis of her activity, claiming for herself the supreme sum of powers, and seeking more and more to become the term of unification in the international diarchy of Papacy and Empire.

§ 11.—Before Gregory VII there had been other popes who proclaimed their power to be above that of kings and emperors, or threatened to depose princes, whatever their rank. But when Gregory VII, in fulfilment of the threat, deposed Henry IV, released his subjects from their oath of allegiance and made him go a penitent to Canossa, the concrete and resounding fact threw the theory of papal power over kings into such relief (especially in the century following), as to create a belief that Gregory was its author. It was thus made to appear as an unheard-of novelty, to be considered (according to the point of view) either as the logical culmination of the supreme *Sacerdotium*, or else as a usurpation of powers, an arbitrary abuse, an act of violence.

The deposing of kings or princes was a structural element of the teutonic political community. The idea of the divine right of kings had not yet entered the consciousness of feudal society; instead that of community or corporation had taken shape, grafted on to the Christian conception of the religious community, the Church. Although the deposing of an emperor would stir the whole of Europe, the action of Gregory VII did not go beyond the sociological framework of the time; it was an historical development, which would subsequently be crystallised in juridical form.

Henry IV in his defence, contesting Gregory's right to depose him, admitted that kings might be deposed for heresy, according to the tradition of the Fathers, which taught, he said that he 'could be judged only by God' and 'could not be deposed for any offence, save touching faith'.[1] The fact remains that traditionally, and in the parlance of the time, simony was called heresy. Gregory's argument begins where that of the Emperor's advocates leaves off. He worked out his idea not so much on the plane of the penitential laws of the Church (though he quotes Theodosius and St. Ambrose and inflicted on Henry the harsh penance of Canossa), as on the plane of the religious social order. 'The Christian religion so proceeds that the royal power is steered, after God, by the care and dispensation of the apostolic dignity'.[2] Thus his Epistle VII. And while Leo IX, in order to uphold the 'earthly Empire' and the 'royal Priesthood' of the Apostolic See of Rome, appeals to the pretended Donation of Constantine,[3] Gregory VII eschews such arguments, since for him the universal social authority of the Church is founded not on any human concession but on a divine dispensation. The power given to St. Peter to bind and loose leads Gregory to see the Papacy as the apex of all powers on earth. Turning

[1] Soli Deo judicandum docuit, nec pro aliquo crimine, nisi a fide, quod absit, exorbitaverim depondeum asseruit.' (*Mon. Germ. Hist.*, Legum, Sec. IV, Const. Vol. I, p. 62.)

[2] Religio sic se movet christiana ut cura et dispensatione apostolicae dignitatis post Deum gubernetur regia. (Greg. VII, Ep. Coll.)

[3] Epist. C. to the Patriarch of Constantinople.

to the members of the Roman Synod of 1080, after the second deposition of Henry IV, he adjures them thus: 'So act, I beg you, most holy Fathers and Princes, that the whole world may understand and know that if you can bind and loose in heaven, on earth you can grant or withhold—according to each man's merits—empires, kingdoms, principalities, duchies, marquisates, counties and the possessions of all men. For you often take from depraved and unworthy men patriarchates, primateships and archbishoprics, to give them to men of religion. If then you judge in things spiritual, should you not be deemed competent to judge in things temporal?[1]

Between the conception of Peter Damiani and that of Gregory VII there was a notable difference. While conceiving the imperial or royal power as within and not outside Christendom, like all writers from the IX century onward, Peter Damiani held to the Gelasian theory of the relative independence of two co-operating powers, so that the secular power was subordinate to the ecclesiastical simply and solely in spiritual matters. Gregory VII, on the contrary, holding that the independent and co-operant duality of *Sacerdotium* and *Regnum* led to the preponderance of the latter (as had happened from Otto I to Henry III), and hence made the Church in practice dependent on the secular power, introduced the theory that the secular power was dependent on the Church. He thus transferred the preponderance from Empire to Papacy, not only in theory but in fact.

To this conception he was impelled especially by the idea of Christendom that had taken shape from Charlemagne onwards, as the unity of Christian society under the two-fold order, spiritual and temporal. This unity could not be real unless the *Sacerdotium*, pre-eminent in dignity and ends, unified the diarchy as ultimate and resolvent power. Therefore he did not feel he was encroaching on the royal or imperial power; on the contrary he believed that he was remaining within his

---

[1] 'Agite nunc quaeso, patres et principes sanctissimi, ut omnes mundus intelligat et cognoscat, quia si potestis in coelo ligare et solvere, potestis in terra imperia regna principatus ducatus marchias comitatus et omnium hominum possessiones pro meritis tollere unicuique et concedere. Vos enim patriarchatus primatus archiepiscopatus frequenter tulistis pravis et indignis, et religiosis viris dedistis. Si enim spiritualia udicatis, quid de saecularibus vos posse credendum est?' (Greg. VII, Ep. Coll., vol. VII, p. 14.)

own religious sphere. The struggle upon which he had entered had a religious character and ends. The power he claimed to him was sacerdotal, in its highest and fullest expression. If he claimed the right to depose kings, release subjects from their oath, allocate kingdoms to those who were worthy, arbitrate on political or economico-political questions (the attribution of fiefs), he did so for religious ends. And thus he widened the significance of St. Peter's power to bind and loose, making it extend to temporal matters. This cannot be said to be a Hildebrandine invention, for various pronouncements of popes and writers in the previous period tend towards such an extension. Nicholas I (858-67) had seen in St. Peter's two swords a symbol of the corporal sword with which he struck Malchus and the spiritual one with which he struck Ananias. Peter Damiani himself, who did not like to see popes and bishops involved in worldly matters, had written that Christ 'committed to the blessed Bearer of the Keys of eternal life the rights of both the earthly and heavenly empire',[1] but he did not mean to extend the 'rights of earthly empire' to cover the temporal power of kings.

But controversy over the acts of Gregory VII led still further, and both powers were called in question. Henry IV in his letter to the Bishops of Germany in 1076, interpreting the symbol of the two swords, attributed the spiritual sword to the pope and the temporal sword to the emperor, while he denounced the 'madness of Hildebrand' in 'destroying the economy established by God'.[2] Gregory for his part the same year was writing to Bishop Hermann of Metz : 'But perhaps they think the royal dignity excels that of a bishop. From the origins of these they may gather how much each differs from the other. The former was invented by human pride, the latter instituted by divine piety. The former is incessantly seeking vain glory, the latter always aspiring to celestial life'.[3] To the same bishop he wrote in 1081, in-

[1]'Qui beato vitae aeternae Clavigero terreni simul et caelestis imperii jura commisit.'

[2]*Mon Germ. Hist.*, Const. I, p. 112.

[3]'Sed forte putant quod regia dignitas episcopalem praecellat. Ex earum principiis colligere possunt quantum a se utraque differunt. Illam quidem superbia humana repperit, hanc divina pietas instituit. Illa vanam gloriam incessantur captat, hæc ad coelestem vitam semper aspirat.' (Greg. VII, Registrum IV, p. 2.)

sisting on the historical origin of the secular power: 'Who does not
know that kings and dukes originated with those who, ignorant of
God, by pride, rapine, perfidy, homicides, in a word by almost every
crime, egged on by the prince of the world who is the devil, in blind
cupidity and intolerable presumption affected dominion over men
their equals?'[1] This thesis of the origin of power (which is a clear echo
of certain Fathers and ecclesiastical writers who made it a consequence
of Original Sin) was inspired merely by polemical motives, but it
obscurely precluded the thesis of the necessity of priestly mediation if
worldly power was to become moral and Christian, a thesis that would
be worked out with its full bearings by Inocent IV. In the meantime the
conception of papal power in temporal matters on a religious and
ecclesiastical basis (which would be known as 'direct power' *in temporalibus*) was taking shape.

On the other side, the resistance of the imperialists to the decisions of
Gregory VII accentuated the theory that the power of kings comes
from God, to the point of making it imply (as it had not done before)
that the king's conduct could not be called in judgment and that the
person invested with such power could not be removed. With time
these elements would form the theory of the Divine Right of Kings.
The starting-point of the two juridical theories, the 'direct power' of
the popes and the 'divine right' of kings, is to be found in the positions
taken up by Gregory VII and Henry IV. This does not mean that we do
not encounter vague indications of these theories in the preceding
period, and we have noted traces of them here and there. But events
precede juridical formulas. The unification of the international diarchy,
first in the Empire then in the Papacy, anticipates the conflict and
creates it ; the successive theoretical formulations lay down the limits
of the actual positions reached by Papacy and Empire. Juridical recognition is posterior to the trend of the diarchy towards unification
and to the necessity for unification felt now by vigorous emperors, now
by combative popes of genius. It is this necessity that is reflected on

---

[1]'Quis nesciat reges et duces ab iis habuisse principium, qui, Deum ignorantes,
superbia, rapinis, perfidia, homicidiis, postremo universis pene sceleribus, mundi
principe diabolo videlicet agitante, super pares, scilicet homines, dominare cacca
cupidine et intolerabili praesumptione affectaverunt?' (*Id.* VIII, 21.)

the religious plane as the theory now of the divine origin of royal power, now of an unlimited concession made by Christ to St. Peter.

In the Gelasian period, when for the unification of the Christianised Roman empire men looked towards Byzance, it was not long before the position was legally formulated in Justinian's *Corpus Juris*, and other books assembling and welding together the principles of a Roman Law combined with Christian law. Again, in the Carolingian period the principles of the *Liber Canonum* given by Adrian I to Charlemagne become general; it is followed by the *Pseudo-Isidoriana*. In the same way in the Hildebrandine period, when the unification of Christendom comes to focus round the Papacy, the result is the canonical collection that would serve as basis to the culture of the age and form the juridical groundwork of the West for many centuries, indeed, up to the modern legal codes. The *concordia discordantium canonum* of Gratian, a monk of Bologna, which appeared between 1140 and 1150, while not authorised was received and adopted as though it were, and became the standard work under the name of Gratian's *Decretum*. It was followed by various *Collectiones*, made by private authors for the use of the schools, and finally by the official codification of Raymond of Pennaforte (1234) compiled and arranged by order of Gregory IX, to be followed in its turn by yet others equally official, up to those of Boniface VIII and John XXII.

The culture of the centuries that saw the opening of the chief universities of Europe was prevalently religious, based on Scholasticism on the one hand and Canon Law on the other, and this culture formed the battlefield for intellectual and practical combats up to the Renaissance. Dante would complain that the clergy instead of studying the Scriptures and the Fathers studied the Decretals. In this there was some polemical exaggeration; in actual fact the Decretals constituted the legal crystallisation of the ecclesiastical power.

From Frederick Barbarossa onwards, the emperors and kings sought to counter Canon Law by a series of constitutions and affirmations vindicating their independence and even superiority. Legists had an important place in their suites and animated the controversies of the time. In such documents the renaissance of Roman Law and re-affirmations of feudal law combined with scriptural exegesis and echoes of the Fathers. But it would take two centuries of controversy and conflict to change public opinion. In these two centuries the consolidation of Canon Law and of the unification not only moral but also juridical of all Christendom in the Papacy, though opposed on particular points, from the point of view of the social organism would become complete.

§ 12.—Between the end of the XI century and the beginning of the XII we find various factors at work that would alter the social structure of the age. Above all, the expansion of municipal life which helps to give the burgess class a personality and initiative of its own, making it independent of the armed aristocracy and of the feudalised and court-bound circles of ecclesiastics. The communal corporation or 'universitas' as a federation of the various guilds or corporations of arts and crafts, the distinction between categories of citizens, each sharing in a diverse manner in civic life, the development of the Commune into a political State and the federation of the Communes for war and peace are a specifically Italian product. But under different aspects and with varied interaction of feudal, ecclesiastical and burgess forces, we find similar phenomena in Provence and in parts of France and Spain, in the Rhineland and in Central Europe—in the countries where small civic industries, trade and traffic, schools and universities were growing up, for all this demanded classes unhampered by feudal subjection, and an articulated economy.

As little by little the Communes emerged from the economic and municipal sphere into that of politics (as they were driven to do by the situation of the time, the need for security and the jealousy between neighbouring cities), they were drawn into the orbit of either Empire or Papacy, no longer as feudal vassals but as partisans or allies. The idea of liberty that grew up in the Commune was that of the freedom of the communal body, a corporate freedom, that rendered it self-governing in its administration and free, by right of immunity, from the feudal system. It meant the conquest of economic freedom within the guild, of municipal freedom within the Commune, of political freedom in the City State, and even of a certain religious freedom, both in the sense of non-dependence on the Church as a politico-ecclesiastical power, and also of a practical freedom in giving shelter to the heretical sects that grew up within them.

The very necessity of guarding these conquests and defending them against troublesome and overweening neighbours, as well as against pope or emperor, divided the communes according to whether they looked to pope or emperor as protecting power. In half a century the municipalities of Northern Italy would be in a position to face Frederick Barbarossa and force him to surrender. The moral starting-point of the transformation comes from Gregory VII. He more than once released the subjects of Henry IV from their oath, appealing to the people against their king and emperor; he increased the papal power in Central Italy with the help of the Countess Mathilda; he gave new consciousness to the people and burgesses, rousing them against feudal lords in conflict with the Church and against the simoniac bishops.

The old seafaring cities of the Mediterranean and Adriatic, which had kept their autonomy and personality through the centuries, whether under Byzance or under the Franks and Germans, now received a new strength and a new impulse from the municipal movement of Northern and Middle Italy, and they too took part in the struggle between Guelf and Ghibelline, with a colouring now orthodox now heretical.

Another factor of change was the Crusades to free the Holy Sepulchre from the Mussulmans and to check their advance, which threatened the Greek Empire. The Crusades on the one hand diverted the energies of the nobles and military classes of feudalism, and this facilitated the development of industrious classes of craftsmen and traders and swelled the ranks of the bourgeoisie. On the other hand they enhanced the prestige of the Roman See and made the Papacy the authorised champion of the West against the infidel peril, and the representative of Christendom before all faithful peoples, princes and emperors. And since the main contribution to the Crusades came from the Franks, these would later become the founders of the Latin Empire of the Levant (in spite of the fact that emperors such as Frederick Barbarossa and Frederick II were leaders of Crusades); in Europe the predominance of the Kingdom of France is already foreshadowed.

The foundation of the orders of chivalry of an hospitaller character (the Templars are of 1123, the Hospitallers proper of 1130) was the beginning of those active, autonomous confraternities which, whether military or purely religious, would acquire an important function in the XIII century through both their numbers and character. Directly or indirectly they would contribute to the disintegration of the feudal structure, just as the municipalities so contributed from the XII century onwards. The orders of chivalry regimented many members of the feudal nobility in autonomous organisms that would soon become rich and powerful. Also the colonising monks and the religious brotherhoods would acquire autonomy and power among the people of the countryside, who because of their lamentable economic situation were often in ferment against the big feudatories, whether lay or ecclesiastic. The struggle of the popes and monks against simoniac and concubinary bishops and prelates was a popular struggle, for such clerics held church property and benefices, and made themselves odious to the people by their exaction of tithes, tolls and other feudal dues. Commune, people, monks and friars, were shaking the foundations of the society of the time.

Another factor of remarkable importance was the schools, which in the XII century multiplied rapidly—a mixture of individualism and of a corporatism *sui generis*—attracting youth that was athirst for knowledge. The intellectual reawakening had unlooked-for consequences. All traditional knowledge is re-examined, the principle of authority is re-debated, human society analysed afresh. Culture is religious and will remain so; hence the intellectual, moral and social problems are seen in the light of religious values. In spite of this, there is a tendency towards an autonomy of reason, which at once alarms the rulers of the Church, even though often they too hunger for the new. The forerunners of Scholasticism, Anselm of Aosta, Roscelin, Gilbert de la Porrée, William of Champeaux, and, with wider influence, Peter Abelard and Peter Lombard, dominate the culture of the age and represent the innovators and renovators of culture, in the face of the patristic and mystical tradition of the Victorines and of St. Bernard.

The last-named had a special role and a special influence. The formation of the ever-growing group of Cistercian monks, detached from honours and office, brought into touch with peasants and serfs (who were often abandoned or at the mercy of inhuman lords, lay and ecclesiastic), intent on the colonisation of the land and the development of agriculture, was of great moral and economic benefit and contributed to social evolution.

Bernard, while not ceasing to be a monk and a rigorous ascetic, stood in the midst of a world in ferment. In the humble work of his agricultural monks, in the preaching of the Crusade for the liberation of the Holy Sepulchre, in the foundation and development of the knightly orders, in the rebirth of the Communes, in the debates of the schools, in the repression of heresies whether intellectual or popular, in the struggle against lay investiture or against schisms, in all that was seething in the first half of the XII century we find Bernard taking up position, encouraging, resisting, anticipating, foreseeing, fighting. His figure is gigantic, in its lights as in its shadows; he was able to unite in himself the two permanent forces of the Church, the mystical and the organisational, and to impel them to mighty realisations.

He might seem a grim conservative in his struggle against the new elements that were arising, rational scholasticism and the free communes, but it was principally a religious defence that drove him against Aþelard and against Arnold of Brescia. His patristic and mystical culture cuts a deep furrow; it would remain fruitful for centuries by the side of triumphant Scholasticism and would provide a vital nourishment when Scholasticism had become an arid concatenation of syllogisms. To the Communes Bernard would bring forces of renewal and vital elements, through the agricultural and artisan classes redeemed by the numerous colonies of Cistercians. The failure of the Crusade was the grief of his last years, but by the impulse he gave to the foundation of the chivalrous Orders (to which he gave powerful support and wise rules), he prepared the way for the subsequent crusades and wars against Islam.

The figure of Bernard assumes a singular aspect in the controversies of the time over the *Sacerdotium* and the *Regnum* and over the spiritual position of the Papacy. As champion of the unity of the Church and of Christendom, he fought vigorously against the schism of Anacletus

II and ensured the triumph of the legitimate pope, Innocent II. He sought always to reconcile the dissident princes of every country with the Papacy. His conception was prevalently religious, like all the con- ceptions of the age, but he does not reach the complete political unification of Christendom in the Papacy; he sees the two powers, the spiritual and the temporal, as distinct and co-ordinated within the Christian unity, neither confounding them nor making one derive from the other.

Bernard is on the lines of Peter Damiani, both in proclaiming the spiritual superiority of the pope over princes, kings and emperors and in refusing to the Church the direct use of material power. The famous passage that has divided St. Bernard's commentators, who have used and abused his immense authority, runs as follows: '*Uterque Ecclesiae, et spiritualis scilicet gladius et materialis; sed is quidam pro Ecclesia ille vero et ab Ecclesia exercendus; ille sacerdotis manu, is militis manu, sed sane ad nutum sacerdotis et iussum imperatoris.*'[1] St. Bernard inserts this passage in his *De Consideratione* where he is speaking of the pastoral ministry of the Pope in Rome towards his people and his court, where there are many who are not sheep but 'dragons' and 'scorpions'. These must be attacked 'by the word, not by the sword—*verbo non ferro*'. It is here that Bernard opens a parenthesis to say that the Church has the power of the material sword, to be wielded by the hand not of the priest but of the warrior at a sign from the priest and on the order of the Emperor.

He is referring rather to the coercive power of the Church than to her political power, though the passage was interpreted to extend to the political power. This seems foreign to Bernard's mind, as mani- fested in other passages of his writings. But since this idea had been ripening for two hundred years, his symbolic crystallisation of it in the two swords would henceforth remain, as a theological proof drawn from the Gospel, while the interpretation, as was natural, would be swayed by subsequent polemics.

If the passage is compared with the similar one in the Bull *Unam*

[1]*De Consideratione*, Bk. IV, Ch. III, p. 7. 'Both are of the Church, the spiritual sword and the material, but the one is to be exercised only for the Church, the other also by the Church, the one by the hand of the priest, the other by the hand of the warrior, but at a sign from the priest and on the order of the Emperor.'

*Sanctam* of Boniface VIII, we see that this follows it word for word, but there are two changes that reveal a diversity of thought. Where Bernard writes '*militis manu*' Boniface corrects it to '*manu regum et militum*'—in the hands of kings and warriors, so that kings are reckoned as executors. And where Bernard writes: '*ad nutum sacerdotis et iussum imperatoris*'—at a sign from the priest and on the order of the emperor, thus marking the duality of powers and functions even in their co-operation, Boniface corrects it to : '*ad nutum et patientiam sacerdotis*—at the sign and on the sufferance of the priest.' For Boniface, the supreme function remains with the pontiff alone.

St. Bernard in his letters and in the treatise 'On Consideration', which was addressed to his beloved disciple Paganelli of Pisa, when he became pope under the name of Eugene III, subjects the Roman Curia and the Roman people to pitiless criticism, and attacks the system of centralising all kinds of temporal business. Certainly he would have agreed with Paschal II over the feudal rights of the popes and bishops. In the first pages of his treatise he notes satirically that no apostle sat 'as a judge of men or a divider of boundaries or a distributor of lands— *iudex hominum aut divisor terminorum aut distributor terrarum*'. As an ascetic and mystic, on the lines of Benedict, Romuald and Bruno, he wanted a detachment from the earthly world that seethed round popes, cardinals and bishops. But, unlike those others, as an active organiser and keen fighter, standing at the side of the authorities of the Church or of the Empire, sitting among them as an abbot of his age, he sought to harmonise detachment with action, spirituality with power, humility with authority, frank and free criticism with respect for the hierarchy. According to him popes and bishops should not concern themselves with secular questions nor trespass on the domain of kings and emperors, but the latter should be subordinate to the spiritual principles of the Church. When the Emperor Lothair II met Innocent II at Liege and, to the consternation of the Roman clergy in the papal suite, asked him to restore the rights of investiture, Bernard alone stood up to him with authority and boldness, and avoided the new ambush.

The *De Consideratione* in medieval patristic culture took a place immediately after Augustine's *Civitas Dei*. A book of less breadth and brilliance than that of Augustine, it was still the voice of a great saint and of a genius, who stood for the reform of the hierarchy and of the clergy, who anticipated the criticisms of orthodox faithful and fanatical heretics, and who in the moment of great earthly power recalled popes and prelates to the reality of their spiritual function and of the necessity of moral detachment and ascetic purification to raise them up to God. In his treatises and in his letters we do not find the wide politico-religious vistas of the canonical construction of the time, but the chief place is given to the spirit of religious reform and to the renewal of the pastoral ministry of bishops and popes. Bernard's activity, his thought, his teaching, impregnated with mysticism, would remain fruitful in the centuries to come, but in the period immediately following him, the politico-organisational stream in the Church, through the practical demands of society, was becoming ever stronger and seeking to achieve the widest possible power over the world.

# CHAPTER IV

## PAPACY AND EMPIRE

### SECOND PERIOD (1153-1313)

§ 13.—The year of the death of St. Bernard nearly coincides with the accession to the throne of Frederick I of Swabia, known as Barbarossa. A new and more serious conflict was shortly to arise between Papacy and Empire. A first foretaste of it was the dispute with Pope Adrian IV (the English Pope) over an ambiguous phrase, which irritated Barbarossa and his legists and agitated Germany and Italy for a year. Pope Adrian IV in 1157, in recalling the favours received by the Emperor from the Papacy in regard to his election and coronation the previous year, used the word *beneficium*, which had then a double sense, and Barbarossa resented it as implying that the Empire could be considered a papal fief and the Emperor a vassal. He took the occasion of asserting his independence of a pope who did no more than give religious consecration to the Emperor-Elect, and he explicitly re-affirmed the divine origin of the imperial power. But though such questions were of considerable significance, for the moment they gave place to others more strictly political, which concerned Italy.

The Norman conquest of Southern Italy and Sicily from the Byzantines and Saracens, was a cause of much anxiety to the Popes, who in defence of their own possessions, or because of local religious interests, or in assertion of various titles of feudal sovereignty, had shown themselves now hostile, now favourable to the conquerors. Above all, they had always opposed the formation of a single kingdom embracing the whole of the South. Nevertheless, after Roger II had been invested with the entire kingdom by the anti-Pope Anacletus, Pope Innocent II, in order to avoid any prolongation of the schism, was forced to bow to circumstances and grant him recognition. The more so in that the legacy of Countess Mathilda was still a burning question between

Popes and Emperors, and other problems were arising through the communal awakening in the North and the revolts of the barons of the South. Communes and barons turned now to the Pope now to the Emperor, seeking protection and aid. Little by little the local factions under the aegis of Papacy or Empire assumed a general character and became known as Guelfs and Ghibellines. In their turn, the Macedonian Emperors of Byzance sought on several occasions to drive the Normans from their positions in the Adriatic. While the Germanic emperors thrust towards the South and Sicily, by armed force and intrigues and marriage, in order to ensure dominion over all Italy, the popes, who as temporal sovereigns now possessed the whole of Central Italy and were feudal lords of the South, Sicily, Sardinia and Corsica, and who as pontiffs politically controlled all Christendom, were constrained to take part in the game of influences and wars of which Italy was the theatre.

Such was the political background of the struggle between Frederick I and Alexander III, which would last from 1159 to 1177. Alexander was accused of complicity, before he became Pope, in the conspiracy of the Normans and the city of Milan against the Emperor. He was therefore to be deemed a felon and ineligible. A minority among the Cardinals chose another pope, Victor IV, and battle was engaged over the most delicate of questions, which was the true Pope. Barbarossa, a belated Constantine, called a General Council at Pavia to judge between the two. It was only natural that the true Pope should refuse so uncanonical a judgment; the Council was held and decided in favour of the anti-Pope. Though both Council and Frederick protested that there had been no lay interference, the Acts of the Council show plainly a political anxiety at the separation of Italy from the Empire and the dualism between Imperial Germany and Guelf Italy. This dualism persists through the whole period of the conflict, which became a schism with the various anti-popes. Gerhoh of Reichersberg, a contemporary writer, though a champion of the papal authority, took the side of the anti-popes. He attacked, as St. Bernard did, the morals of the Roman Curia, maintained the Gelasian thesis of a duality of powers, and was hostile to the whole political movement of the Normans in the South and of Milan in the North, which the popes of the time encouraged.

He approved of the calling of the Council, because he saw no other way for Alexander to clear himself of the charge of having intrigued against the Emperor by promising the Sicilians and Milanese to excommunicate him if he himself were elected Pope.

Alexander III is the true successor of Gregory VII. On the one hand, he asserted his papal right not to be judged by either Council or Emperor. One the other, he based his resistance on the people and the Communes in the name of religion and freedom. He thus struck a formidable blow at the old feudalism; an organic, communal conception replaces the purely hierarchic and feudal one. The burgesses and craftsmen become classes fighting in the name of liberty; the war is waged not by nobles and professional soldiers alone, but by the people.

The Lombard League put up a tenacious resistance to Frederick Barbarossa. Milan was razed to the ground, but Barbarossa was defeated at Legnano. In 1177 he was reconciled with the Pope at Venice. As he submitted, he pronounced the famous sentence: '*Non tibi sed Petro!*' To which the Pope replied: '*Et mihi et Petro!*' John of Salisbury, interpreting events as a theologian, enlarged on the theory of the papal supremacy. He approved the deposition of Barbarossa by Alexander III: '*Eius est auferre qui jura conferre potest*'.[1] But if John of Salisbury has a religious conception of the papal power as supreme and derived from the privilege granted to St. Peter, he, like St. Bernard and Gerhoh of Reichersberg, bitterly deplores the avarice of the clergy, the ecclesiastical wealth employed in struggles and wars, the disputes over feudal and material questions, the relaxation of discipline, the crumbling, abandoned churches.[2] But the rebuilding of the churches, with popular

[1] 'It is for him to take away rights who is able to confer them.'

[2] It was during the papacy of Alexander III that the conflict arose between Henry II of England and Thomas Becket, Archbishop of Canterbury, over the competence of ecclesiastical courts in criminal matters. Henry wished that any ecclesiastic recognised as guilty of an offence should be handed over to the royal power and condemned as a layman. He forced Thomas to subscribe to the Constitutions of Clarendon, which settled the dispute in accordance with the King's wishes. But the Archbishop was able to get the Pope to release him from his oath, as forced from him under threat of death, and fled to Vézelay for refuge. In his absence the bishops took the side of the King, whereupon the Pope sent letters depriving them; these he had consigned to Thomas who, returning to England, began to put them into execution. It was then a Norman law that no one might communicate with the Pope without the royal consent, a law

fervour, artistic ideals and generosity of offerings, was even then beginning, coinciding with the renewal of communal life and the re-assertion of ecclesiastical independence. It is the period of the Norman cathedrals, soon to be followed by the first ogival cathedrals of France and Germany and those of the Lombard-Romanesque school of Northern Italy.

Barely twenty years separate the reconciliation in Venice (1177) from the election of Innocent III in 1198. It was then that the theory of papal dominion was most precisely formulated and most fully carried into effect. After over a century of struggle, from Gregory VII on-wards, the idea of the subordination of the royal or imperial power to the Pope had penetrated the consciousness of the time. The opposition of jurists or dissenting canonists was on the juridical plane of limits and facts, but did not prejudice the prevailing conception, to which kings and emperors submitted, even while they fought against it. The deposition of Henry IV and of Frederick Barbarossa were still living examples, though judgment on the facts might be favourable or un-favourable. Innocent III could without difficulty become the arbiter of the whole of the West, overcome opposition and reassert the rights of the Holy See against princes and hostile peoples. The social structure corresponded to this concept of religious unification, while already local forces were developing, kingdoms and communes gaining in cohesion, the burgess class organising, and the populace in ferment.

Innocent III defined the character and limits of the papal power in unequivocal terms[1]—The papal power over temporal things is great and

that the Church had always refused to recognise. Henry II, who was in France, was enraged at the papal intervention. And four knights, believing they were serving the King, left the court, went to Canterbury, and ordered the Archbishop to absolve the bishops and to restore them to their sees. When Thomas refused they killed him. The people were on the side of the Archbishop, and Henry II, to avoid a conflict with the Pope, gave way over the Constitutions of Clarendon and promised to restore the property he had confiscated from Canterbury—he submitted to the penance of the scourge, laid on his naked shoulders by seventy monks.

[1](i) 'Romanus Pontifex . . . non solum in spiritualibus habet summam, verum etiam in temporalibus magnam ab ipso Domino potestatem.' (Ep. VIII )

(ii) 'Non solum in Ecclesiae patrimonio, super quo plenam in temporalibus, gerimus potestatem, verum etiam in aliis regionibus, temporalem potestatem casualiter exercemus.' (Ep. V.)

was given by the Lord, (St. Peter's privilege). It is complete over the Patrimony, and over other countries is to be exercised as occasion arises. The basis of this power is not feudal (save in the cases of special privilege or custom), but moral and religious: *ratione peccati*. The Empire, in its origin and its *raison d'être*, derives from the Papacy. Such are the main lines of the thought of Innocent III.

In modern times an attempt has been made to find in the famous sentence, '*Non intendimus iudicare de feudo . . . sed decernere de peccato*',[1] the theory known as that of 'indirect power', that is, that the Church possesses power *in temporalibus* only indirectly and as necessary consequence of her moral judgment. But neither the thought nor the practice of Innocent III bears out this theory. The Innocentian conception is the logical outcome of that of Gregory VII and other predecessors, who always claimed a wide and decisive power over Christendom, as unifying the social structure in a religious centre which, inasmuch as religious, was also political. This power does not suppress but integrates that of the Emperor. The duality does not disappear but acquires distinct characteristics. The diarchy is international, but unified by the religious spirit, and by the dependence, organic and finalistic, of the Empire on the Papacy.[2]

(iii) 'Non enim intendimus iudicare de feudo, cuius ad ipsum (regem) spectat iudicium, nisi forte iuri communi per speciale privilegium vel contrariam consuetudinem aliquid sit detractum, sed decernere de peccato, cuius ad nos pertinet sine dubitatione censura, quam in quemlibet exercere possumus et debemus.' (Ep. VII.)

(iv) The Empire depends on the Papacy 'principaliter et finaliter.' (Reg. super Neg., R., Imp. 29.)

[1] 'We do not intend to judge of feudal matters, but to sift out sin.'

[2] To the pontificate of Innocent III (1198–1216) belongs not only the crusade against Raymond of Toulouse and the Albigensians but that against King John of England, which ended in his submission. John claimed that since the Archbishop of Canterbury was nearly always Chancellor of the Realm, he should be appointed by the King. The monks of Canterbury wished to elect him, as their head; so too the Bishops of England, as their primate. All three appealed to the Pope, who himself made the choice, excellent in every respect, of Stephen Langton. As an answer, John confiscated the property of the Archbishopric. Innocent III laid an interdict on the kingdom, and since John would not give way, excommunicated him and finally authorised Philip Augustus of France to lead a crusade against him. John was forced to surrender his crown to the Pope's Legate (to receive it back as a vassal of the Holy See), and to accept the new archbishop the Pope had appointed.

It is to this episodal conflict that England owes *Magna Carta* and the beginning of

§ 14.—In the conception and activities of Innocent, in spite of the experiences of Gregory VII and Alexander III, the people have no place. They had acquired a consciousness of their own in the Communes, as an *élite* in process of selection, an organism in process of formation, but the masses were still amorphous, uncertain, suffering from the economic and legal conditions in which they were placed by feudalism, and aspiring to a liberation which, given the mental habits of the time, was conceived in religious terms. In this atmosphere there was a widespread flowering of such movements as the orders of friars on the one hand, culminating in Franciscanism, and on the other the heretical sects, secret or public.

The reappearance of heresies in the XI century, when the old heresies could be said to be extinct and the Latin world had been able to hold its own against the subtle and restless thought of the Greeks, was not due to theological controversies or currents in the schools, but sprang from mystical and social factors among the people.

The Cathars of Northern Italy, who in Provence and Languedoc were known as Albigensians, present themselves as anti-social secret sects infected with a combination of Manicheanism and Gnosticism. The tenuous veins of such infiltrations go back to the IV and V centuries; but in the XI century social factors giving a new impetus and wide development to the old theories were ripened by events. The struggle of Peter Damiani and Hildebrand against the married and simoniac clergy was extremely popular for various reasons. Such clergy were often rich and powerful, they took the tithes (always hateful to the people) and other dues for maintaining numerous families and a re-

her liberties, and France the beginning of the unification of the realm under the Capets. John thought to revenge himself on Philip Augustus and entered into coalition with Otto of Brunswick and the Count of Flanders, but his barons refused to follow him because he had not yet been absolved from excommunication. In spite of this he pursued his campaign and was defeated in 1214 at Bouvines. It was this defeat that enabled the King of France to regain a large portion of the lands possessed by England (except Gascony and the port of Bordeaux), and the English barons to oblige John to sign the Great Charter in 1215—a thing he would never have done had he returned victorious from France. John appealed to Innocent III to release him from his oath so that he could withdraw his signature. The Pope was indignant at the armed revolt and laid an interdict on London, but Archbishop Langton took the part of the burgesses and did not observe the interdict!

tinue of servants and men-at-arms, according to feudal requirements. Such clergy, in the period of the Investiture Conflicts, were often excommunicated; they were centres of party strife; the reformers, priests and laymen, instigated the people not to receive the sacraments from simoniac and concubinary bishops or priests. Popular agitation in this delicate matter often led to unheard of excesses and sacrileges. On the other hand, it was debated whether the sacraments could be validly administered by excommunicated clergy, or even those who were simoniac, or reputed as such. Naturally there were no bounds to the discussions and popular agitation that ensued. Doubt was cast on the spiritual value of liturgical worship, on the Sacraments themselves, on purgatory, on the hierarchic order of the Church. And since the abuses came from the wealth of the clergy, the reformers preached against their avarice and in favour of Christian poverty. The attack on ecclesiastical riches was general. With the poorer people were united the lower clergy, often wretched, treated as serfs by the lay or clerical patrons of churches and chapels. Reform was preached in the market-places and streets; even women joined the throngs preaching the reform of the Church. It was not hard for even orthodox reformers to touch the borders of heresy. The Patarines of Northern Italy, who were originally anti-simoniac, came to mingle with the Cathars and other heretics of manichean tendencies. In France towards the end of the XI century and the beginning of the XII, Peter of Bruys and Henry of Toulouse stirred up Dauphiné and Languedoc, while in Champagne and Flanders there were Eon de l'Etoile and the Apostolicals.

The leaven was everywhere working, and was chiefly anti-social, that is, contrary to the social structure seen under a religious aspect. The economico-political order of the time was repudiated by anti-Catholic and anti-dogmatic arguments. At bottom, there was a repudiation of the Church as a hierarchic and social order and of her sacramental institutions, because of her predominant share in wealth and in political and worldly life. This anti-social reaction easily combined with the instinct of secret societies, and manichean negations of the family and the very propagation of the species, through the pessimistic sense born of the dualistic conception of good and evil as of two absolute entities in perpetual conflict.

For over a century and a half—from the Council of Orleans of 1022 to the Council of Verona of 1184—the struggle against heresy was conducted case by case by the application of local penal laws, disqualification from public office, confiscation of goods, banishment and, occasionally, the stake, which had been introduced by German legislation as the punishment for coining and necromancy. Lucius III, concerned at the spread of heresy, determined, in agreement with the Council of Verona, to send episcopal inquirers—*inquisitores*—to take cognizance of the situation and suggest the most suitable remedies. It was thus that the name of Inquisition arose. The same pope agreed with Frederick Barbarossa on measures to arrest the spread of heresy. The religious interests of the Pope and the political interests of the Emperor coincided; in the struggle against heresy nearly always the kings and emperors showed themselves more zealous and more relentless than the bishops and popes. Frederick II would accuse Gregory IX of protecting heresy because he protected the Communes of Northern Italy, where Cathars and Patarines were numerous and influential. The clergy of France and Germany, likewise, looked with suspicion and disapproval on the support given by the popes to the Italian Communes; for some time these had been the most active centres from which the heretical and reforming currents had spread, invading France, Catalonia, Aragon, Flanders, the Rhineland, Bavaria and Switzerland.

Under Innocent III the struggle against heresy was intensified, especially in Languedoc, whither in 1206 he sent Cistercians in the quality of papal legates to act as inquisitors. This the bishops resented as lessening their authority, and the Count of Toulouse, Raymond VI, adopted so ambiguous an attitude as himself to fall under suspicion of heresy; he was finally excommunicated by the papal legate Pierre de Castelnau. Shortly after, the legate was murdered. It was then that Innocent III proclaimed a war against the Count of Toulouse, and since the King of France had refused to intervene, and, on the other hand, it was necessary to induce lords and followers to take up arms, for the first time the system of a crusade, which up till then had been preached only against the infidels and for the liberation of the Holy Land, was applied to a Christian country. A crusade implied that the war was not only just, according to the theories of the time, but of a sacred character, for a religious end, proclaimed by the Pope and rewarded by spiritual concessions to the crusaders, over and above the temporal advantages they might win by its favourable outcome.

In this particular case, the Albigensian Crusade, led by Simon de Montfort and fought with considerable ferocity, was directed not only against the Count of Toulouse but against the population of heretics or sympathisers with heresy. These were either killed or banished or dispersed, while the dispute that ensued with the Count of Toulouse and the King of France, over the ownership of the captured towns and occupied fiefs, was settled (to the advantage of the King of France) by the Treaty of Paris of 1229.

Historical judgment on the Albigensian War has been rightly severe. Other crusades against heretics or enemies of the Papacy would be proclaimed, among the most notable that of Boniface VIII against the Colonna and those of Martin V against the Hussites of Bohemia. The essential principle of a crusade (against heretics or infidels) as a war justified in itself has been frequently called in question, and there are theologians whose answer is definitely in the negative. For our purposes it is sufficient to ascertain how it was that this new form of crusade could arise, and what were its sociological and historical effects.

In the logic of the thought of the time it was easy to transfer the juridical criteria of a religious dispute with kings and emperors to a religious dispute with a city or people. The popes used spiritual weapons against kings and emperors, but they had to defend themselves on the plane of force, on which the feudal structure of society obliged them to fight. In the consciousness of the time both heretical kings and emperors and heretical countries were beyond the pale of Christian society, in the same way as infidels or Saracens. A crusade against the disturbers of Christian order was on the same plane as a crusade against the infidels. The Count of Toulouse was an heretical or semi-heretical prince, his lands were infected with heresy, he was reputed a miscreant and a felon, and since he could not be punished by normal means, war was declared on him. The novelty was not the war in itself; in the past there had been politico-religious wars, but what was new was to apply the system of a crusade to a Christian country, for the purpose of striking down heretics and rendering them powerless. The religious motive and the lack of a direct territorial interest, which only the King of France could claim, were the determining factors.

The heretical currents continued to stir the urban and rural populace throughout Europe. It was Gregory IX who finally transformed the Inquisition from an episcopal into a pontifical institution, organised it in a permanent form, and entrusted it to the Dominicans. Thus all inquisitorial matters were withdrawn from the competence of the bishops and secular courts.

Heresies and erroneous tendencies among the people had another character and bearing from those that came from the professed theologians and the Schools. Yet there was a kind of intrinsic convergence, an unconscious logical nexus that made them akin. Berengarius's error on the Eucharist (1050) and that attributed to Abelard on the Trinity (1121) were certainly far removed from the heresies of the Cathars, but the eucharistic question involved the position of the priesthood as a distinct order of society and that of the Trinity the problems of divine revelation and human reason, of good and evil.

The mystical, apocalyptic movement, which Joachim de Flora (d. 1202) aroused in the second half of the XII century, was not simply a religious dream on the part of the Calabrian Abbot, but a sign of the disquiet of the Christian spirit in an age in which the higher clergy and even the old monasticism were drawn into worldly and secular life by wealth, power, strife, contests and wars. The power of the Church was juridically strong, but from the Christian standpoint it was weak. The papal authority had reached its highest peak in an earthly sense, but this very fact involved heavy counterweights. St. Peter Damiani's harsh reproaches to the avaricious and loose-living clergy, the warnings and lamentations of St. Bernard, summoning bishops and popes to simplicity of life and spiritual detachment, had not sufficed to provoke a reform. The renunciation of feudal power advocated by Pasqual II had come to nothing through the obstacles placed in its way by the clergy themselves, allied with the emperors and kings. The concentration of earthly powers and medieval pomp in the Papacy did nothing to awaken feelings of poverty and detachment in the popular imagination, even though there had been Popes of virtue and sanctity, such as Leo IX, Gregory VII, Victor III, Urban II, Eugene III, and later St. Peter-Celestine. Abbot Joachim de Flora, by an apocalyptic interpretation of Revelation, came forward as the herald and prophet of the *Third Kingdom*, that of the Holy Spirit, in which the Church would have no more wealth and material goods, nor political or coercive powers, but would be spiritualised, in pure poverty, detached from earthly things, in manifestation of the Spirit of Truth. This Third Kingdom of the Holy Spirit was to begin at once, and would be differentiated from the Second Kingdom, of the Son (Christianity of Grace), as this was differentiated from the First Kingdom, of the Father (the Judaism of the Law). The influence of Joachim was extraordinary, in spite of an intricate and over-elaborate symbolism and an apocalyptic vision of history remote from reality, and although the prophesied opening of the Third Kingdom would appear neither on the date fixed for it, nor as an immediate future. Actually, Joachim's conception through his messianic expectancy nourished and sustained the spiritual need of an age in quest of detachment, poverty and abnegation.

It was thus that early Franciscanism arose like a living flower, which cannot but be linked to the potent influence of Abbot Joachim. Together with Franciscanism, other forms of popular associations came into being, based on detachment from the world, but soon to be coloured by another influence, that of the heretical currents or sects and of the anti-social movements seething all over Europe. The spirit of poverty combined with a denunciation of the use of earthly goods; it became a communistic spirit, awakening among the poorer masses, and which by an easy transition became a negation of priesthood and all religious authority. Franciscanism itself had two branches. The chief was the orthodox branch, which while keeping its own personality and popular character, gradually tended to conform to the organisational, intellectualist, ascetic and practical character of the other orders which had arisen or been regularised during the same period, like the Trinitarians, Dominicans, Augustinian Canons Regular, Carmelites, Mercedarians and Servites. The other branch, that of the *Fraticelli*, gradually severed itself from the first, in order to maintain the purity of the Franciscan tradition, but little by little it was tending to become assimilated to the heretical, protestatary, anti-social currents among the people, which adopted various names such as the Hallelujah Brothers, Flagellants, Brothers of Sion, Joachimites, and many others, promoting public penances, preaching reform, and working on the feelings of the masses. Sincere men in good faith and turbulent rogues were confounded in this heated mystical atmosphere, the explosion of which taxed the resources of ecclesiastical discipline and penal rigour.

The anti-social spirit and propaganda against the ecclesiastical structure, together with the ready affirmation of principles held to be heretical, alarmed the established powers, whether popes, emperors, kings, feudal lords or governments of cities. All were agreed upon repression. The Inquisition, unified in the hands of the Pope, had gained considerable power and influence. In this agitated setting, the example of the crusade against the Albigensians weighed heavy. The Bishops had adapted themselves to the régime of the Inquisition. It was a case, in the opinion of the ruling class, of saving society from the peril of the insurgent masses. The words *Fraticelli, Hallelujah Brothers, Apostolicals* sounded then as Communism and Bolshevism sound to modern ears. But a century more would be required before that mass movement, which left behind it notable traces and active ferments, could be suppressed in the name of orthodoxy and social order.

§ 15.—After the reconciliation of Barbarossa and Alexander III at Venice, there had been no further motives for great disputes between Papacy and Empire. Nevertheless, in view of the ever-increasing economic and political progress of the Communes of Northern and Central Italy, and the power of the Normans in the South and Sicily, the Papacy had to concentrate its energies on maintaining a constant balance of forces of which Rome was the hub. The marriage of Henry VI with Constance of Sicily, sister of William I and heiress presumptive to William II, changed the position. The popes feared an encirclement by the Hohenstaufens, and the struggle that ensued became, willy-nilly, more through force of circumstances than fault of men, a war to the death, ending only with the extinction of the race and the passing of Sicily to a Valois king.

Innocent III defended the right of Constance's son Frederick II, who was his ward, to the kingdom of Sicily. But when Frederick was elected King of the Germans and Emperor, in 1212, Innocent ensured that the kingdom of Sicily, under a regent appointed by himself, should pass to Frederick's son Henry. Henry later became also Duke of Swabia (1217), Regent of Burgundy (1219) and King of the Romans (1220). But Frederick, with his extraordinary activity, the fascination he exercised on court and people, and his unbridled ambition, was to overthrow the papal plans and disturb the whole of Europe for thirty years.

Pope Honorius III, cautious and temporising in policy, did his utmost to avert long and irremediable conflicts, even while he resisted Frederick's demands. On the other hand, he could not but encourage the formation of a second Lombard League against the Emperor. This was a necessity of papal policy, corresponding to the communal spirit of the time. Gregory IX, who succeeded him, a sturdy old man who, as pontifical legate, had co-operated in the formation of the League (1226), was not made for a waiting policy and, on the contrary, himself precipitated events. Frederick was excommunicated in 1227 for his failure to leave for the Crusade and to furnish the troops he had promised, for his spoliation of the Templars and of the Crusader Roger, who was under papal protection, and for other misdeeds enumerated in the Bull. The reasons for excommunication were evident and adequate, but it cannot be denied that, in excommunicating him, Gregory weakened Frederick's position in regard to the Communes of Northern Italy and in the South and Sicily.

In 1230 Frederick was reconciled with Gregory, but the situation remained unaltered. Frederick's constant dream was to unify the Germanic Empire and to form a real Italian Kingdom. He was forced first of all to face the rebellion of his son Henry, then, returning to Italy, he mustered his forces against the leagued Communes. After three campaigns in Northern Italy, when his fortune was at its height, Gregory excommunicated him afresh, for a whole list of particular causes, among them his behaviour in the Holy Land, his heretical reputation, and also the occupation of territories of the Holy See in Sardinia and the district of Ferrara. No mention was made of the situation of the Communes of Northern Italy, but to the aged Gregory this was a matter of deep concern. This time Frederick had his revenge. Continuing his successful campaign in Italy, he occupied cities and provinces, winning victory on land and sea and taking prisoner prelates and Cardinals. Gregory had sought in vain for help in France and elsewhere; he had hoped in vain to be able to call a crusade against Frederick, with the support of the Hungarians. St. Louis of France, while he caused the Bull excommunicating Frederick to be promulgated throughout his territories, refused to join in the war, and forbade the collection of money for the assistance of the Pope. When Frederick, who had gone from victory to victory, was on the point of laying siege to Rome (1241), Gregory died with all the appearance of defeat.

After a vacancy of nearly two years, Innocent IV was elected. He too was one of the mighty Popes of the Middle Ages, and fully equal to facing a Frederick II. The latter was ready for peace with the new Pope, but not for submission to him. The temporary peace signed in 1244 was short lived. It was hoped that order and peace would be restored by the Council of Lyons; instead, from that Council came the final decision to depose Frederick. The last five years of his life were a savage and desperate struggle. He was believed and called Antichrist. Even his own subjects rebelled against him. His defeat was total, and the ascendancy of the Guelfs in Italy became practically general.

Frederick died in 1250, but the struggle against the Hohenstaufen house continued. Manfred was slain at Benevento in 1266, Corradino executed at Naples in 1268, Enzo, after long imprisonment, died at Bologna in 1272. Over a century of warfare between the popes and the House of Swabia—from the treaty of Benevento, between Adrian IV and the Normans in 1156, which brought the first clash with Barbarossa, to the battle of Tagliacozzo in 1268—represents the effort of the Papacy to defend itself against imperial encirclement, to safeguard the Patrimony and its feudal rights over Southern Italy and the Islands, and to affirm its predominance over the Empire. The struggle of the Guelf Communes against the Empire, and the defence of their liberties, the popular basis of this policy and the growth of the Italian burgess class, entered directly or indirectly into the orbit of papal policy.

This policy could not fail to be mainly religious or directed towards religious ends. Yet in the fight waged by Gregory VII the reform of the Church and the question of her spiritual freedom had prevailed over other less general or immediately political aims. Little by little, as the Papacy came to lean on the material support of alliances, leagues and wars, and disposed readily of royal thrones and imperial crowns, political factors became confused with religious factors, and sometimes overshadowed them. The popes, obliged to run the risk entailed by alliances and the use of armed forces, had often to anticipate it or face it on a plane that tended to adhere more and more closely to that of politics; by then the politics of nearly all Europe had become papal politics.

Frederick II, oscillating between the role of God-Emperor, in the oriental and pagan fashion, and that of a devoted son and protector of the Church, introduced not a few elements of a secularisation of power, law and State. While his coronation in Jerusalem, excommunicated as he was, assumes the significance of an oriental rite for the divinisation of his power, his insistence on the autonomy of royal power, deriving direct from God without priestly intermediary or limitations by the Church, bears the stamp of the theory of absolute power by Divine Right. On the other hand, in his *Liber augustalis*, in which we may note an idea antagonistic to the *Collection of Canons and Decretals*, he seeks to put forward a civil and political code based on *Law*, *Nature* and *Reason*. Gregory IX reproached Archbishop Giacomo of Capua for his share in Frederick's collection of laws, saying that these did not 'co-operate in salvation but call down evils upon many'. Frederick's struggle against the supremacy of the popes was that of a disorderly genius, who passed down to posterity as a heretic, a renegade, an Antichrist, but his theories and his legal experiments were garnered by the already flourishing universities, in spite of the fact that he ended his life as a beaten man and the Guelfs emerged victorious from the struggle.

It is the period when the juridical formulation of papal power reaches its widest extension. Innocent III, as we have seen, had defined the distinction between the *ratio feudi* and the *ratio peccati*, between papal intervention in politics *casualiter*, and by *plena potestate*. Gregory IX holds to the formula of his great predecessor, but he insists also on the Donation of Constantine and the transfer, effectuated by the Pope, of universal empire from the Greeks to the Romans, It is, however, Innocent IV, who gave the papal power its widest interpretation, juridical and theological, such as was never known before or after.

He is a jurist and does not forget it. In his *Apparatus ad Quinque libros Decretalium* he recalls that the Emperor's power is derived from the Roman people, through the *Lex regalis*, which Justinian reiterated in his Codex. But this historico-legal origin of the transmission of power from people to emperor does not contradict his own theologico-metaphysical theory, which is founded on the idea, of which there are traces in the Fathers, that coercive power, like private property, is a result of Original Sin, and therefore in itself, in the material sense, something illegitimate and an abuse, which can never be free from hatred, violence and misdeeds. Gregory VII and his successors had frequently insisted on this concomitance of power with injustice, murders, wars and tyrannies, which accompany its historical origin and its practical development, in order to proclaim the power of the Church, not only as moral teacher but as having the right and duty of intervening to correct kings and princes and to deprive them of power should they prove incorrigible and harmful to the community. In the XI and still more in the XIII century power and the Empire could not be conceived as extraneous to the Church (given the evolution of Christian thought from the IX century onwards, for which kingdoms and Christian empires were within the Church and part of the Church). It would have been foreign to the spirit of the age to carry such a theory to the pessimistic conclusion, which might have led to an irremediable dualism (of which there are hints in the Fathers), that the civil power was caused by Original Sin and closely connected with crime in its formation and exercise. The dualism of power from Gregory VII onwards resolves itself into the power of St. Peter.

Hence the distinction, which Innocent IV clearly establishes, between the original power deriving from sin, illegitimate, an abuse rather than authority, and legitimate power, deriving from God, to be wielded in the Christian world for the common good and under religious control. This power is to be found *naturaliter et potentialiter* in the Church, not as a gift from the emperors, not through any Constantinian concession, but of itself, from the day the Church was founded. The popes represent this true power, 'as legates of God on earth', '*Generali legatione in terra fungimur Regis regum*'. Thus the letter to Frederick II in 1245, in which Innocent IV symbolically expounds the Donation of Constantine.

In the paganism from which Constantine came there was but one earthly power, which, unlegitimised and unennobled by Christianity, was permitted by God only as a consequence of sin. When Constantine became a Christian, he resigned his earthly power to the Church, to receive it back from the Church renewed by Christianity, that is, as legitimate power, recognised as such because recognised as coming from God. In Constantine in his quality of Emperor all human power is symbolised; through the Church the Empire became Christendom. The secular power might be acquired through a variety of human forms, succession, election, nomination, popular choice, but its legitimation came through the intervention and consecration of the Church. Power proceeds from no one but God, but it is through the Church that its divine origin is proved, rendering it theologically lawful. That is why the Pope, as legate of God, has a general authority over the earth.

By this process ecclesiastical mediation is carried to its fullest expression by Innocent IV. The metaphysical conception of power in a natural society is transformed into a theological one in a Christian society, hence in the authority of the Church all human power is unified. And since Christianity had to be preached to the whole world, the Church, in virtue of her religious mission, *naturaliter et potentialiter* has authority over the whole world, as she had over the Roman Empire even before Constantine turned Christian. From this sprang the right, recognised in those days and maintained by Innocent himself, to make war on infidels, occupy their territories, and dethrone their kings if this were necessary either for the moral and religious good of their Christian subjects or for the preaching of the Gospel. This extension of the power of the popes led to the opinion of the legists that the Emperor too had a potential authority over the whole world and could therefore make war on the infidel, a right Innocent IV and other canonists explicitly denied. This thesis would be revived after the discovery of the New World and be debated in a new light from the legal and theological standpoint. The Brief of Alexander VI which, dividing the regions of America between Spain and Portugal, recognising the occupation and authorising its expansion, is based on the Innocentian theory, which had remained part of the canonical traditions of the Church.

Innocent's conception attenuates but does not alter the diarchy Papacy-Empire, or *Sacerdotium-Regnum*. The new element is the priestly mediation, which subordinated civil power not only spiritually but also politically to the Church. The diarchy persists, for civil power, where its exercise is concerned, resides wholly in the Emperor or King, save in cases of papal intervention. Papal intervention, in actual fact, did not overstep the limits already defined by Innocent III, of an intervention *casualiter*, whenever it might be required, not *ratione feudi* but *ratione peccati*—to-day we should say for moral and religious reasons—apart from intervention of a more strictly political nature, resulting from privileges, customs, special rights or full sovereignty; the last was the case in St. Peter's Patrimony.

While canonists and legists disputed over the juridical formulas of their theories of power, the scholastic philosopher-theologians seem to us to have stood spiritually aloof from the impassioned debate; maybe it appeared to them mainly a controversial and legal issue. In general they confined themselves to reflecting the traditional theories of the Church on a metaphysical, moral, or dogmatic plane. In the contemporary theologians, the greatest of all being St. Thomas Aquinas and St. Bonaventura of Bagnorea, we find no echo of the Innocentian theory of the Donation of Constantine, which belongs to the period of their youth.

The schoolmen of the time, with a few exceptions, follow rather the lines of Gelasius I and Peter Damiani, or else they repeat the famous passage from Bernard of Clairvaux, as does St. Bonaventura;[1] it is repeated also by St. Thomas[2]: '*Habet spiritualem (gladium) tantum quantum ad executionem; sed habet etiam temporalem quantum ad eius jussionem*'.

For the church to have a temporal power of which the executor

[1] IV. Sententiarum, objection IV.
[2] Also in a Commentary on the Sentences (IV): 'She has the spiritual sword even for execution, and she has also the temporal sword, but only as under her order'.

was the prince (as was then generally admitted) did not at all imply the theory of priestly mediation if the secular power was to become legitimate from the Christian standpoint. St. Thomas, without discriminating between the time before Christianity and the time since, admits that the secular power comes straight from God, just as from God comes, though with diverse character and diverse derivation, the spiritual power of the Church. He has no mention of the mediation of the Pope, either as a means of transmission of power or as legitimising it, but only as consecration. According to St. Thomas, the secular power is subject to the spiritual only in what concerns the salvation of souls. Hence he asserts that in what concerns the civil weal the secular authorities should be obeyed before the spiritual ones. He mentions only one exception: when the two authorities are united, as in the Pope. In making this exception St. Thomas was perhaps alluding not only to the Pope but to the many Prince Bishops who had sovereignty over cities or territories, as the Pope had over the Patrimony. But he attributed to the Pope alone the right to depose sovereigns by penal sentence in the case of an excommunication 'for heresy or for other causes, as has actually happened'. This is St. Thomas's sole reference to the historical events of his time; we believe that it is as a concession to the canonists that he extends the right of deposing sovereigns, traditionally admitted by the Church for motives of heresy, to include 'other causes', which he does not specify. St. Thomas explains that the Pope's punitive power in the case of heresy in a sovereign is not political but religious, since, he says, *convenienter in hoc puniuntur quod subditis fidelibus dominari non possint*[1].

§ 16.—From the deposition of Frederick II, the imperial power begins to wane. There is a vacancy for twenty years, which shows the general turmoil, disorder and clash of interests, and also the diminished exigency of such an office. Finally Rudolph of Hapsburg is elected Emperor. After prolonged controversy, and almost against his will, Gregory X recognised Rudolph as King of the Romans and promised to nominate him as Emperor (1277). His successor, Innocent V, de-

---

[1] 'It is fitting that they should be punished in that they may not hold dominion over faithful subjects.'

layed still further; finally John XXI nominated Rudolph after the latter had declared that he would *submit his will to the Pope*. It was Rudolph who issued the famous Privilege of 1279, in which, while admitting the distinction between the two powers, he recognises that the Romano-Germanic Empire owed its historical origin and its authority to the Church, who granted the German princes the right of election and the Emperor the supreme rulership of the world. Rudolph accepted the Innocentian idea that his authority came through the mediation of the Church, to which it was subordinate as the moon to the sun.

Events and juridical affirmations favoured the complete authority of the popes, but the scholastic theories and those of the legists, circulating in schools, courts, monasteries and populace, undermined its foundations. Thus, when a fresh and resounding conflict arose between the *Sacerdotium* and the *Regnum*—this time no longer with the Emperor, but with a powerful and obstinate king—the positions established by Innocent IV half a century earlier no longer found the same response in the new environment that had come into being.

Boniface VIII was of the stamp of the pontiffs in direct descent from Gregory VII. His conception of the papal power is theological and legal, with complete fusion of spirit and form. The Bull *Unam Sanctam* remains the clearest and soundest document of his mentality, and the historical conclusion of the struggle between *Sacerdotium* and *Regnum*.

But times had changed since the days of Gregory VII, Alexander III, Innocent III, or Innocent IV. The imperial power, which had not succeeded in unifying Europe politically, was already on the wane. Italy had become autonomous; to Italy, Pope and Emperor meant factional rallying-cries or symbols of local interests. The Communes were falling into the hands of nobles and tyrants. National spirit was growing up where kingdoms were becoming consolidated, and the interests of the nascent burgess class demanded strong central authorities to cope with popular turbulence. The universities had grown in number, importance and autonomy, and the intellectual class counted already as a Third Estate.

More than any other European country, France for the past century had consolidated her structure and made herself mistress of the other parts of the Kingdom and the vassal countries. The Crusades, the struggles against the English and even those against the Albigensians had given her a distinct personality. The influence of ecclesiastical France, with the University of Paris and the Cluniac, Victorine and Bernardine traditions, was potent throughout Europe. The conflict with Boniface VIII, and her subsequent control of the Papacy when it was driven to Avignon, made France the first nation in Europe.

Although Boniface VIII, like Innocent III, distinguishes between the *ratio feudi* and the *ratio peccati*, he too makes the papal authority cover the whole political activity of the time. He orders the King of France to make a truce with his enemies; he protests to the German princes against the deposition of Adolf of Nassau and the election of Albert of Austria as King of the Romans; he sends Charles of Valois to Florence; he resists the Sicilians, who, having driven out the French, would have Frederick of Aragon as their king; he protects the rights of the infant Carobert to the throne of Hungary, and so forth. Throughout his pontificate he vigorously upheld the tradition of a politico-religious unification of Europe in the papal power.

He met with resistance nearly everywhere, in the realm of theory and the realm of action, from kings, princes, and bishops, in the same way, indeed, as nearly all the great popes of the three preceding centuries, and certainly to no greater degree. But whereas popes like Gregory VII and Alexander III could count on support and help from people, communes and princes, Boniface VIII found no effective support outside the ecclesiastical organism, the Roman Curia and the canonists. He had not with him even the new burgess and intellectual forces, which had grown up as a third element, driving a wedge between the ecclesiastical and military powers of feudalism.

The people were in majority opposed to Boniface VIII. They were at that time swept by the currents of the Fraticelli, in whom were united three tendencies capable of moving the emotions of the populace—the spiritual apocalypticism of Joachim de Flora, the poverty of St. Francis, and the anti-social and anti-ecclesiastical theories of the heretical sects. Pietro di Morone, who became Pope as Celestine V, was one of the most fervent champions of poverty and spiritual asceticism, and his followers outstripped him, to the point of fanaticism. All these currents were hostile to Boniface VIII, guilty of supplanting Celestine, and accusations against him were the more constant the more rigorous his conduct towards those who wished to profit by the simplicity of the deposed Pope to make him a pretext for warfare. Boniface ended by imprisoning the ex-Pope, for fear lest his fanatical supporters, allied with Charles of Naples, should promote a schism. When Celestine died, from a tumour in his right side, his devout followers decided that his head had been pierced by a nail on Boniface's orders.

Boniface dealt harshly with the Fraticelli, who were excellent men, though perhaps unbalanced, like Blessed Jacopone da Todi, and who were persecuted together with others who were genuinely heretical, or evil-livers and instigators of disorder. The poorer people, whether from admiration for men who lived in perfect poverty, or incited by their preaching against the wealth and power of the clergy—which could create an unconscious hope of a more equitable distribution of goods—for the most part supported the Fraticelli and imitated their exalted frame of mind. In a period which had seen the revival of an ampler urban and personal life, tending therefore to break through the hundred-and-one economico-social bonds of feudalism, the problem of property had become actual and urgent.

The dispute over ecclesiastical immunities, in France and elsewhere, as a result of the Bull *Clericis Laicos* of 1296, found public opinion highly unfavourable to the Papacy. Not that the ancient right to fiscal immunity was denied, but because the weight of taxation in the more unified and belligerent countries like France, England, Aragon and Bavaria had become overwhelming. The laity did not want to bear the burden alone, and saw with resentment how ecclesiastics evaded it through papal protection when without this they would often have been unable to resist the kings' demands. Nor did the kings look favourably on a lofty control that made it difficult for them to help themselves to the revenues and properties of the churches, which would have been far easier than helping themselves to the revenues of laymen. Philip the Fair, against whom, though without naming him, the Bull *Clericis Laicos* was directed, riposted at once by forbidding the export of moneys out of France (*i.e.* to the Pope). Edward I of England, too, felt himself injured, through the refusal of the clergy to pay the war taxes; he at once sequestrated their revenues and seized the wool of the wool-producing monasteries.

Between those who preached evangelical poverty, criticising clergy and bishops, and those who despoiled them in the name of royal rights and fiscal equity, the attack on church property became at once a popular emotion and a court matter. And this attack went far further, for it struck at the very authority of the Church, who found in feudal property the basis of many rights, and in political and religious power the moral justification of such property-holdings.

In the controversy between Philip the Fair and Boniface VIII we find proclaimed for the first time that the Pope, in claiming universal authority, meant to assert a kind of universal property-right, and that, on the other hand, the King of France claimed the right of levying dues on ecclesiastical possessions inasmuch as the whole kingdom was his property. There is here a mixture of the idea of the paramount feudal property-right of the medieval sovereign and that of the patrimonial or dynastic State which peeps out, in contradiction to the idea of the political Community, which is the juridical principle of the Middle Ages. If we correlate the conception of the patrimonial State of Philip the Fair (a notorious debaser of the coinage), with that of the secular State of Frederick II and that of the divine right of the royal power, so emphatically asserted by Frederick Barbarossa, we find the elements that will develop in the modern State from the beginnings of the Renaissance onwards.

Boniface certainly did not pretend to universal ownership in a real and effective sense. He considered his power to spring from the source of all pontifical rights, the keys of the Kingdom of Heaven given to St. Peter and the Two Swords he retained. But the subjection of the whole world to the Papacy implied for him, as a kind of paramount or dispositive right, the right of the Church, not only over men but over human possessions, kingdoms and wealth, through the general subordination of all temporal things to the higher order of the spirit. Therefore he believed it his duty to resist the kings who violated the immunity-rights of Church property, and to strike down the fanatic good or bad, who wilfully or otherwise instigated the people against the right of churches and clerics to possess property.

On the other hand, both regalists and spirituals and all Boniface's personal enemies of every kind vigorously attacked, in the person of the pontiff, the sovereign power he had proclaimed over the whole world, declaring it a distortion of the Gospels and a usurpation of the rights of others. No one denied the Pope's spiritual power, but in the asperity of debates and the frenzy of the struggle no one was capable of defining the exact boundary between the spiritual and secular powers; each side overpassed the limits, to the detriment of the other. The champions of Philip the Fair, starting with respect for the Pope's spiritual power, ended by asserting instead the King's rights over even the spiritual domain. Cardinal Matteo d'Acquasparta, Boniface's Legate, on the contrary, affirmed that the Pope could judge every temporal question *ratione peccati*, and that temporal jurisdiction belonged to the Pope *de iure* and to the King only *quantum ad executionem actus*.[1] In any case, a short time before, the celebrated Ostiensis (Cardinal Henry of Susa) had written: '*Unum caput est tantum, scilicet Papa, unus debet tantum esse caput nostrum, dominus spiritualium et temporalium.*'[2]

Both sides were equally powerless to determine any theoretical or practical limits, and, driven by the urge towards unification, they came by diverse paths to the idea of a universal Council, superior to pope, emperor or kings. The Pope could not be said to unify what was already divided for and against him, nor the Emperor, who no longer stood for a directing authority over all Christendom, nor the several kings, who could aspire to be the expression of unity only in their own kingdoms. The idea of a Council above the Pope, able to judge the Pope, a supreme politico-religious assembly of Christendom, which had been mooted in Barbarossa's day and proclaimed at Pavia, re-emerged in the last years of the XIII century, to evolve during the next till the decisions of Constance.

In this disquieting atmosphere three historical documents stand out:

---

[1] In what concerned the execution of what was done.
[2] There is only one head, the Pope, one alone should be our head, lord of the spiritual and of the temporal.

the Bull *Unam Sanctam* of Boniface VIII, the treatise *De potestate regia et papali* by John of Paris, and Dante's *De Monarchia*.

The Bull *Unam Sanctam* has had undying fame, through controversies that have continued from the time of its promulgation to our own. Although its dogmatic value is confined to the conclusion and do not go beyond the limits of traditional subjection to the Roman Pontiff, without which there could be no Church, yet in the text theological and political affirmations are so intermingled, all on the same plane, as to imply the most absolute subjection of the secular authority to the papal. It can indeed be proved that Boniface VIII did not go beyond the tradition of the two previous centuries, and that his affirmations, compared with those of Innocent IV, are neither further-reaching nor more strongly worded. But the time in which Boniface published his Bull was very different from that of Innocent's letter to Frederick II, and the solemnity of the Bull with its dogmatic conclusion gave a tone of definition to Boniface's teaching, which was lacking in the polemical letters of the popes to the emperors. Moreover, the influence of the jurists and canonists, theologians and schoolmen of Boniface's day was much greater, through the importance and autonomy of the universities, which were assuming a role outside the orbit of the ecclesiastical hierarchy, and what was almost a control of official teaching—as would be still more apparent at the Councils of Pisa and Constance. In this historical setting something hitherto unprecedented was possible, the solemn repudiation by another pope of the acts of Boniface VIII, so that Bulls of his were annulled and erased from the papal registers, and the order given to burn all copies. The Bull *Unam Sanctam* itself was modified, and even in modified form was declared not to apply to France; neither should the other Bull, *Clericis Laicos*, but that instead the whole position of the rights and privileges affecting France should be as it was before, as though Boniface VIII had never been pope. This marked a complete victory for Philip the Fair, and was combined with another, over the Templars, wrung from Clement V. These were suppressed, and the order given for the confiscation of their goods in favour of the *manu regia*. The presence of the popes in Avignon, the nomination, even though barren of result, of a Valois prince as Emperor of Byzance, and many other favours and forms of support on the part of the Papacy to the House of France, displaced the centre of European politics, at a period in which the formation of nationalities and the development of absolute sovereignty tended to weaken the unity of Christendom and the papal-imperial diarchy. It may be said that ecclesiastico-political Gallicanism becomes conscious with the conflict between Philip the Fair and Boniface VIII.

John of Paris, in his treatise *De potestate regia et papali*, is the interpreter of French thought, which for five centuries would correspond to the spirit and practice of nearly the whole of Christian Europe in respect of the Papacy. While according to the most widespread conception of the medieval canonists, the popes derived their power in temporal things from the spiritual basis of their supreme ministry, John of Paris makes it derive instead from historical causes or from the concessions of princes, or from necessity, usurpation, or other human deeds, which might or might not be lawful. Thus on the one hand he opposed the Spirituals who denied to popes and bishops any power at all *in temporalibus*, and on the other he returned to the position of Gelasius I, in recognising the two powers as distinct and autonomous, the spiritual directed to spiritual ends, the temporal to ends of the earthly common good. The two powers alike derived from God, and, in speaking of the relations between them, save for particular details of fact, the conception of John of Paris tallies with that of St. Thomas, where he writes: 'In tantum saecularis potestas est sub spiritualis, in quantum est a Deo supposita, scilicet in his quae ad salutem animae pertinent; et, ideo in his magis obediendum potestati spirituali quam saeculari. In his autem quae ad bonum civile pertinent, est magis obediendum potestati saeculari quam spirituali, secundum illud Matth. xxii. 21. Reddite quae sunt Caesaris Caesari.' (*Com. Sent. P. Lombardi*, ii, 44, 2, 3.)[1]

On the Pope's special power derived from the Donation of Con-

---

[1] 'The secular power is under the spiritual in as much as it is sustained by God, *i.e.* in those things that concern the salvation of souls; and therefore in these the spiritual power is to be obeyed rather than the secular. But in those that pertain to civil good, the secular power is to be obeyed rather than the spiritual, according to Matth. xxii, 21, "Render unto Caesar the things that are Caesar's."'

stantine, John of Paris, while not denying the fact, favours the opinion
that holds it juridically invalid. In any case, he limits it to Italy and to
other provinces, which certainly did not include France. On the Pope's
power over the Empire, he notes that Constantine did not cede away
the Empire, but merely transferred its seat from Rome to Byzance.
But above all, John of Paris is anxious to show that the Franks were
never subject to the Roman Empire. In substance, the papal and
medieval, Italian and Germanic idea of a universal Empire embracing
all Christendom holds no place at all in his conception; what concerns him is to place France beyond any political subjection either
papal or imperial.

Against the opinion of the heretics of the time, he admits that the
Church has the right to own property. He holds, what in substance was
in the spirit of the Church itself, that such ownership should not be
vested individually and personally in the Pope, bishop or beneficiary,
but in the community, for which the prelates were merely stewards.
He too is against the abuse of wealth by the clergy, in this agreeing
with Peter Damiani, Bernard and many others. He does not admit that
even the King should be considered as owner of the realm and lands,
but as the steward of the community; thus the King can neither be
considered as arbiter of the laws of the realm nor *solutus a lege*, but
under the law. This, an echo of the medieval conception of the political
Community, is lost in his exaltation of the power of absolute and
limitless monarchy.

Therefore, he not only contests the Pope's right to interfere in the
affairs and laws of the kingdom, but, while admitting the papal right
to ask the King for help and intervention in religious matters, he
denies the Pope the faculty of constraining the King by canonical
penalties should he refuse, or deposing him should he resist. Indeed, if
the Pope oversteps his religious authority and invades the civil domain,
he can be deposed by a Council. Thus John of Paris combines the
theories of Gelasius and Thomas Aquinas with Gallican principles and
the theory of the Council superior to the Pope.

The *De Monarchia* has a broader and nobler purpose than the defence
of the rights of any monarchy or kingdom. Dante seeks to re-establish
the spiritual, juridical, political basis of the universal Empire, precise

at the moment of the decline of the Romano-Germanic Empire. The absolute independence of States would destroy the unity and disturb the peace of Christendom. Dante maintains the necessity of a single Empire (*monarchia*) within which the individuality of each kingdom shall be respected, but through which all kingdoms, principalities and free communes shall have a supreme regulator, judge and arbiter in politico-civil matters; the Empire is thus an international organism for co-ordination and unification.

According to Dante, this Empire belongs by historical and providential right to the Romans. By the Romans the world was conquered, to prepare it for the advent of Christianity. The Empire itself became Christian. It is not the popes who are the heirs of the Monarchy of the Romans, but Rome is the perennial title of the Empire. Christ confirmed this juridical title by His birth under Augustus and His death by sentence of the Roman Praetor. Dante goes so far as to attribute a natural perpetuity to an historical event, where in showing the natural necessity of human society and extending it to universal or international society, he confuses the principle with the concrete fact of the Roman Empire. But what he sought was a juridical title, and he could not but find it in the will of God, providentially manifested, even with the support of miracles, in favour of the Romans.

It is naturally in the economy of Dante's thought that the Emperor's authority derives from God, without the mediation of the Pope, and hence without the right of the Pope to intervene in civil matters. He contests all the arguments advanced by the popes in support of their thesis, and which the canonists reiterated in their writings. The comparison of the sun and moon, which we found in the Privilege of Rudolph of Hapsburg, Dante declares an inapplicable allegory based on false reasoning; so, likewise, with other examples drawn from the Old Testament. Dante does not accept the chief argument, the Keys given to St. Peter, for the keys are those of the *regna coelorum*, that is, the spiritual authority, never the temporal. The *quodcunque ligaveris vel solveris* refers to the spiritual function indicated by the words *regna coelorum*. Nor does Dante accept the current interpretation given to the two swords, as symbolising the two authorities, spiritual and temporal, both in Peter's hands, for this, he thinks, the sense of the

Gospel passage in no wise allows.[1] Finally, he assumes that Constantine could not alienate what was not his own, the imperial power. Nor, for Dante, was any right created by a Pope's nomination of Charlemagne as Emperor, just as no right could be created by the fact that on occasion the Emperor had nominated a Pope. Dante vehemently denies that the Pope is cause and originator of the Empire, that the Emperor receives his authority from the Pope, that to him appertains only the exercise of power, not its fullness; this would be contrary to the nature of the Church. The relation between the two world authorities, the Pope and the Emperor, is, he declares, necessary and must correspond to the respective ends of the spiritual and temporal good of mankind, which is placed under two universal rectors in order that it may thus attain the good and find the way to salvation in God. In Dante the universal diarchy is perfect; unification is only original and finalistic, that is, only to be found in God. Therefore he writes in the last paragraph of the *De Monarchia*: 'Illa reverentia Caesar utatur ad Petrum, qua primogenitus filius debet uti ad patrem; ut luce paternae gratiae illustratus, virtuosius orbem terrae irradiet, cui ab Illo solo praefectus est qui est omnium spiritualem et temporalium gubernator.'[2]

Dante's defence of the Empire was closely connected with the disordered state of Italy, the captivity of the Papacy in France, the disunion of the German kingdoms and the impotence of the popes to restore the unification of Christendom. The chivalrous Henry VII, elected as Emperor, became an ideal in Dante's thought.

Like the Ottos and Henries of the past, Henry VII would have reorganised the Empire, pacified Italy and the other warring peoples, brought order into the Roman See, and restored the Pope, already in Avignon, to Rome. A legendary figure of medieval Emperor, come three centuries too late, Henry did not see the impossibility of his mission. Fought by the Guelfs, ill-advised by the Ghibellines, opposed

---

[1]St. Peter, he says, was of too impulsive and simple a nature not to have 'answered merely to the obvious aspect of things,' and in any case, if the two swords were to have a symbolic sense, they would mean the sword of words and the sword of deeds.

[2]'Let Caesar use to Peter the reverence that a first-born son should use towards his father; so that, illuminated by the light of paternal grace, he may the more virtuously shine upon the round earth, over which he has been set by Him alone who is the ruler of all things, spiritual and temporal.'

by France, forsaken by the Pope, discouraged by his very friends, he died in Italy (1313), carrying his ideal with him into the grave. It may be said that his death was the death of the old Romano-Germanic Empire. His successors would become, little by little, mere shadows of an institution that, with all its defects, had done great service to feudal Europe.

Dante's *De Monarchia* is not a realistic or legal treatise, like those of John of Paris, Ptolemy of Lucca or Egidius Romanus. It is an idealistic and polemical treatise, scholastically conceived. It aims at proving by logic, law and scripture the necessity of a supreme power, political and moral, uniting Christendom and through Christendom the world, in harmony with the Church, but independent by nature and functions. The duality of powers, tempered by Caesar's filial sentiments towards Peter, is no negation of a spiritual unity in God, which Dante seeks with all the strength of his faith and genius. On the earthly plane unification was for him real in the Empire and mystical in the Church.

This conception he rendered immortal in the Divine Comedy, thanks to which the *De Monarchia* is still remembered, and it is in the Divine Comedy that Dante introduces human personality as a living element into temporal and spiritual life. This element, of which we had lost sight as though it were hidden away in the monasteries of the early Middle Ages, we found emerging at the beginning of the struggles between Papacy and Empire, in the formation of the Communes, the creation of the craft guilds, the Franciscan movement, Scholasticism and the Universities, and in the political struggle itself. But for the value of this emergent human personality to ripen required two hundred years, culminating in the most mature thought of the Middle Ages and its synthetical and artistic expression in the divine poem.

Dante rediscovers individual personality which had been swallowed up in the earthly Empire and the spiritual Church, and he refashions it as at once human and celestial. In his thought and art he synthesises the mystical apocalyptic stream of Joachim de Flora and the ascetical stream of St. Francis of Assisi; in his struggle against the wealth and power of the clergy he becomes prophet of the reform of the Church. Soaring from earthly science to theological heights, he turns scholastic speculation into poetry. He is a forerunner of the renaissance of classicism, which he sees as an historical reality and as the seal of the Empire. And he quickens the whole by a supernatural faith tried in combat, by the hope of the militant Christian and by the absorbing contemplation of theology and mysticism.

The personality of man and Christian as sung by Dante has continued its unceasing evolution up to our own time, and will develop still further. For man and Christian the *Divine Comedy* remains the book of art nearest to our spirit and our faith. But the Dantesque synthesis of the universal Empire, of a single Christian and Roman Monarchy, was belied by events. The Empire closed with the dream of Henry VII. And in the same way the synthesis of universal papal dominion, unifying all Christendom, nay, the world, and of which, in the medieval struggles between *Sacerdotium* and *Regnum*, Boniface VIII was the last exponent and one of the greatest, closed with the tragedy of Anagni.

The international diarchy of Pope-Emperor would last at least in name for over a hundred years more, a ripening-time for the period of the great transformations that would lead to the modern State and national churches, against which the Papacy—once the crises of Avignon and of the Schism of the West had been surmounted —would begin a struggle of a very different character.

# CHAPTER V

## FROM THE MIDDLE AGES TO HUMANISM

§ 17.—Dante belongs to two epochs—to that which, chronology apart, we call the Middle Ages, and to that of the movement known under the name of Humanism. The *De Monarchia* belongs to the Middle Ages that were passing away, the *Divine Comedy* to the Middle Ages as they live on, to dawning Humanism, and to what the Middle Ages would hand on to Humanism.

It is one of the most common distortions of our attitude towards history, and one of the hardest to correct, to look upon Humanism as the negation of the Middle Ages. For this state of mind the two epochs appear in perfect antithesis, the one a revolt against the other, with a total opposition of values; as though there were an actual historical discontinuity between the Middle Ages and the Age of Humanism. Certain historians go so far as to cut away the entire Middle Ages from the process of human thought, joining up Humanism to the thought, art and culture of the classical period, and taking early Christianity into account only in so far as it was influenced by Greco-Alexandrian philosophy. On the other hand, not a few Catholic apologists not only extol the Middle Ages beyond what reality warrants, but minimise the negative aspects of a civilisation they believe to have been purely Christian. They too admit of a discontinuity between one epoch and the other, with the difference that for them the join has yet to be effected—notwithstanding the attempt of the Counter Reformation and the less effectual one of Catholic Romanticism.

Apart from polemical motives, *hinc et inde*, with which we are not concerned, such a conception prevents any sociologico-historical interpretation of human process. History is process without discontinuity; the past resolves itself into the present bearing with it the good and

127

the evil realised by events; the trend is always towards the rational, either truly such or so believed; the process is not always progress, it admits of stasis and involution, which can never be complete because there is always a constant grade of rationality and of tendency towards unification. New elements brought into history by men of genius, sages and saints, those who by virtue and mind are or seem to be the expressions of potent personalities—through whom we best see the divine imprint in history—or even by anonymous multitudes impelled by exceptional happenings, are always living elements within the social whole. Even in the periods of moral eclipse the sense of an origin other than ourselves and of a goal outside ourselves is never wholly lacking; we are never deprived of an effectual intuition of our contingency and of the original and finalistic exigency of the Absolute. This, the basic idea of our 'historicism', is not belied by the facts, not even by the affirmation of humanism or by any other revolutionary affirmation, such as have occurred in periods of fruition like that of Socratic Hellenism or of the French Revolution.

From their opposing camps, historians and apologists declare that Humanism brought a reversal of values, that what in medieval thought might be called theocentrism, individual and social, was replaced by anthropocentrism, likewise individual and social. Hence the word 'Humanism', understood as though the idea of man or 'humanity' was now fundamental, resolving all other ideas into itself. Even when the humanistic conception was at its height, this alleged anthropocentrism in thought, art and life—as the opposite of theocentrism—seems a facile and inappropriate synthesis of so varied and complex an age. One series of manifestations is taken into account and the rest ignored; intellectual and artistic motives are over-stressed, at the expense of all the others prevailing in the social life of the time. Especially in philosophy or art the Greco-Roman period and the Italian Renaissance are compared and welded to form an historical pseudo-synthesis. Thus the idea of a cleavage gained credit, an idea that only the anti-historicist rationalism of the XVIII century could have conceived as corresponding to reality and which has been repeated ever since through a kind of mental inertia.

What most distinguishes the humanistic age and its later developments, through the Renaissance and the modern conception of life, is the quest for the concrete in philosophy, art, politics and religion; an attitude of mind in contrast to the abstractionist formalism that at that very time was reaching its worst excesses. The quest for the concrete did not stop short at manifestations of thought, but created realistic currents in every department of life, in regard to nature and its conquest, to man and his history, to God and communication with Him.

Theocentrism and anthropocentrism, if so presented that one is the negation of the other, falsify the comprehension of history, which has never been wholly humanised or wholly divinised. Understood as two poles of the spiritual dynamism of man, to be found in each one of us and in social life, they cannot be made to indicate different ages, since in every age as in every person the two tendencies now blend, now conflict. If, indeed, we wish merely to underline a prevalence in the significance of given historical events, in such a case accuracy should compel us to take into account all the features of the period, not forgetting that the two tendencies, albeit with varying efficacy, are always working in the dynamism of history, so that we shall never find a cleavage and discontinuity produced by the disappearance of one or the other.

The leaning of the cultured classes of the latter Middle Ages towards classical antiquity has three distinct aspects. The first is the revival of Roman Law, which coincides with the birth of the universities, contributing strongly to the formation of a legal mentality, to the institutional growth of Church and State, and to development of corresponding theories. A second aspect is the philosophical, which stretches from the triumph of an Aristotle made Christian (a task accomplished, in so far as it was possible, especially by St. Thomas Aquinas), to the triumph of Plato (the divine Plato of Marsilio Ficino), surviving the phases of a nominalism that touched the two extremes of material concretism and symbolistic abstractionism. Finally there was the philological or archaeological aspect, which would come to predominate as the revival of classical languages, the imitation of classical art, and the translation of the ethico-political thought of the classics into realities of experience.

These three aspects, though not concomitant, are interchained by a basic value, that of the quest for concrete reality as a human synthesis, against the ideological and logical abstractness of the currents of the past. To such currents those of scholastic realism and juridical theory came to be assimilated, through their ready recourse to aprioristic and abstract methods, which still prevailed in the mental formation of the time. For this reason the philological and artistic aspect of the humanistic movement seemed at variance with the others, and this has led many to misconceive its real and historical substance.

There are two phenomena that strengthen the illusion of a contrast between the various aspects of Humanism. Above all, there is the entry of the laity into the lists of culture, on an equal footing with the clergy, not only as legists and notaries but as philosophers, men of letters, teachers and moulders of public opinion. The second phenomenon, related to the first, is the growth of a cultured class (composed indiscriminately of laymen and clerics), which as such overshadows and dominates public institutions—Church, kingdoms, lordships, cities, guilds, monasteries—either by occupying the posts of command and counsel, in their quality of learned men or philosophers, or else by their powerful contribution to the orientation of thought and to the spiritual transformation of the age. It is this 'Republic of the Learned' that dominates the conciliar movement at the end of the XIV and beginning of the XV centuries; it is this class that becomes powerful in the princely and papal courts, centres of culture and the arts, hubs of political activity, where, as the organism of an *élite*, it evolves with its own autonomy and personality, as above the law, of all laws, political, ecclesiastic and moral.

The tendency to the affirmation of personality, which showed itself potent in Dante with the *Divine Comedy*, and which originates mainly in the spiritualistic movement of the XII and XIII centuries, expresses itself in the humanistic period as the formation of the cultural and political *élites*, embracing the two camps of laymen and churchmen. Truth to tell, these camps were none too clearly differentiated, and could be distinguished neither by mental tendencies, nor by detachment from the world, nor by the institutions they defended. Laymen, religiously minded, and clerics, worldly in feeling and life, laymen who for the sake of reputation and power turned cleric or obtained benefices, clerics who played the part of laymen, all intermingle. The world is still so penetrated by the organisation of the Church, by the influence of the friars and other religious corporations, that the layman as representative of an *élite* apart does not exist. The Captains of the Free Companies or the lords of cities and castles are laymen (when the lord is not a bishop or abbot, or the captain an ex-friar); the legists and notaries are laymen, but the *élite* in itself, whether in the courts or in the universities, is still a clerico-lay amalgam. The basic economy of the time is still feudal (save that of the cities, which was slowly throwing off feudal bonds), with a predominance of ecclesiastical mortmain and an ecclesiastico-administrative organisation of an international character. The humanist class brought about a flow of wealth towards cultural and artistic tasks, with a munificence that could only come from papal and royal courts, from princely and religious centres, from friaries or from rich and prosperous cities.

These cultural and ruling *élites*, influenced by the study of classical antiquity—which appeared to them as a world of lofty, profound, and beautiful thought—assimilated from it all that corresponded to the mind and need of the time, to the hunger for knowledge, to a facile reaction against the past, to a new fulfilment of political and religious aspirations. The medieval language, a conventional and formula-ridden Latin, ceased to correspond with the new humanistic thought and with the classical influence. The use of the Latin of Virgil and Cicero was not, in Humanism and the Renaissance, a mere literary exercise, but the expression of a living thought. These learned men, all the learned men of the time, were forging a mentality that required a suitable linguistic instrument. The vulgar tongues were still in their infancy; Italian, which had reached maturity through Dante, Petrarch and Boccaccio, was not yet general, nor had it emerged from the domain of the people; it was, moreover, limited to Tuscany. Culture at this time was European. National boundaries were no obstacle to cultural contact; the Roman See was first in France, then in Italy; the Councils gathered together men of culture from all countries at Lyon, Vienne, Pisa, Constance, Bâle, Florence. This universal, European culture—lay-ecclesiastical, pagano-Christian, philosophico-philological—found a language suited to its dominant class in Ciceronian Latin.

Philology at this time was not literary pedantry, but meant a spirit of research, of rearrangement, of philosophical co-ordination, of historical re-orientation, of reconsideration of ethical and aesthetic, political and religious values. These aims, of course, did not show themselves in the thought of every humanist, but taken as a whole these men were more or less clearly aware of their mission and of their reasons for a fight against a past that was becoming ever more obscure and incomprehensible to them. With their philological platform, seeking to reconstruct the ancient world, pagan and Christian, they lost sight —through lack of historical training—of the value of the Middle Ages, but they bore within themselves all that had remained alive and operative from the Middle Ages, and which could not fail to influence their minds and constructions. The classical past, which through them was coming back to life, did not come (except for a few narrow and unimaginative minds, such as are to be found in all periods) as a mere re-evocation of a bygone world, but as a new factor that took its place in the historical process, seeking to shape it to a synthesis with the elements that had survived from the Middle Ages.

Every historical synthesis is elaborated through a long period, with a multiplicity of factors not easily analysed. It is always dynamically in process through fresh disintegrations and re-integrations. We seize hold of given aspects of such syntheses and name them according to the predominance of such factors and phenomena as strike us most or are best known to us; thus we speak of Humanism. This restoration of man as the centre of historico-social life, in thought, art and politics, meant not a reaction against medieval theocentrism, but a deeper study of the natural life of man and its repercussions on the spiritual life. Thus the humanistic conquest is not at all the negation of theism as origin and end, but an attempt at a co-ordination, now inward to the point of immanence—these are the days of the German mystics from Meister Eckhart to Nicolas of Cusa—now external to the point of the most excessive religious legalism, which leads to the theory of the two truths and two moralities. In this wide region between theocentrism and anthropocentrism, Humanism was the expression of an exigency that sprang not only from the development of culture but from evolution in the economic, political, national and social fields, the evolution and persistence of those same elements that the Middle Ages had ripened and quickened. The philological, historical, and ethical contact of these elements with ancient classicism would produce a synthesis at once fruitful and disturbing, which stretches from the beginnings of Humanism to the late Renaissance.

§ 18.—It might seem at first sight as if the dispute between John XXII and Ludwig the Bavarian, which lasted through the whole of the latter's reign (1314–47), had the same politico-religious bearings as those of earlier centuries between popes and emperors. But in the new setting, in which humanistic features were rapidly developing, the religious and political questions raised rang different and had effects of quite other range.

After the moral and political defeat of Frederick II the Empire decayed; its function was becoming more and more limited to Germany; Italian affairs were left in the hands of the imperial vicars and petty tyrants, who were appearing, a sinister crop, in every city. Meanwhile the popes, after 1305, preferred to stay in Avignon, under the shadow of the Kingdom of France, sending their legates to Italy to bargain or fight.

During this period the popes had resolved to their own advantage the question whether the King-Elect in Germany could or could not exercise his power without the papal approbation, which implied not only acceptance of him as king but also his nomination and subsequent consecration as emperor. Albert I in 1303 had recognised (it was a victory for Boniface VIII) that from the Pope '*reges et imperatores, qui fuerunt et erunt pro tempore, recipient temporalis gladii potestatem ad vindictam malefactorum, laudem vero bonorum*'.[1] This was the most resounding practical recognition of the theory of the priestly mediation of the secular power. Clement V in his turn, after the death of the Emperor Henry VII, maintained that during the vacancy of the Empire its administration should pass to the Holy See, and this gave the popes, during such prolonged vacancies, a free hand in Italy.

---

[1] 'Kings and emperors, who have been and will be, shall receive the power of the temporal sword for the punishment of evil-doers and for the praise of the good.' *Mon. Germ. Hist.*, Const. IV, 1, p. 155.

These were the politico-legal elements of the beginning of the dispute between John XXII and Ludwig the Bavarian, whose election was strongly contested by Frederick of Hapsburg. Frederick too considered himself as King-Elect; the votes of the electors had been divided between the two and both had had themselves crowned. The war that ensued, which lasted seven years, was not so much a war of the Empire as a local war between the House of Wittelsbach and the House of Austria. Beyond the local interests of the two Houses, their partisans showed little warmth for a future emperor, who outside his own domain was no longer important and, if he went to Italy, knew he would put his hand into an adder's nest and would easily draw down upon himself the fulminations of the Pope—as had nearly always happened.

John XXII, elected Pope in 1316, was in no hurry to recognise either of the two contestants, and remained neutral, turning his attention to Italy, which in that period more than in the period previous was torn by local wars. To prevent any exercise of the imperial power John, in 1317, published a Bull threatening with excommunication all those who in a period of imperial vacancy might assume the title of imperial vicar without his sanction; in the meantime he appointed Cardinal Bertrand du Pouget his Legate in Italy. But when the Bavarian, after the victory of Mühldorf, considering himself now unchallenged, and exercising a power that had not yet been recognised, sent Berthold of Neiffen into Italy as imperial vicar, to the help of Can Grande and the Visconti, the quarrel with the Pope was bound to come to a head. John XXII ordered him to appear at Avignon to clear himself. Since he paid no heed, in March, 1324, he was excommunicated. The Bavarian replied, the following May, by the manifesto of Sachsenhausen.

It can serve no purpose for our study to follow the ups and downs of this dispute. The events that followed Ludwig's excommunication would have remained within the picture of the age and had a merely episodal character, if in support of the emperor's action and opposing the policy of the Avignon popes, there had not been three currents, the philosophical, the mystical, and the juridico-political, eminently represented by Ockham, by Michael of Cesena and by Marsilius of

Padua. Their activities and their influence go beyond even the quarrel between Papacy and Empire; they extend beyond their period and establish new elements that for another century would have a notable historical development.

William of Ockham was the greatest intellect of the time; his activity in every field of thought was extraordinary, and he took a lively part in the polemics and struggles between popes, emperors and friars. He may be taken as representing that intellectual class that was having so potent an influence on social evolution. The pupil and follower of Duns Scotus, he developed the anti-intellectualism and voluntarism of his master, moving towards a nominalism which he revived and made a living stream of thought. Those who do not see the relation between philosophical theories and historical realities often confuse the philosophy of the study or lecture hall with representative and constructive philosophies, arm-chair philosophies with vital philosophies. The former often remain barren individual speculations or else the repetition of ideas that once had life in them and have become empty of reality; the latter are potent ideas that reflect the consciousness of the time and impel it on new paths through profound experiences; they have thus an historical life.

After the triumph of Thomistic intellectualism, which represented the finest balance between thought and reality that the Middle Ages had ever known, the Franciscan school of the XIV century gained the ascendancy. In the world of nature their voluntarism drove them towards experimental reality, considered as the effect of an absolute Will not bound to intellective necessities; in the theological world it made them accentuate positive revelation, as made by the divine Will, minimising any effort at rational interpretation.

Ockham emphasised still more the anti-intellectualistic voluntarism of his order in the direction of a nominalist metaphysic and an 'acosmistic' system. Creation is simply one of infinite possibilities, and was willed by God by His absolute power. Both the cosmic order and the ethical order are such because God willed them so, never by an intrinsic rational exigency. Since there are no universals, neither as essences of reality nor as laws of morality, everything is particular and concrete, everything is the product of the pure act of the Divine will.

Even the natural law is but the abstract form of the decalogue, which itself is nothing but a positive law, the law given by God. On this nominalist basis, Ockham in the religious field opposed a fideistic traditionalism to rationalising theology. The repercussions of his metaphysic and of his theology on the politico-social system were so remarkable that they largely supplanted the already widespread influence of Thomism. They corresponded more closely than Thomism to the social evolution of the XIV century

The voluntarist system, released from the idea of intrinsic rationality, harmonised well with the conception of the absolute and tyrannical lordship that was taking shape on the ruins of the communal democracies and of the already decadent feudal constitutionalism. The idea of the *bonum commune*, the common weal, as the aim of political society, was replaced by that of will as power, which in fact if not in law annulled the participation of the popular classes in affairs of State. The struggle of the princes against the Curia assumed a spiritual character, aiming at disentangling it from earthly interests, but it was also the beginning of a breach between the two powers that would logically resolve itself into the control of the Church by the State.

Neither Ockham nor many others of his time were anti-constitutionalists, in favour of the absolute power of the prince against the rights of the people and of the various social bodies. Indeed Ockham, good Englishman as he was, was a supporter of the Great Charter. But in the thought of the time these were problems of what we should call private law, of the relations between the prince and the persons subject to him. Every country had its traditions, its forms of safeguard, however their efficacy might vary, against infringements on the part of the secular or the ecclesiastical power; franchises, immunities and local or personal rights still formed the basis—legally speaking—of the society of the time, in spite of the increasingly marked tendency towards an absolute power. The questions that we should define as being of public law were then those that referred to the ecclesiastical power, to canonical laws, to the Papacy as the supreme politico-religious authority over all Christendom and to the relations of the Church with the secular power. Against the power of the popes, as expressed in international, legal, political form, Ockham fought, and with him w the whole Spiritual Franciscan stream, momentarily allied with the legists.

Both were declared adversaries of the canonists and fought the tendency of the Roman Curia to transform religious and political relations into legal relations. Ockham, carrying the legal controversies into the realm of theology, denies plenary power to the Pope, denies that he has power over temporal things by divine right, and will grant only that he has been invested with such power by the faithful and that it resolves itself merely into an historic right. Considering the organisation of the Church in voluntaristic terms, not as an *a priori* rationality, but as something shaped by circumstance, he favours a tempered papal monarchy, with a system of national churches which, under certain aspects, would be autonomous. He admits the intervention of the Emperor in exceptional cases, such as that of an heretical pope. This was then a topical question, for John XXII was accused of heresy by the Franciscan Spirituals because of his pronouncements in the dispute over poverty which was then raging, rousing even the lowest strata of the population and bringing disquiet into the whole Church.

The movement of the Spirituals in the XIV century is in a manner connected with the popular and heretical movement of the century before, but differs from it in several respects. It had grown up within a recognised and approved Order, and hence brought profound division into an organism belonging to the Church. Though at odds with the popes (as happened often enough in those days, to churchmen of all ranks), the Spirituals wanted to remain within the Church. In spite of polemical excesses they considered themselves orthodox and their lives conformed to a high standard of purity and austerity. The people followed them, no longer with the fanatical exuberance of the previous century, but with the confidence inspired by their religious spirit and goodness.

The quarrel of the Spirituals with the moderate section of their own Order centred in the interpretation of St. Francis's message on poverty. They condemned as hypocrisy the papal concession by which property could be held in trust for them through the intermediation of the Holy See. In support of their thesis they adduced two erroneous principles:— that the Rule and Testament of St. Francis of Assisi, inspired directly by

Jesus Christ, was to be considered as of the same value as the Gospel; that neither the Church nor the true follower of Christ could possess goods of any sort, just as Christ renounced all right of earthly possession.

The question of Church property, when so much of the wealth of the time was administered by the Church or held by ecclesiastics, had now been troubling Christendom for three centuries. All the movements that had arisen, whether anti-ecclesiastical and heretical or orthodox and reformist, considered the social problem of property in religious terms, and thus interpreted the immense economic disproportion and agitated to amend it. For the most part these currents, permeated with apocalypticism, found no solution in social and political terms, but reached the pure negation of all property. The difference between the earlier movements and this was that now the laity, lords, traders, craftsmen, peasants, approved the action of the Spirituals as tending to disentangle the Church from wealth and power, and not as the advent of the Kingdom of God for the poor alone, in a world that would renounce all private property. The theorists of the movement, like Ockham, differentiated between the Church (which included the friars and the true followers of Christ), to whom the law of poverty would apply in its entirety, and the world which would remain dualistically in contrast to the Church, in its quest and possession of wealth. The communism of the early Christian communities, on which there was so much discussion, could not be applied either in the Church alone, as a body isolated from the rhythm of society, nor to the whole of society as such. The problem of those days was not conceived in the terms of modern Communisn. The compromise of Ockham and others, of a poor Church which would abandon wealth to the world, had no social foundations. Unable to see the problem in terms of an asceticism freely chosen, and faced by an ecclesiastical organism sustained by power and riches, they sought to isolate the Church from all realistic contact with the social life of the world.

For a time the popes used mild measures against the Franciscan dissidents. There were prolonged arguments. Ubertino da Casale took part in the discussion at the Council of Vienne, and the Decretal of Clement V, *Exivi de Paradiso*, was not a condemnation but confined itself to calling upon the superiors of the Order to punish the guilty.

But John XXII thought to make an end of an agitation that was steadily widening and was troubling the relations of the Holy See with princes and peoples. He condemned the declaration of the Franciscan Chapter that had been held at Perugia in 1328, he proclaimed the Spirituals to be heretics, and caused them to be imprisoned, tried, sent to the stake. Driven out of the convents, which were held by the moderates, the Spirituals gathered together here and there in friendly centres, or else scattered over the countryside, living the life of hermits and nearly always keeping alive their influence over the poorer people and the lowest social strata. On the other hand, Fra Michele of Cesena, the head of the Order, in a circular of 1331 addressed to all the friars, defended the Chapter of Perugia, confuted the assertions of John XXII on poverty, denied that Christ had held universal dominion over temporal things, and accused the Pope of heresy. This charge was exploited by the opponents of John XXII from another and wholly theological motive, that of his opinion on the Beatific Vision. He had said, (as a theologian before he became Pope), that this would not be granted to the elect in heaven before the Last Judgment. This opinion was not peculiar to John, and was held by several theologians, but it served the purpose of his adversaries, especially of Ludwig the Bavarian under whose protection Michele of Cesena had taken refuge in the Franciscan convent of Munich, together with the most celebrated Franciscan dissidents, Ockham, Buonagrazia of Bergamo and others.

These did not belong to the Spiritual party (except for Ubertino da Casale, who had already left the Order), but they joined forces with it in the struggle against John XXII and in favour of the Bavarian, whom they inspired with the idea of schism. They did not consider John a true pope, deeming him a heretic, and they raised up against him Peter of Corvara, a Franciscan friar like themselves, who, though not of the Friars Minor nor belonging to the Spirituals, promised to disengage the Church from wealth and from the secular power that riches demanded and at the same time assured.

The election of Peter of Corvara as pope, in Rome (whereas the popes were still at Avignon), with the intervention of the Roman clergy and people and of Ludwig, elected Emperor by the Roman people on the same occasion and crowned by the new Pope, had neither legal basis nor general moral assent. In spite of the support of the Emperor, the *mise en scène* of the election and the propaganda of the Franciscans, it was clear that this was merely an attempt at schism, which, after certain phases of struggle, collapsed of itself. Moreover, Ludwig the Bavarian was not the right man to uphold the thesis of the Spirituals on poverty and the reform of the Church, which he had adopted as his own from the time of the Sachsenhausen manifesto of 1324. The inward conviction, religious spirit, force of character, and intellectual level required for such a position were lacking him. For him the arguments of the Spirituals were of the worth of those of his legists, that is on the legal and political plane of the dispute and never on that of an inner reform of the Church.

Ludwig, in accordance with the imperial tradition, had no lack of legists in his service, among them Marsilius of Padua, Rector of the Sorbonne, who together with John of Jandun had written the *Defensor Fidei*, and who, having fled to Bavaria, took part in the Roman revolt against John, stage-managed the election of the Bavarian as Emperor, and became his Vicar-General. His writings are characteristic of his period, and his fame came late. He follows the tradition of the legists placing the Emperor's authority even in ecclesiastical matters above that of the Pope; he revives the heretical theses against the authority of the Church, such as had been circulating from Arnold of Brescia onwards, and he proclaims the superiority of Council over Pope. This last theory was then accepted even by the orthodox party, but in the writings of Marsilius it has a different ring, since he did not admit of a real ecclesiastical hierarchy.

He was, however, not a legist in the true sense of the word, but a political philosopher, and his groundwork is taken from Aristotle who dominated the general culture of the time as an undisputed authority. Marsilius provided the arguments for a naturalistic conception of society, which was creeping in, in opposition to a Christian and religious conception. His political polemic against the Church was based on the conception of human nature as self-sufficient and complete, able to rule itself and develop itself, even while he admitted a supernatural religion as an exigency of the other world, which is reflected on this world, but does not subject it to a system of order and coercion.

This naturalistic separation of the earthly society from the Church, integrally presented for the first time in Marsilius, corresponds, in its political consequences though not in its theoretical premises, to the separation Ockham advocated, on the basis of his political voluntarism and religious fideism. Both, therefore, reach the same conclusion, the strengthening of the secular power to the point of absolutism and of complete control of the Church, which would become no more than a spiritual association. Marsilius maintained that the Church had no legal character, and hence could not constrain men to follow the Christian law by a punitive system; she should only teach, exhort, correct and intimidate by eternal penalties. In any case, he adds, for the salvation of souls, which is the only aim of the Church, external punishment is no use, but only good conduct followed through conviction. On the other hand, as a man of his age, he declares that the prince may make laws punishing heresy with banishment, confiscation of goods and other temporal penalties, for the security of the State; the punishment inflicted on heretics would thus be not of a religious nature but solely political.

Marsilius from the politico-legal standpoint, Ockham from the philosophico-religious standpoint, in substance both tend to unite all powers in the single power of the State. The Emperor was still symbolically the apex of power, but both were aware of the evolution towards the national State or towards separate principalities. Nationalities were gaining substance in the thought of the time, not only in language, or as kingdoms freed from feudal ties, but also as moral entities. Feudal constitutionalism, communal democracies, the corporative conception of public bodies, local and general, within Christendom, no longer corresponded to the Romanised legal conception, nor to the Aristotelian scaffolding of so much political culture. Not only do we catch glimpses of the constituent elements of the modern state, but it begins, more or less unconsciously, to be a reality.

The idea of sovereignty which a century earlier meant only the independence of a kingdom or of a people (the two terms were often interchangeable) from a higher political authority—*universitas superiorem non recognoscens*—now comes to mean plenary and absolute powers. Sovereignty belonged originally to the people: this idea is now associated with that of a contract between the people and the sovereign. The idea of a contract as the practical origin of society is not a new one; its roots are to be found in all the endeavours to reconcile the rights of the many with the authority of one. But whereas in the Middle Ages the rights of the many were expressed in those of groups, rendered effectual by the corporation, from the beginning of humanism the rights of the many are conceived as standing by themselves, though ineffective without their transformation into sovereignty. Marsilius had already the idea of the sovereignty of the people, realised and expressed by the majority. Actually, such sovereignty is not immanent, but transient. The idea of the ancient *Lex Regia* returns, by which all the powers of the Roman people were transferred to 'the imperial authority'. This principle in its revived form is presented as a kind of political obligation of the many towards a head, a social contract in which the personal right of the contracting people—even if occasionally exercised—always resolves itself into the absolute power of the sovereign.

What we are here analysing is a tendency, which does not mean that in the XIV century corporate rights no longer existed or that medieval political society had disintegrated into a system of individual rights resolving themselves in practice into the right of the head. It is the idea that is creeping in, even while parliaments, such as that of Westminster, universities such as the Sorbonne, municipalities such as Florence, and above them all, the Papacy, even though enclosed in Avignon, resist as best they can the invading absolutism of princes and kings—when they themselves do not fall into absolutism in theory or practice.

The idea of sovereignty brought with it an extension of the ends of the State and an identification of the ends of the community with the ends of the sovereign. And since the concentration of resources in a single person, sustained by force, brought the widest extension of power, thus it widened still further the ends of power itself. The sole theoretical check, in the constant opinion of the schools of the time, was the natural or moral law and the law, positive and divine, represented by the Church. Yet the plenary powers of the Church are challenged, especially that of controlling and checking the power of kings and emperors and of deposing them if they are unworthy (according to medieval theory and praxis). The political community is dissolving into its elements, individuals and rulers, and is unable to resist the advancing tyranny, while striving painfully to safeguard corporative, particularist and traditional rights.

The decline of the supremacy of law over power—law being considered an abstraction, and power a concrete fact; 'quod principi placuit legis habet vigorem', echoed the exponents of Roman Law—rendered power increasingly personal. Even the canonists and theologians, like Ptolemy of Lucca and Egidius Romanus, while recognising the right of the corporative systems of the past, leaned towards pure or absolute monarchy. Liberty was conceived as in Cicero, as a participation in political life; hence in the absolute, monarchic régimes, there was no longer any room for liberty in the absence of any participation in power.

In the face of the tyranny that was growing up at the expense of liberties and which sought to evade the moral limits of the natural law, practical legal resistance grows weaker and weaker. Force prevails, local wars, rebellions, assassinations spread. The Free Companies are coming into being, supporting petty lords in their ambitions and rivalries and intimidating town and country. The ecclesiastical princes do the same as the lay princes, and the popes of Avignon too have recourse to arms and intrigue to maintain their dominion in Italy and to make their authority felt. It is no wonder that in such an environment anti-authoritarian currents appear; against the excessive powers of the Pope they maintain the superiority of the Council or secular sovereign (when they do not wish to see him deposed); against the kings and princes they have recourse to the theory and practice of tyrannicide.

The Curialists, who defend the papal theses against those of the Franciscans and jurists and against the propaganda of the Spirituals, hold fast to the medieval tradition, while the popes assemble their acts in Decretals, such as the Clementine Collection of Clement V and the Extravagants of John XXII, in which the rights of the Papacy are asserted to their full extent. Henry of Cremona returns to the thesis of the direct temporal authority of the popes, and their sovereignty over all goods or paramount universal property-right, and Agostino Trionfo champions the juridical absolutism of the Papacy.

Thus at the entrance to modern times, while the dissident Franciscans and the Spirituals, in their struggle to purify the Church from the defilement of earthly power and riches, form the religious basis of the absolutism of the princes, the Curialists and the organisational part of the Church tend more and more towards a juridical and centralising papal monarchism.

§ 19.—The administrative centralisation of the Church was the special achievement of the popes of Avignon, and above all of John XXII. The tendency had already started in the XI century, with the great Investiture conflicts, and it had gradually taken shape, now in the secular, now in the ecclesiastical sphere, according to the phases of development of the international papacy of the great centuries. In spite of this, the local churches still enjoyed special rights of nomination and important autonomies or exemptions, either by ecclesiastical tradition or as concessions from prince or king. But it is at Avignon that the papal Curia reaches a stage of centralised organisation such as it had never known. Officialdom is generalised and regulated down to the smallest details. The popes intervene frequently in the domestic affairs of the local churches, of the monastic orders and guilds. They confer university degrees, distribute prebends, overrule elections, handle benefices directly, while appeals, suits and pleas rain upon Avignon from all over the world.

The right of reservation, which in the past had been the exception, under the Avignon Popes became a custom. In virtue of this right the popes reserved to themselves the direct appointment to vacant benefices or in anticipation of their vacancy, overruling rights of presentation of patrons or electoral rights of religious bodies. As the practice of papal reservation became general the electoral rights of the local bodies were either contested or fell into decay. Such reservation was very useful to the papal Curia, enabling it to allocate benefices to its functionaries, thus lightening the expenses of administration; the bishoprics and other minor benefices remained for long periods without resident titularies, and their revenues accumulated in Avignon.

Protests, often vigorous protests, were not lacking, especially since often the charge of abusive centralisation was doubled by one of simony and nepotism; too often these charges were founded on fact. Edward III protested in strong terms against Pope Clement VI and the parliaments incessantly demanded a return to local nominations. Resistance sometimes took an active form. The dispute with Ludwig the Bavarian was the occasion for the Germans to refuse to recognise the papal nominations and to proceed to fresh nominations either by election or by imperial collation. This continued under Ludwig's successor Charles IV, in spite of promises made by him to Clement VI.

The struggle went on for some time and the popes, not wishing to compromise either their authority or their right, sought by means of understandings with kings and princes to keep the electoral bodies in subjection. These, caught between two fires, the Pope on one side and the Prince on the other (who was only too pleased to take a direct or indirect part in clerical appointments), ended by giving way and adapting themselves to the new trend.

Another activity of the Avignon popes was to reorganise their fiscal system. Besides reservation of benefices (productive of important resources in an economic structure still based on mortmain) many new taxes were created or revived from the past. Some were paid directly to the papal Curia, among them that of a third of the revenues of a benefice (not to speak of minor taxes on the occasion of ordinations, paid as honoraria to the personnel employed); other dues were collected on the spot by the papal collectors, especially the tithes, death dues and so forth. The fiscal methods of those days were primitive and detestable; in the present instance they were aggravated by ecclesiastical penalties, excommunications and other censures, of which the papal tax-gatherers made uncontrolled abuse. These reached the point of refusing ecclesiastical burial to the body of a bishop whose heirs had not paid the death dues. The peoples often grew exasperated, and what with the general wretchedness and the lack of currency, fiscal vexations became unbearable. Resistance frequently took the form of revolt, when papal agents were seized and imprisoned, or mutilated or killed. Excommunications and interdicts multiplied and fiscal motives overruled those of worship or cure of souls. Lamentations became general, so that to-day when we read the writings of the time and the later chronicles, we feel it hard to believe that they are not exaggerated.

On the other hand, the system was not wholly without justification. The Curia was a necessary organism for the government of the Church. Its centralism served to create a unitary discipline at a time when factors of disintegration were everywhere operative. Much money was needed for the wars in Italy, to regain St. Peter's Patrimony and other provinces, to maintain the feudal sovereignty of the Pope and to prevent the encroachments of the Empire. Moreover, the popes were making every effort to prevent the advance of the Mussulmans in the Mediterranean and in the East, and were working for union with the Greek Church. Here were reasons enough for the Curia to seek to have adequate resources, but so hateful a fiscal system produced lamentable effects on the populations, which grew increasingly disaffected towards a Papacy ill-represented locally and towards the Curia itself which through excess of wealth had fallen into moral decadence. The political result of the Avignon system was important. The Papacy was the first modern fiscal State, the only power with a monetary treasure, helping to generalise the use of money as means of exchange, the only power able to make large loans to kings and princes and which, combining economic and religious resources, from a small French city could still make itself felt in a disintegrating world.

The papal power was rendered stronger by the absolutism of its procedure, which whittled away all forms of consultation and collaboration. This was evident in the Council of Vienne under Clement V. Although the Cardinals had an important place in the Curia and often formed divided and turbulent factions, papal intervention and the administrative system steadily gained in vigour through a sound and vigorous canonical legislation. The Inquisition was strengthened and rendered more organic by means of a more constant procedure and the collaboration of the papal inquisitors, who were friars, with the local bishops. It functioned ruthlessly against the Templars, the Fraticelli and the dissident Franciscans, and later against the Flagellants. The propaganda against the excessive power of the popes and their riches weakened their spiritual force but not their canonical, penal, economic and administrative force. At the basis of society there was a conformity, religious and political, which, in spite of all, was not shaken. The social structure was still built on the unitary conception of Christendom and on the international, organised diarchy of Church and State.

The death of the Bavarian in 1347 coincided with the rising of the Romans and the tribunate of Cola di Rienzi, who for a brief while seemed to awaken the memories of the republican liberty of ancient Rome. Humanism had revived the cult of Rome; the Roman plebs had always liked to remember that it was the heir of the ancient Romans. The episode of Cola di Rienzi, notwithstanding imperial and papal support, soon fell into discredit, and on its repetition ended in blood. The remoteness of the popes from Rome was a great evil, religious and political; the Papacy suffered from it, and Italy fell more and more completely into the hands of tyrants and became the prey of factions and of local wars. The Free Companies devastated the country and sacked the towns. The popes, in order to maintain their position from a distance, to regain provinces that were either lost or in a state of anarchy, and in order to face the manœuvres of the imperialists, were driven to use the same means as the other Italian princes—wars, waged by mercenaries and the Free Companies, with which they combined the missions of preaching friars, indulgences for their followers, and excommunications and interdicts against rebellious chiefs and cities. Cardinal Albornoz, whom Innocent VI sent to Italy in 1353, was an able administrator, who certainly achieved much for the pontifical dominions and for Italy, but his action was compounded of compromises, adaptations, struggles and resistance, wars and truces, on the insidious platform of realistic politics. The religious reflex came from the hope of a return of the Pope to Rome and from the endeavour to pacify the populations and to restore order. But the very absence of the Pope from Rome was a source of disturbances and disorders. To many it seemed as though the Papacy were eclipsed not only from Italy but from the world.

Several times in the Middle Ages had the popes left Rome for other Italian cities or crossed the Alps for prolonged periods, holding assemblies and councils and going to and fro in the world, now triumphant as fathers, now as fugitives, and now trailing in the wake of armies sent to subdue their rebel subjects. In ancient days some had taken the road of exile, to die in the East Yet never had the Papacy itself seemed failing or the Roman See tottering. But since the popes had established themselves at Avignon with all their court, buying the city and building there palaces and fortresses, it seemed as if there were no longer a universal Papacy, but only a Curia for dealing with Bulls and business.

This period was styled 'the Babylonish Capitivity'. The mystics, the Spirituals, the poets, the polemists made the name a symbol. The Italians who felt most keenly the remoteness of the popes and who suffered from the moral and political crises more than any other people of the time, hated Avignon. With all allowance for heated passions, the reminder of Babylon was not unfitting; the francophil policy of the Avignon popes touched servility. No pope has sunk so low as Clement V, who to please Philip the Fair allowed the trial of the corpse of Boniface VIII and ordered that his acts should be erased from the Pontifical Register; who also decreed the suppression of the Order of Templars. The chaos into which the Germanic Empire and Italy fell comes partly from the captivity. And if it cannot be said that the moral decadence of the papal court at Avignon was the effect of forsaking Rome, we can assuredly say that the formation of a court similar to those of the princes of the time, under the influence of the early Renascence and in a period of great affluence of riches, contributed largely to the corruption of the clergy who had gathered round Avignon. Even if Petrarch be accused of exaggerating, it is not possible to reject his testimony or that of other contemporaries.

In this period the mystical element, pure of all defilement, is represented by two women of the highest worth, even from the human standpoint, Bridget of Sweden and Catherine of Siena. Unlike the rebellious Spirituals, these two women are faithful to the authority of the Papacy, both pray and labour for the return of the Pope to Rome, Catherine with a special mission that certain French writers have sought in vain to minimise. But both have a keen sense of ecclesiastical decadence and the faults of the popes; they are in the line of Dante. In a letter addressed to Pope Clement VI, St. Bridget makes Jesus say to the Pope: ' . . . I will punish thee for having pursued thy goods wit' unworthy means and for the evils by thee unchained on the Church in the days when thou didst enjoy peace . . .' And as the Pope did not reply to her, she heard Christ speak these words: 'The earth hides heaven from such prelates.' One of Bridget's most lively pages on the conduct of the priests ends with the Dantesque words: 'May they be accursed by heaven and by earth.'

No less bold in deploring and commanding was Catherine of Siena. She speaks in the name of God and manifests His will with extraordinary firmness to popes, kings, princes, peoples and magistrates. She has a mission, as even her adversaries recognise. It seems as if in the defection of men God had raised up women to be His prophetesses (soon a third extraordinary woman would appear on the national, political, military plane, she too divinely inspired—Joan of Arc), as though to usher in modern times under an influence at once mystical and active, religious and political, with their sacrifice as a pure holocaust.

Unhappily the gulf between the mystical currents, (whether faithful or dissident) and the organisational forces of the Church grew ever deeper, even when a saint like Guillaume de Grimoard was elected pope as Urban V, and attempted a reform of the clergy. The idea of a reform of the Church was not new, and was beginning to be keenly felt, but the anti-papal campaigns of the Spirituals and the continual attacks on the fiscal policy of the Curia directed the reform towards a disintegration of the Church. The awakening sense of nationality helped to make local churches conscious of themselves as national churches, and the efforts of clerics to defend themselves against the fiscal burdens laid on them by the papal Curia drove them more and more into the arms of the secular authorities. Kings and princes for their part sought to subjugate the clergy to their will, and to profit by benefices and ecclesiastical wealth. The Assembly of Vincennes in France (1329), the *Statute of Provisors* in England (1351), followed by the *Statute of Praemunire* (1353) limited the rights of the local clergy, hampered their relations with the papal Curia, and laid the foundations of national churches. In Spain too the trend is towards a close association of the clergy with the court, and this is facilitated by the struggles against the Moors and against the Jews.

In the Empire there is no tendency towards national churches, nor in Italy. Among the innumerable kingdoms, principalities and free cities, there were no centres of polarisation like Paris or London. On the other hand, the Empire had become a shadow of what it had been in the past. In Germany there was no longer any true bond, moral, political, or economic, between the various parts of the Empire; the break-up was complete. Charles IV the Moravian sought to install a new order by his Golden Bull of 1355, but actually it consecrated the existing anarchy. What was remarkable, and shows the spirit of the time, was that the Golden Bull omitted any right of the Holy See to sanction the election of the 'King of the Romans' and Emperor. This omission was made with the active consent of the ecclesiastical and lay Electors, and with the implicit assent of the bulk of the German clergy. Innocent VI protested in vain. The Golden Bull remained the title-deed of the new Empire, which had been grafted, for a brief space, on the old, already withered stem.

Henceforth neither Empire nor Papacy would be those of the Middle Ages, interwoven in organisation and power at the summit of an ecclesiastico-feudal society. The world had changed. The most tangible effect of the Golden Bull concerned Italy, which now escaped almost entirely from Germanic influence and from the claims of the Empire. At the same time Italy lost a political orientation, and divided as she was into so many local principalities, would be torn more and more by internal conflicts, the intrigues of powerful families and partisan passions, without an effectual power to hold them in check or to maintain order and give a unity of purpose. The evolution of Italy towards autonomy of the Empire and, under certain aspects, of the Papacy also, had not waited till now to begin, but the policy of Charles IV and the absence of the Papacy in Avignon eased its progress.

All the movements of the time, political, religious and cultural, were at bottom a breaking away from the oneness and universality of the medieval conception, towards a particular and individualistic localisation. And at the same time they were a quest for other motives of coalescence and of a solidarity more living and more profound. Hence a seething of new elements which would find formal expression in humanistic culture but not yet a decisive orientation.

The forces of decay were reinforced and social anarchy increased by the Black Death which invaded Europe in the middle of the XIV century, decimating it and scattering the incipient nuclei of the new social and intellectual classes that were rising. The effects were terrible—everywhere famines and popular risings in both town and country. The necessity of order and the instinct of conservation rendered ruthless those who wielded power and force. The Church suffered as much as other social organisms and perhaps more. The need to restore the nuclei of the local churches and to resume a normal rhythm of life brought a carelessness of relations with the centre; both the sense of independence and the pressure of the secular power grew more marked. Discipline everywhere became lax and vanished, especially in the decimated convents. The brothers scattered and resumed their freedom, or else acted on personal initiative, reviving the ideas of the Spirituals and the dissidents. The plague gave a pretext for all the apocalyptic movements, which coloured generous impulses and fervent asceticism.

The return to normal life was hampered for some time by the Free Companies, by the vagabond troops of workless men, by an unchecked brigandage and by all sorts of anarchic movements, which were favoured by the renewal of the wars, especially in France. One of the most natural outcomes, given the memories of the past and the apocalyptic temperament of many friars which was excited by the terrible advent of the plague, was the movement of the Flagellants. These thought to appease divine anger by scourging their naked bodies, praying and singing through the streets and market-places in an exaltation half mystical and half fanatical. The crowd followed them and felt the contagion of their excitement. Once again there was preaching against the wealth and immorality of the clergy, anti-social proclamations against authority, the hierarchy, property. Moreover, a violent hatred broke out against the Jews, who were accused of spreading the pestilence, and this led to horrifying assaults and massacres. The repression of the Flagellants also by the ecclesiastical and religious authorities was violent and cruel. Here and there the custom of flagellation remained as an ascetic practice, which St. Vincent Ferrers revived a few years later in his popular and famous preaching. He was the last representative, and an orthodox one, of a movement soon to disappear.

# CHAPTER VI

## THE GREAT SCHISM AND THE RENAISSANCE

§ 20.—The return of the popes to Rome in 1377, so longed-for by the Italians and for which both Petrarch and St. Catherine had done much, unfortunately led—on the death of Gregory XI in 1378—to the Great Schism, which lasted about forty years. This event did not remain within the bounds of an ecclesiastical controversy between legitimate popes and illegitimate, but had an immense effect on the relations between Church and State, which were now set on a new course, both in theory and practice.

The immediate effect of the Schism was to divide Europe into two 'obediences'—the legitimate obedience of Rome, to which belonged the Empire, Northern and Central Italy, England and Wales, Ireland, Flanders, and the dissident obedience of Avignon, comprising France, Savoy, Scotland, Castille, Aragon, Navarre, Portugal, Naples and Sicily. When the Council of Pisa elected Pope Alexander V, he too illegitimate, and the popes of Rome and Avignon (Gregory XII and Benedict XIII) would not give way, there was a fresh scission. Several nations of either side, including the Empire and part of Italy, supported the pope of Pisa, other nations stood neutral, till John XXIII—who succeeded Alexander V—had the greater part of Europe in his obedience, and, yielding to general desire and to vigorous pressure from every side, summoned the Council of Constance. Gregory XII, the legitimate pope, who had retired to Venetia, sent his envoys to Constance, and these, in order to give the council canonical legitimacy, repeated the acts of convocation in his name; thereupon he resigned. John XXIII was obliged to a like renunciation, and consented unwillingly. Benedict, who persisted in refusal, was deposed by the Council, though he never surrendered and to his death the kingdom of Aragon remained faithful to him. Thus in 1417, when Martin V was elected at Constance by a special conclave of Cardinals and other delegates from the various nations, the Great Schism came to an end.

In forty years of uncertainty about which pope was the true one, when support for one or the other was determined by external, mainly political criteria, or the king's pleasure—for the kings decided to which obedience their kingdoms should belong—the tendency that had already asserted itself during the Avignon period, of the local churches to withdraw upon themselves and buttress themselves by the secular authority, found the way made easy. Where the clergy of their own initiative wished to support another pope than that supported by the court, or to hold themselves neutral, they were faced by either secular repression, when this was possible, or by the intrusion of other bishops and beneficed clergy appointed by the court or by the pope the court favoured. Thus to uncertainty about the head of the Church was added unrest among the clergy, an increased secular interference, and the multiplicity and opposition of bishops and chapters.

In this situation many countries sought a new basis for their churches, releasing them from the many canonical and fiscal ties binding them to the papacy, and substituting national or provincial councils and royal sanction. In this the clergy of France led the way, in the period after 1394 when the kingdom followed the way of neutrality between the various popes fighting for power. They held synods and councils, they fixed the rules for collation to benefices, made ecclesiastical laws, and, in the spirit of tradition that went back a hundred years, to Philip the Fair, they laid the organisational foundations of Gallicanism. The English clergy had already won autonomy; the *Statute of Praemunire* of Edward III was of 1353. The same course was followed in the countries with a certain national unity, such as Aragon. The growth of nationalities was already such at the end of the XIV century as to weaken the sense of universality, characteristic of medieval Christendom. In the Council of Constance, organisation by 'nation' prevailed over the more rational system of organisation by matter.

The Councils of the first half of the XV century did not meet, like the great Oecumenical Councils, primarily to define some revealed dogma that had become an object of theological controversy, but rather to regulate practical problems that affected both the Church and the politico-ecclesiastical organisation of the time. It is therefore not surprising to find at Constance nearly 18,000 ecclesiastics and over 50,000 laymen, while during the three years of the Council more than 150,000 foreigners passed through the city. The lay princes, and above all the Emperor Sigismund, through the multiplicity of popes and the depreciation of their personal authority, played at Constance a part of the highest importance; but the ruling section of all three Councils (Pisa, Constance, Bâle), was formed by the educated men, the new university class, which, with its rationalism, stood inter-mediate between ecclesiastical dogmatism and popular feeling.

There was nothing new in the intervention of elements extraneous to the hierarchy in Church Councils; what was new was the important and decisive part played by the universities. This may have been oc-casioned by the multiplicity of popes and favoured by the national tendency that was now asserting itself openly, but its basis was the Conciliar Theory, which had taken shape in the previous century and in the XV century had become almost general, and was defended by the freest spirits, the most vigorous intellects and the most zealous reformers of the Church. The university made this theory its own and sought its practical realisation.

In 1394, when the Schism had been ravaging the Church for sixteen years, the Sorbonne organised a kind of referendum on how unity could be restored. It received over 10,000 replies, which were classified by Nicholas de Clémangis. There were those who advocated the method of arms, which had already been tried: let war decide which was the true pope. Others proposed arbitration, and there were some who suggested direct conversations between the two claimants. There was the wish to avert war. Arbitration was desired by neither party. Direct conversations were a failure. Therefore, then, the majority in-clined towards the summoning of a General Council, which would settle the dispute between the various popes by an act of authority. There were plenty of experts to examine the legal questions involved and to propose reforms for the future, and the secular authorities could be expected to ensure respect of the decisions of the Council by force. (There is a curious similarity to the position after the Great War, and the creation of the League of Nations.)

The referendum of the University of Paris paved the way for the idea of the Council as superior to the Pope and hence also for that of a Council without the Pope or not summoned by the Pope. The greatest theologians of the time, Jean Gerson, Francesco Zabarella, Baldo di Perugia, Pierre d'Ailly, Henry of Hesse, were for the superiority of Council to Pope. Popular opinion favoured the conciliar movement, so that a Council could assemble at Pisa without any papal convocation, in spontaneous form, and be considered as a true oecumenical council, invested with authority. It declared the two popes of Rome and Avignon heretical and deprived, and proceeded to the election of a third pope. All this in perfect good faith, with the intent of serving the Church, ending the Schism, initiating the reform and giving peace to Christendom.

The theory of the Council as superior to the pope began to make its way from the day the two terms were presented as in opposition. Frederick Barbarossa, after instigating the election of the anti-Pope Victor IV against Alexander III who was accused of felony towards the Emperor, called a council at Pavia to judge which of the two was true pope. The conciliar thesis was then maintained by the famous Gerhoh of Reichersberg.

This precedent three centuries removed from the Council of Constance would have had no intrinsic connection with the conciliar theory had it not been for the dispute of Boniface VIII with Philip the Fair, who after the pope's death made Clement V accuse him to the Council of Vienne, and for the conflict of the Spirituals with John XXII and the writings of the anti-papal publicists, culminating in Ockham and Marsilius of Padua. The great Schism incubated such historical elements, so that the conciliar theory triumphed over the opposition of the Roman Curia, and was not only for a long time accepted by theologians and canonists, but would form the basis of the claims of Catholic princes and national clergies.

There are those who see in the conciliar theory a democratic content, holding that it represented within the Church, from the canonical standpoint, a development of the system of popular election of the hierarchy, with the establishment of a real ecclesiastico-lay parliament. To our mind the theory that the Council was above the Pope, that it should be periodically summoned, that it should act as supreme tribunal for all disputes affecting the Church and Christendom, is not of ecclesiological but of political origin. It is true that theologians of the XV century did their utmost to find reasons in support of such a thesis in early Christian tradition and in the Scriptures, with a rationalist incursion into the constitution of society, but at bottom the problem was of a political nature, even though carried on to an ecclesiological platform, for the fabric of society was still interwoven with that of the Church.

Society was then identified with Christendom. Pope, bishops, kings, emperors, universities, immunitary bodies, clerical and lay vassals, free cities and independent principalities were all operating within the Church, each with a special function, each as a living corporation, inter-related and with a common end. The decline of the medieval Empire and Papacy, the consolidation of the Monarchies, the rise and development of Humanism, the consciousness of the new-born nations, had displaced the focal points of society. A new class dominated, the men of the universities, which without much opposition was assuming control of religious and political thought. The whole effort of the theologians and *universitaires* of the time (learning was still theological, even if philosophical and philological) was to bring an order into this complex society, which was falling apart and fostering the germs of a profound division both between the various parts of Christendom, as the politico-religious unity of Europe, and between the Papacy and the national clergies and their realms.

Most of the men who assembled at Pisa, Constance and Bâle believed that the greatest disturbance came from the popes, both through their exaggerated claims to secular power, the memory of which had not faded, and still more through their direct interference in the ordering of the national clergy and through their fiscal exactions: the riches these brought them were a cause of venality, struggles, immorality and simony. The efforts of the councils were not confined to the particular case of the Schism, but sought a new order and a general reform of the Church. Such councils were therefore not strictly ecclesiastical assemblies (apart from their canonical procedure), but all the various orders of Christendom took part, the university class predominating. This predominance made them at once fruitful and barren.

The theologians of Pisa, Constance and Bâle did not take their stand on ecclesiology; a true ecclesiology, in the two-fold sense, philological and theological, which would shortly come into being under the pressure of other thought and other struggles, as yet did not exist. As yet the Papacy, the various churches and the secular rulers all turned for the defence of their rights to the collections of Canon Law, the papal bulls, the decisions of general and local synods, pragmatic sanctions, privileges of exemption, the whole network of positive law which, despite appeals to tradition and to the Scriptures, was taken as a legal and social construction often of diplomatic character, and entered into the theological and scholastic construction only where the two chanced to overlap.

The papal power as the Power of the Keys, in the religious sense, was not brought under discussion save by heretical currents or by Catholics carried away by controversy. The problem of the papal infallibility was then not raised, as it would be in the years before the Vatican Council of 1870. The problems of the papal power were attacked in a political spirit; the Council became a kind of mediating centre between the Pope and the nations, in such a manner as to limit the papal faculties to the advantage of the local churches, of particular kingdoms and of special bodies, and of that politico-social whole that was then understood by the word Nation.

It was for these reasons that the conciliar theory prevailed over the praxis of the Curia, which was founded on the Pseudo-Isidorian Decretals and had created the tradition of the medieval Councils from that of the Lateran in 1123 to that of Vienne in 1311. The influence of nominalist logic, founded on a basically naturalistic concept, (since the whole is greater than the part, the Council is greater than the Papacy), combined with the influence of Humanism, which tended for preference towards the concreteness of a particularised society (rather than towards one tending to universalism), and the rise of the intellectual classs which had taken control of collective life, carried the theory to its extreme conclusions. The Council of Pisa was not convoked by either pope and ended in the nomination of a third. The Council of Constance, summoned by an illegitimate pope (John XXIII), and regularised by the spontaneous and subsequent act of the legates of the legitimate pope (Gregory XII), in its IV and V sessions ended by proclaiming the superiority of Council to Pope as a doctrine of the Church and by establishing that the Council should meet periodically as a permanent institution. The Council of Bâle did without the legitimate pope, declared him illegitimate and nominated an anti-pope. In all three Councils the experiment was made of a direct administration of the Church, whether with the Pope, without the Pope or even against the Pope.

It must not surprise the reader if we attribute the same sociological value to the three Councils, though well aware that from the canonical standpoint that of Pisa is not recognised as regular, that in the Council of Constance the decisions of Sessions IV and V are reputed invalid, and that the Council of Bâle was valid only up to the time when it was superseded by the Council of Ferrara and later of Florence. From our standpoint, the spirit of the three Councils was the same, in all their phases, whether legitimate or illegitimate. The discrimination from the point of view of legitimacy was made later, when the post-Constance popes reassumed their monarchic power in full, and the canonists could appraise the past at their ease and classify it according to the prevailing canonical praxis; the theologians and university doctors themselves could then better sift the conflicting theses and find, according to their various schools and tendencies, those compromises that would save both the orthodox theory of papal authority and local rights.

The reform of the Church had been talked of for over a century. At Constance it was discussed at length, and the necessity of a reform 'from the head to the limbs' was solemnly proclaimed in a famous canon. This reform was envisaged more in respect of relations between the national churches and the Papacy than as a real moral renewal of the clergy; it was more on the administrative plane, with political effects, than on a religious plane. There is no doubt that there were not a few who aspired to a complete reform, and many provisions of all three Councils were directed to this end, but the prevailing tendency was an endeavour to shake off the centralising yoke of the Papacy in the administration of benefices and ecclesiastical revenues, in the heavy dues going to the Curia through the annates, in the judicial system and the granting of spiritual and temporal favours—a whole system that led to intrigues, simony, and impoverishment of local resources which accumulated at the centre.

In this spirit the Concordats of Constance were drawn up in 1418, between the new pope Martin V and the various nations. They were the ripest and most interesting fruit of the movement towards de-centralisation, which marks the passage from the medieval papacy of a united Christendom to the super-national papacy of modern times. But at Constance the Concordats with the nations—that is, with the clergy, secular authorities and university doctors—were given a temporary form. They are a prolongation of the new type of Council. These concordats were to be revised and readapted in successive Councils. Indeed, they were spoken of again at Bâle. But it was not long before papal reaction against this transposing of powers and of ruling and administrative organs. Eugene IV, who succeeded Martin V, and who summoned the Council of Bâle (1431) in the hope that it would raise a dyke against the ever growing disorder, ordered its dissolution. The Council resisted, and the Pope, abandoned by nearly all, after a year and a half of struggle had to give way. The Council then superimposed itself completely on the Pope, to the point that many prelates and laymen felt it had gone too far and rallied to Eugene IV. The Pope seized this moment of uncertainty and disorder to send a *Liber apologeticus* to the secular princes, denouncing the abuses of the Council and vindicating the rights of the Papacy. This was the beginning of a revival, with new elements, of the centralising action of the popes, and of a system of direct understandings no longer with the 'nations' or with the local clergy, but with the princes. These indeed had profited by the Schism and the conciliar disputes to take up a commanding position in respect of the Papacy.

Charles VII of France, in the period when France was recovering national consciousness after the Hundred Years War (which had ended through the heroism and sacrifice of St. Joan), in order both to obviate religious disorder and to defend the autonomy of the local clergy against the Curia in Rome, had the idea of a royal Council, composed of ecclesiastics and laymen. After hearing the delegates of the Council of Bâle and those of Eugene IV, this Council issued, in 1438, the famous ordinance known as the Pragmatic Sanction of Bourges, which laid the foundations of the rights of the Gallican clergy. Naturally it was in favour of the superiority of Council to Pope, and was opposed to papal reservations and provisions in the collation of benefices. It re-affirmed the right of chapters and religious houses to elect their bishops or abbots, and it added—what is significant—that the kings and princes of the realm might recommend their nominees '*par des sollicitations bénignes et bienveillants*'. These 'sollicitations' at once became commands and interference. The system became general; the kings took the place of the Pope in respect of the major part of beneficiary and fiscal rights in the national churches.

The Pragmatic Sanction of Charles VII was imitated by the new Emperor of Germany, Albert II, who promulgated a similar ordinance the following year at Mainz. The other kings and princes of Christendom, by analogous systems or by practical action, invested themselves with many papal rights, especially in regard to benefices, and this no longer as in the XI century with the feudal concept of investiture, but as benevolent and authoritarian intervention to defend the State and religion from papal interference and to prevent revenues from being sent out of the country.

The popes, from Eugene onwards, protested and resisted, and never recognised such pragmatic sanctions or similar acts as legal, however they might have to tolerate them in practice. The kings and princes used them as a political weapon in their relations with Rome, especially the King of France with whom the dispute was keenest and most prolonged, and who would now promise the popes to abolish them, and now give them renewed vigour. From that time forth understandings were arranged directly between the popes and the princes. The agreements between the Pope and the 'nations' were at an end. The local clergies often found themselves between the double pressure of popes and monarchs, who sought more and more to take control of the churches and to abolish in practice and by agreements between themselves any rights of election or presentation to benefices held by religious bodies in the various countries.

§ 21.—Among the exponents of the conciliar theory, as it was held i the second half of the XIV and the first half of the XV centuries, there were both those whose Catholic orthodoxy remained unshaken and those who deviated towards heretical currents. Between these two groups there was neither religious solidarity nor political community of interest. The Councils of Pisa, Constance and Bâle, while professing bold and untraditional theories on the Pope, the Council and the Church, were no less rigorous than previous Councils in their dealings with heretics. The reiteration of the condemnation of Wyclif, the condemnation of John Hus and Jerome of Prague, and even the condemnation of tyrannicide in the form in which it was defended by Jean Petit and John von Fulkenberg,[1] took place at Constance, when advocacy of the conciliar theory was at its height. The same atmosphere is to be found at Pisa and at Bâle.

The great heresies of the Middle Ages from the Cathars and Albigensians to the Spiritualists and Flagellants had been not so much clearly formulated theories as popular and social movements, that had assumed a religious aspect and a dissident and sectarian character. Theoretical affirmations on authority, the power and wealth of the Church, marriage, the political society, circulated among the people as practical impulses, driving them to seek a new moral and economic order in mystical exaltation and social revolt. The heresies of the Schools, though not uninfluenced by this environment, remained extraneous to it. Apocalyptic Joachimism was never clearly formulated as a theory; it remained as a tendency of which there are many traces in later writers, even in St. Bonaventura and Dante. The exaltation of ecclesiastical poverty found its great theorist in Ockham, who maintained the conception of a separation of two distinct worlds, that of the Church, founded on poverty and hence deprived of all social power, and that of the laity to whom possession of goods and of external power was permitted. It must be remembered that then public power was not conceivable otherwise than strictly bound up with the possession of goods and the principle of property, in whatever form this might be envisaged, and even if such property was merely paramount or symbolic.

This compromise between the principle of absolute poverty and the economico-political ordering of society was lacking in dynamism and

[1] See Finke, *Acta Concitii Constanciensis*.

in intrinsic logic. The question still remained in the doctrinal and university domain. It was revived by Wyclif, he too an Englishman from the university of Oxford, which for more than a century had rivalled the Sorbonne. Wyclif united on a common ground what Ockham had separated, forming an irreconcilable dualism. Wyclif's common ground is the principle of Grace: no possession and no power is lawful save for those, whether clerics or laymen, who are in a state of grace. With Wyclif the problem of Grace is seen in its social aspect, the ultimate term of all the other problems of collective life, of the relations between the individual and society and between the spiritual power and the secular power. He sought, by his numerous and unequal writings, to systematise the whole theologico-social problem that was occupying the thought and activity of his time. He reacted against Ockham's nominalism, to the point of reaching an extreme realism. For him the Ideas are realities in the very Essence of God; God does not work through His dominant Will, free from all rationality, but instead God is an ordered and rational power, His activity is determined, and we by Grace are part of the divine determinism, either as predestinate or foreknown as reprobate. In this iron system of divine determinism Wyclif sought to save man's inward moral freedom by a dialectic in which the free resolves itself into the necessary and the necessary into the free. The predestinate of necessity seek good, they do not commit sins and mortal sins are not to be imputed to them. On the contrary the reprobate are bound to evil, and their sins are sins indeed.

The social development of this system, and it was the motive of the Wyclifite reform, is inset in his theodicy. The Church is the society of the predestinate. Salvation comes by Faith; Scripture alone and not tradition is the law of Christ and all can read and interpret the Scriptures. (It was he who made the first English translation of the Bible and circulated it among the people.) Priesthood, the Sacraments, the teaching and ruling authority of the bishops and the pope, the religious orders are all attacked by Wyclif, who wishes to restore the Church to her primal poverty and to a purely interior religion. Under this aspect he is a precursor of the Reformation. Buttressing himself by the royal power in the struggle against the mendicant Orders and the Papacy, he maintains that Church property should be secularised.

But on the other hand, by maintaining that only the predestinate might hold possessions, offices of magistracy and dominion over others, since they alone are participant by Grace in God's possession of earthly things, he gave an impulse to the communistic currents that were creeping among the people in a latent state, through the old influence of the popular heresies, bringing from time to time an explosion of discontent among peoples stirred by apocalyptic mysticism and oppressed by the fiscal régime, by feudal servitude and by the appalling crises that followed the Black Death. The nobles had then brought in the Statute of Labourers which reinstated a real form of serfdom.

Wyclif's action was confined to England where the protection of the Court enabled him to spread his doctrines among the lower clergy, and among the bourgeoisie and people. The Wyclifite controversy was the result of practical antagonisms between the secular clergy, the friars and the laity, and of the clashes between the Curia at Avignon, the English episcopacy and Court. The story of the strife between the King of England and the Papacy over episcopal appointments, tithes, papal reservations and ecclesiastical dues is a long one. For their continual wars at home and abroad (the beginning of the Hundred Years War came almost immediately after the conquest of Wales and the English defeat in Scotland) the English kings had great need of money and also of papal support and protection. Hence conflicts alternated with restoration of peace and agreements with the papal Curia. The popes for their part in moments of peace sought to recover the ground they had lost, so long as they did not meet with resistance among the upper clergy.

This environment was highly favourable to Wyclif when he defended the secular power against the Papacy and against the upper clergy and the religious orders. (It may be noted that Chaucer's picture of friars and monks and bishop's agents—the Sompnour in the *Canterbury Tales*—is much the same as Boccaccio's.) The Court in London, and especially the brother of Richard II, John of Gaunt and his party, which was hostile to the clergy, took Wyclif under protection. The people saw the corrupt life of the secular courts and of not a few of the ecclesiastical courts; through the thought and writings of Wyclif which were spread among them by the 'poor priests', who were nick-named

Lollards, they learned of corruption and simony in the papal court; as a result they drew the conclusion that all by their sins had lost the right to possession of goods and of civil and ecclesiastical office, and that the whole of society must be permeated by reform in the most drastic and substantial manner, beginning with the sharing of the masses in the goods of the earth.

It is usual to minimise the influence of Wyclif's theories on the Peasants' Revolt of 1381, and indeed its causes were various and complex. But if we note how in those days social and economic theories were expressed in religious terms, we shall see the importance of their influence on hungry peasants, crushed by taxation, forced to work at the same wages as before the plague and doubly oppressed by the lay and clerical powers, so that mystical and psychological motives would rouse them more potently than purely material ones. Certainly after the Black Death savage revolts were a melancholy feature all over Europe. The Jacquerie in France is of 1358; in 1378 it was the revolt of the *Ciompi* in Florence; in 1381 the Peasants' Revolt in England, to mention only the most famous, but everywhere distress was terrible, the masses were restless, a brutal violence ravaged civil life, and anti-social theories found a soil prepared for them.

Certain of Wyclif's theses were condemned by the Council of London and afterwards by Gregory XI in 1378; this did not prevent their spread in England and in certain foreign universities. The marriage of Richard II with Anne of Bohemia brought the two countries into contact. The University of Prague was a fairly recent one; it was the first university of Central Europe, founded by Charles IV in 1347. The Wyclifite theories there found a soil suited to their wide development. In Prague too motives of Church reform are at the basis of the intellectual trends of the university. The great wealth and wide power of the clergy here as everywhere led to scandals, simony and conflicts. Added to this was the Great Schism, the influence of the conciliar theory, the struggles between clergies and courts over the choice of the pope, and over nomination to benefices. Bohemia was then divided, a part for GregoryXII and a part for Alexander V; the university stood for reform and the Council. John Hus, an austere priest, professor and then rector of the University, urged reform from chair and pulpit, drawing his inspiration from the theories of Wyclif and developing them to suit the intellectual or popular circles he was addressing. The position was complicated by national issues. The University of Prague was composed of Bohemians, Moravians, Poles and Saxons. In founding it the King had allotted three votes to the Bohemians, who were to include Moravians and Slavs (or Slavonians), and one to the Germans, who were to include Poles and Saxons. But subsequently since there were large numbers of Germans, these had usurped the three votes and formed the majority. Jerome of Prague, bound to Hus by friendship and following his theories, wished to vindicate the ancient rights of the Bohemians, and Hus, who was confessor to Queen Sophia, obtained a rescript restoring their three votes. The result was the exodus from Prague of German and Polish professors and students, numbering about 36,000, and in a few years rival universities had been founded at Cracow, Leipzig and Ingolstadt. The Germans took with them a violent resentment against Hus, and were in a strong position because Hus's theories were erroneous and heretical and led to rebellion against the Church and against the Empire. The animosity of the German university class found fruitful soil in the political endeavours of the new Emperor Sigismund to lay hold on Bohemia. These questions were certainly marginal when Hus led his campaign of reform, but they had an unexpected outcome when he was tried and burned alive at Constance in 1415.[1] Then for the Bohemians who had flocked to the Council, the imprisonment of Hus, in despite of his imperial safe-conduct, the behaviour of Sigismund and the Germans, and finally the bearing of Hus himself at the stake (which roused many to admiration), laid the foundations of a national Hussitism, which was heretical as Hus was heretical, who at the stake had become its hero and its martyr.

Hus's theories were not very different from those of Wyclif, nor were they systematically presented. He continued on the same themes, giving them a popular colour and national emphasis and relating them to the Schism that was disturbing Europe. For Hus the Church as a doctrinal and sacramental public order vanishes in an ethical mysticism; the use of the chalice for the communion of the laity was principally

---

[1] In England the statute De Heretico comburendo had been passed in 1401.

intended to strip the priesthood of the character of a separate and hierarchic class. The chalice became a war standard and a source of division among the Hussites themselves. The central point of Hussite teaching is a deterministic predestination, which makes of the elect the sole ruling element of society, the propertied class, the men invested with authority. This predestined election is the mainspring of action of Hus's followers, who turn against the upper clergy and the court, their local adversaries, and against the central authority of emperor and pope, in order to vindicate the independence of the Bohemian nation. To subdue the revolt the Pope calls a Crusade. Three wars in succession are ruthlessly waged, till Bohemia is conquered, and the scattered Hussites take refuge in inaccessible places. The crusades in the hands of Sigismund were at once a vindication of the dominance of the German people over the Slav Czechs, and of the dominion of the reigning house over the Bohemian nobles who sought support among the insurgent masses. The ferment of reform remained in the centre of Europe in a latent condition. The Hussite theories were never stamped out, and circulated in secret. The causes of the moral and economic crisis remained, together with the national spirit which had been rendered keener and more effective by the wars.

The sense of nationality that was developing all over Europe between the XIV and XV centuries had a religious character, since the social structure was still religious. Therefore the Christian uniformism, which produced the persecution of heretics even by burnings and crusades, was reinforced by a national intolerance, which produced an expulsion of dissidents and defeated rebels. These could not remain in their own country; they were considered a danger to the social order. Europe was still wide, not all regions had been explored or inhabited, and they could find sure refuges. They migrated from one region to another, from one kingdom to another. The Hussite wars were a mixture between religious and national. The pursuit of dissidents involved the Jews as well, who were spread over Central Europe. The Jew was alien to the social body. On all occasions of conflict or popular effervescence the Jews were victims. National sentiments intensified the persecutions from the standpoint that nonconformity was becoming a religious and political peril.

The Jewish people from the time of their dispersion by the Romans had found it hard to live in Western communities, remaining everywhere distinct, as a racial and religious group, often hostile, as well as through the special qualities that drove them to become a mediating element between the various peoples and various classes. Thus through the centuries they had suffered the ebb and flow of popular tides of religious hate and political persecution.

The first outburst of popular hatred in the Christian West coincided with the first Crusade, when in France and Germany the armies and the mob turned to massacre the Jews, in spite of the fact that these were defended by bishops and monastic Orders. It was a blaze of mob frenzy, a blind fanaticism, due to morbid forms of religious feeling and popular resentment. The same happenings marked the second Crusade, in spite of St. Bernard's efforts to prevent them. In the wars against the Albigensians and in those against the Moors the Jews suffered as hostile to the established order, infidels dangerous to the faith and to the realm.

Popes and emperors sought to safeguard the Jews through regulations that at the same time limited their activities, impeded their influence on Christians, and struck at their methods of usury. There came to be even a physical separation of Jews from Christians, by means of the ghettoes and a special political supervision. The dependence of the Jews directly on the pope, emperor or king was a legal institution indicating that their lives and the rights recognised to them were inviolable. None the less where the peoples were in ferment, where kings feared for the stability of their thrones, in periods of social anarchism (as during the Black Death, which the Jews were accused of spreading), anti-Jewish feelings reawakened in the most violent form. In England it was Edward I who in 1290 expelled the Jews, but he allowed them to take with them their portable property and money. They would not return till the time of Cromwell.

In Spain the Jews were objects of special mistrust in the wars against the Moors, for the liberation of the provinces still occupied by Islam. As a remedy, and as a means of obviating popular massacres, 1391 saw the promulgation in Castille of one of the most unreasonable and unjust of politico-religious enactments. The Jews were forced to choose

between baptism and death. It was believed that baptism would ensure their religious assimilation and at the same time their national
loyalty. On the contrary, the result was the crypto-judaism of false
converts, known also as *marrani*, who had loyalty neither towards
religion or nation; both, through the violence of a royal decree, had
become enemies more to be hated than ever before. Thus after a century of conflicts, persecutions and inquisitorial fires, in 1306 the Jews
were expelled from Spain, at the very time of the expulsion of the
last of the Moors.

In France Philip the Fair decreed the banishment of the Jews in 1306,
believing that this would be a means of procuring money. The ban
was extended to the vassal provinces, and in spite of the efforts of kings
and nobles to bring them back, for economic reasons, the people would
have none of them. In Germany there was no general expulsion, since
each of the kingdoms or principalities into which Germany was divided
regulated itself according to its traditional autonomies. But the massacres of the Jews during the second half of the XIV century were
terrible and extended to Switzerland and Savoy.

Italy—except for Naples—was less troubled by the Jewish problem.
The popes nearly always showed themselves more tolerant and even
benevolent; the control exercised by the cities over Jewish activities
tranquillised the populations, and finally, a true national feeling, such
as would make the Jew especially hated, was non-existent in nearly all
the regions of the peninsula. It was in fact the awakening of nationality
which, combined with the principle of religious conformity and the
fears created by the heretical movements, had awakened the anti-
Jewish feeling that reached its height in the Hussite wars in Bohemia
and those against the Moors in Spain.

The sense of nationality, as particularism and political conformism,
after the great Councils of the XV century grows still more marked.
The Christian universalism of the West, the unity of Christendom in
an ecclesiastico-feudal order, with no rigid frontiers between kingdom
and kingdom, was resolving itself into the particularism of the autonomous States, the evolution of the vulgar tongues into written
languages, and a national feeling that had spread even among the
popular classes. The Christian Middle Ages had inherited the political

and cultural universalism of Rome. Rome had received into its empire many and diverse peoples without demanding any uniformity. The basis of the Empire lay in its administration, its legal system, the cult of *Roma Dea* and of the Emperor. The Roman people ruled, guided and synthesised in itself the subject peoples, who did not by this lose their personality.

Christianity, on the fall of the Roman Empire and through the barbarian invasions, had to refashion the unity of the West on the basis of the Christian faith, the feudal system, and canon law, arriving thus at a moral unification, through the ecclesiastico-feudal ruling class, extending to all countries and solidly established in the unity of Christendom. Although the rulers and heads of countries and even popes and emperors might be divided by struggles and wars, they were always agreed on the religious and juridical substructure of Christendom. The dissidents, the nonconformists, were those who religiously and socially did not accept the pre-established order: both the politico-social dissidents and those who denied religious dogmas were heretics.

As the national sense developed, it came to form a new strand in the conception of Christendom. Kingdoms tend to consolidate themselves as autonomous domains. The peoples assert their personality. The Church begins to be considered as a society not only distinct from the political society but outside or above it as the case might be. The common denominator is no longer the Christian faith and personal fealty to the sovereign; it is also and still more the national personality and the particularity of the State. We are at the beginning of this break-up of the social idea of Christendom and of the deepening of the sense of each nation as a particular group. The struggle against political nonconformists (who would still for a long time be seen under a religious colour) has already begun with the crusades against the Hussites and the banishment of the Jews. Here are symptoms of a particularism that is gaining the ascendancy over universalism.

The system of General Councils, as organs of a politico-religious unification of Christendom, like the Councils of Pisa, Constance and Bâle, had failed. After Bâle national division was still further accentuated in the particularist contraction not only of kingdoms but of the local churches. The unity of the Church, reaffirmed at the Council of Florence in ephemeral union with the Greeks, attained anew with the end of the Bâle schism, proclaimed in the urgent need of resistance to the advance of the Turks, had never been so threatened as now by the development of the sense of nationality. After the death of Eugene IV a great pope appeared, Nicholas V. In him medieval traditions united with the splendour of the Renaissance, but he had not the universal efficacy he would have had a century earlier. The end of the Schism of Bâle (1449), the Great Jubilee (1450), the coronation in Rome of Frederick III as Emperor (1452) were solemn events of a period that had reached its close. The foundation of the Vatican Library and the consolidation of the pontifical State were events of a new period at its opening. Between the two periods there was a spiritual and political revolution that marks the passage from one to the other and creates the difference and opposition between them.

§ 22.—Three outstanding events accelerated the passage from the Middle Ages to modern times. The first, chronologically, is the exodus of the cultured class of Greco-Byzantines to the West, especially to Italy, before the progressive advance of the Mussulmans in the Mediterranean and the fall of Constantinople in 1453. The Turkish menace should have found all Christendom united, together with the Eastern Empire, to avert so terrible a disaster. But in spite of the exhortations of the popes and a favourable public opinion, kings and princes could not rise above the egotistical sentiment that attached them to their own particular policies. Apart from the successive efforts to check the advance of the Turks by land and sea (which would occupy and preoccupy popes and princes for three centuries more), the chief effect of the fall of the Byzantine Empire was of a cultural nature.

The humanism that for over a century had been spreading from Italy to other parts of Europe, drawing to itself the most cultured sections of the clergy and becoming the basis of lay culture, was widened and deepened by contact with the culture of Byzance. A potent aid to its generalisation was the invention of printing, which in a short time had spread everywhere. The Greek and Latin classics, both those already known and those that were being resurrected from manuscripts newly discovered or brought from the East, were circulated, admired, worshipped.

The knowledge of the Greco-Latin world, no longer confined to a few chosen spirits but extending to the whole of the educated classes, was like the revelation of an unknown world. As such it imposed itself on the ideas, feelings and activities of all those whom it touched. Stoicism among the nobler spirits took the place of Christian ethics and spirituality, while Epicureanism spread rapidly among the artists and men of letters. In philosophy, Platonism was opposed to the Aristotelianism of a decadent scholasticism and to a nominalism that had lost itself in hair-splitting subtleties. In art natural beauty and classical imitation banished the last remains of the abstract forms of the Middle Ages. These ferments from the ancient world, which seemed to arouse among the educated class an intellectual and moral fever, were very soon brought into contact with the political and religious realities of the time.

The discovery of new lands and finally, in 1492, of a whole continent that would later be called America, led to a social displacement of the highest importance. The physico-experimental trend, which had begun with Albertus Magnus and Roger Bacon two centuries earlier, though wandering in the mazes of astrology, had led to the first inventions and the first discoveries. Gunpowder changes the aspect of war, the press is extending culture, astronomy brings a knowledge of the terrestrial globe and leads to the discovery of other lands and other peoples. Marco Polo and Christopher Columbus are the beginning and end of a first series of travellers of fortune and genius. By a natural repercussion, moral, juridical and religious problems presented themselves under a new aspect. The universality of the Empire, which in the Middle Ages had been raised to a quasi-dogmatic dignity (according to the celebrated phrase of Bartolo, to deny it was heretical), was plainly paradoxical in the face of an expanding world. It became tangibly apparent that Christianity was still the privilege of the smaller part of mankind. And while missionaries and adventurers set forth for the new lands, which Spain and Portugal divided between them, Europe saw the arrival of cargoes of gold and slaves, pagan expression of a naturalism that was gaining the ascendancy with the splendours of the Renaissance.

The Renaissance was not the result of humanism alone, nor are the two historical phenomena to be confounded, as they are by superficial writers. The spirit of humanism found its full expression in the Renaissance, but it is not the whole of the Renaissance. This, in the strict sense of the word, might be limited to the great efflorescence of Italian art in the Quattrocento and Cinquecento, especially painting, sculpture and architecture, poetry and belles-lettres and lastly, in the following century, the theatre and music. But in a wider sense the Renaissance embraces the whole trend of thought and of cultured and moral activity which from Italy spread over Europe, and through its purely artistic and literary manifestations assumes the significance of a new civilisation. The Renaissance is the key to the new age. Thus considered it is necessary for us to understand its sociological implications and to trace the new factors that are developing in social life and in its religious and political expressions and their mutual relations.

The chief element of the Renaissance is what we have called the revelation of Greco-Roman classicism, not only from the artistic standpoint, but also in culture, religion, and philosophy. The Christian world had never lost sight of classical culture. In the time of Julian the Apostate the Christians both of East and West had defended their right to study and teach the classics. Cicero and Virgil had been considered if not on a par with the Fathers as very near them. Roman law had been in part transfused into canon law and in part had either survived or been later restored with its own autonomous character. The Neo-Platonists and Plato himself were present in the writings of the Fathers, especially in Augustine, the well-spring of the whole of medieval culture and of the Augustinian and Franciscan currents. Aristotle, returning through the Arabs, had been adopted by the Schools and, through the work of St. Thomas Aquinas, christianised and made the philosopher *par excellence*. The Roman world had been glorified by Dante. But in all this classico-Christian tradition the prevailing tendency had been to consider classicism as not only the historical antecedent of Christianity but as a preparation for it, intellectual, moral, juridical and political. The providential conception of history made of the Greco-Roman world at once the antecedent, the antithesis and the preparation of Christianity. From St. Augustine to

St. Thomas and Dante the mental attitude was one of seeking to understand, appraise, interpret, sift and purify that world in function of
Christianity, of its supernatural ends and religious content.

In the Renaissance classicism presents itself as a self-subsistent reality
and truth, complete in itself, as a conception unrelated to Christianity.
Indeed the antithesis of Classicism and Christianity is felt not as a
necessary subordination of the first to the second and the elimination
of contradictory features, but with the attraction of something newly
revealed, to which to subordinate the values of a present that seems
already of the past and which men doubt or no longer cherish, or
would imbue with new life.

This state of mind, whether conscious or unconscious, was widespread in the educated class that now ruled the thought and activity
of Europe, and overflowed into social, political, economic and religious
life, invading even ecclesiastical circles. It is unnecessary to recall that
in those days much of economic life was grafted on to the ecclesiastical
benefice, and that many men came to holy orders and ecclesiastical
offices through family interests and as a career. The individual resistance
of religious men, of austere thinkers and of the people that remained
faithful, was feeble and had little efficacy. The reform of the Church
was envisaged as a legal systematisation and a demarcation of interests.
The triumph of the arts brought the spell of newly revealed beauty,
inventions drew men closer to the secrets of nature, with a thirst to
ask of it an extra-physcial and magical reality, the new philosophy led
to the concrete even in forms and ideas. Christianity for many was
confused with a negation of beauty, with an excessive asceticism, with
scholastic abstractions, with a whole world that was receding.

The classicism of Greece and Rome was saturated with naturalism;
this had an influence on the decadence of morals. The previous period
had not indeed been a wholesome one. Papal Avignon was corrupt,
and the princely courts of the XIV century even more so. But then the
spiritual movement was a popular reaction; Dante thundered against
the avarice and simony of the clergy and against the laxity of custom
of his own Florence; St. Catherine of Siena and St. Vincent Ferrers
were fire and flame against the general corruption. There was a healthy
body that reacted and had influence; now such voices had become

weaker. St. Bernardino of Siena (d. 1444) was one of the last echoes of the Middle Ages.

The difference between early humanism and the Renaissance in the matter of morals lies in the prevalence of a naturalistic and pagan orientation over the Christian one. For many of the educated class and the ruling classes whether clerical or lay, the Christian religion becomes sterile, formal, exterior, a social sheath to be sloughed off by those who would attain to personality, contact with nature, liberation from all moral ties, perfect enjoyment. They are oriented towards the earth, man is his own end, values are transposed into dominion, gold, pleasure. The very anti-ecclesiasticism of the XIII and XIV centuries, which had waged war on Papacy and clergy in the name of poverty and renunciation, in the Renaissance becomes a mundane anticlericalism. Popes and cardinals and bishops (not indeed all of them, nor all to the same degree) are drawn by their very environment and by the general corruption to become like the other great and petty tyrants of Italy, the centres of luxurious courts, rather patrons of the arts than shepherds of souls, pleasure-seeking and convivial, mixing the sacred with the profane without scruple, in a paganisation of life drawing in its wake the people who were eager for amusement, together with the corrupt elements of the cities. These lived on the great or small courts, in which riches, art and dominion had centred.

Thus an exuberance of pagan life burst forth on a soil once saturated with medieval Christian life, and this, though latent and subdued, lived on beneath the surface. Hence we are surprised to find manifestations of pure art and religious ideals together with the triumph of a shameless naturalism, mild and great figures like St. Antoninus of Florence and Cardinal Nicholas of Cusa, side by side with pagan men like Cossa (the illegitimate pope John XXIII), or worse, theorists of immorality such as Panormita.

In all ages good and the evil intermingle and influence thought, customs and social activities, but in the Renaissance the naturalistic trend, as it became autonomous, under the influence of humanistic classicism and through the revelation of beauty in art, passed from antagonism to Christianity to the position of a concomitant and often dominating factor, influencing religious theory, penetrating even the mental habits and feelings of ascetics and mystics. From this standpoint we may classify three currents in the Renaissance, personified, for the sake of simplicity, in three great men, who all three lived in Florence, then the moral centre of Europe, the Athens of culture—Marsilio Ficino, Girolamo Savonarola, and Nicolò Machiavelli.

§ 23.—Marsilio Ficino was the greatest of the XV-century Platonists. His love for Plato was equal if not superior to his erudition. His personal influence, and as head of the Platonic Academy of Florence, extended throughout Europe. In his early period he was a humanist and a philosopher more or less tending to paganism. In the maturity of his thought and life he became deeply aware of the Christian values that many of the learned class too readily ignored. His ideal was to reconcile Platonism and Christianity, pagan classicism and Christian thought, ancient ethics and Catholic morals. St. Augustine fascinated him, but he felt that the Augustinian synthesis could no longer satisfy the world of his contemporaries. Problems were set in other terms, whether they concerned nature, ethics or history, and what he sought was to Christianise Plato and to Platonise the Gospel. Both tendencies are to be found in his *Theologia Platonica*, which he intended as a new *Summa Theologica*, founded no longer on Aristotle but on Plato.

Three elements make the work of Marsilio Ficino representative of his age—the sovereignty or autonomy of philosophy as a rational instrument, no longer the handmaid of theology; a concrete realism as the object of knowledge, in nature and history, as against the universalising abstractions of Scholasticism; an animism, derived from the principle of the 'third essences' (the substructure of the astrology of the time), as opposed to the Aristotelian conception of forms.

The tendency towards concrete reality and philosophical mysticism was not new. Cardinal da Cusa had initiated modern philosophy with his *Docta Ignorantia* and his *Visio Dei*; his immanent principle resolved itself into divine transcendency, his all-but-infinite world lost itself in the real infinity of God. Ficino took a further step towards modern thought in proclaiming the autonomy of philosophy. He would not have it detached from theology, nor does he repudiate theology, but he would reconcile the two in the name of reason, of which the greatest exponent was Plato. Therefore Ficino subjected the dogmas of Christianity, miracles, grace, the supernatural life to a rational elaboration other than that of the Thomist system, and though in matters of faith he kept within the bounds of orthodoxy, he sought to illuminate them by a broad Platonism that had become for him a principle of truth.

All this would be outside the scope of the present work if it did not reveal what for us is the basic tendency of the Renaissance, the effort to reconcile Christianity with classical paganism as religious and moral thought, as culture, as art, as politics, as the whole of associated life. The two elements, Christianity and Classicism, were considered, in the best hypothesis, if not of equal rank at least of equal force and exercising an equal attraction; the synthesis of the two was sought in a harmony that would imply neither subordination nor negation. The attempt would fail and lead to a profound crisis, but the reality of the Renaissance lies in this conscious or unconscious effort to reconcile a radical dualism, which in its precise terms could admit of no reconciliation.

This irreconcilability was exposed by Girolamo Savonarola to Florence, to Italy, and to the cultured world of Europe. Savonarola's political background in Florence has almost the same features as that of Dante, but the ethical and mystical aspect of events throws into relief the impossibility of reconciliation so keenly felt by the Dominican friar. Whereas Dante arrived at a synthesis of this world and the world above, of nature and grace, of philosophy and theology, Savonarola could not do so: the Renaissance prevented him.

Savonarola fought against the corruption of morals, and in this he was not peculiar. Other holy men and women, his contemporaries, among them the great St. Francis of Paola, fought in the same sense with varying success. Savonarola wanted the reform of the Church, and this word was echoing throughout Italy, as in France, in Germany, in England, in Spain, everywhere; zealous men, laymen and men of religion, were convinced of its necessity and urgency. Their voice remained without response among the high dignitaries of the Church and in the courts of the princes. Faced by the simoniacal election of Pope Alexander VI, by his immoral conduct and the corruption of Rome, Savonarola calls for a General Council and works for its convocation, but his action is not enough to create in Christendom a state of mind comparable to that which little more than half a century earlier had led to Pisa, to Constance and to Bâle. The endeavours of the Councils to establish a new order in the Church had been at once wearying and perturbing; now each country was making what arrangements it could for itself, particularism was developing more and more at the expense of universalism, the Papacy itself was becoming diminished, involved as it was in disputes with the tyrants and republics of Italy. The central administration of the Church was becoming more and more bureaucratic, formalistic and fiscal. The wind of great aspirations had fallen.

Above this withering ecclesiastical world and above the other mundane and paganising world the figure of Savonarola rises as that of an ascetic and prophet, who at the height of the Renaissance revives the apocalyptic spirit of the past, framing it in Thomist philosophy and in Catholic orthodoxy. If he makes the Council superior to the Pope and believes that it could be summoned by the King of France in agreement with such cardinals and bishops as were not subservient to Alexander VI, he does not depart at all from the normal thought of Catholics of the time. That theory was then generally advocated and was for a long time taught almost throughout Europe. The name of Gerson was venerated as that of a saint. Pius II, in condemning the principle of appeal to the future Council against papal decisions, had not settled the question or annulled the decisions of Constance. In any case, Savonarola took his stand on a point then universally accepted (and which would be reiterated by Julius II in a Bull of 1505), that a pope elected by simony was no true pope. Savonarola wavered on this point. He recognised Alexander as pope and at the same time maintained that he could not be so legitimately; thus he first felt himself bound by the excommunication and then free to set it aside. But these oscillations came from the whole excitement of his threefold struggle, in the political field in the Florentine Republic, in the religious and ecclesiastical field against Rome, and in the moral and ascetic field against the paganism of the Renaissance. The complication of these three titanic struggles made it difficult for Savonarola always to find a coherent synthesis in his practical action. Yet the spirit that he released in the course of these very struggles was the Christian spirit, seeking to set a check to the paganism that had filtered into thought, art, the administration of the Church and the government of States.

In certain respects Savonarola might be considered the last representative of the Middle Ages that had already closed, the spiritual heir of Dante and St. Catherine of Siena. Under other respects he was the prophet of the forthcoming Protestant rebellion, of the desolation of the Church and of the movement of reconstruction that followed. But his most real aspect is that of one who sought to resolve the problem of the Renaissance in a Christian sense, not repudiating but subordinating to a religious conception of life all that was being achieved in culture, art and social activity through the new experience of Greco-Roman classicism. He sought to purify art, to make Christian ethics inspire politics, to proclaim a freedom combined with religious discipline, to raise the Church above earthly passions, not as separate from the world or alien to it but as a vivifying spirit in the whole of human life. He has been called mistakenly a forerunner of Luther by those who confused his active asceticism with the passive asceticism of the reformers, taking his struggle against Alexander VI for a denial of the Papacy, and interpreting his bonfire of vanities and his preaching against the Florentine carnivals as a condemnation of art. Here are errors of historical perspective. There was nothing of Luther about Savonarola. He was the prophet of the Renaissance, and sacrificed himself to this his mission.

His condemnation, the outcome of political passions and not for religious reasons, while it brings out the spiritual character of Savonarola's mission, fits into the picture of XV-century customs and morals. He is forsaken by his own people and handed over to his enemies, tortured physically and morally, judged by prejudiced judges on documents falsified by bribed notaries; he must die, whatever the cost, because he is inconvenient to the Government of Florence and to that of Rome. In a period of unprecedented violence, poisonings, assassinations, treacheries of every kind like the XV century, the condemnation of the ascetic and prophet to an unjust and pre-arranged death does not move even the people that for years he had carried with him, to the vindication of its own liberty and political personality and the defence of its interests. The very friars of S. Marco deny him, Florence will return to subjection to the Medici, only a few faithful ones will remember him and seek to vindicate his memory. Thus his sacrifice was complete in every sense.

Something profound and perennial would remain of the activity and personality of Savonarola, and this would be indelible. It is not his protest against a pope of the type of Alexander VI, nor the resurrection of the Republic of Florence and the defence of civic liberties and the democratic system against the tyranny of the Medici; it is the fact that all this is carried on to the plane of a spiritual and passionate affirmation of Christianity against the paganism of the Renaissance, the vindication of asceticism against the theoretical and practical hedonism that from the courts was spreading to the people and invading the sanctuary, the championship of a political life, an economy and an art vivified by religious ethics. His thought was saturated with Thomism, warmed by a breath of Platonism, a Thomism not formalistic but substantial, in its effective realism, its ethical and social organicity, its ontological and finalistic transcendency as against the pantheistic naturalism that was making its way—leaving behind the Platonism of Marsilio Ficino— into ethics, politics and art.

Nicolò Machiavelli did not understand Savonarola and judged him a fanatic. He was the man of 'working truth'—*verità effettuale*, as he called it, or Reason of State, as it was called after him, or 'realistic politics,' as we should say to-day. For him politics are nothing but the art of domination. The ends of the ruler, whoever he be, is the rule to which the ends of the subjects must be subordinate. Means are indifferent; if they are honest, so much the better, but even dishonest means, if they are useful, are not to be set aside. Religion, whether true or false, is a good thing, for it keeps the people in check; morality is useful for general well-being, but politics are independent of morals and religion, both as method and as the autonomous aim of the government of peoples.

Never in paganism had the calculated absence of any higher ideal been so complete as in Machiavelli's political conception. In his theory ethical life is separate from political life, the ends of individuals united in a society from the ends of the head of the State as a single person superior to all. The coincidence of these ends in the idea of the prosperity, order, security and greatness of a State means merely the total resolution of the ends of the subjects into those of the head. Subordination to the head is neither ethical nor social, but exclusively political, in the sense that the one criterion is utility. If virtue is useful, have virtue, if crimes, well, have crimes. Machiavelli does not like crimes, but if they bring success he admires their results. Many, to-day as yesterday, agree with Machiavelli without owning to it, indeed veiling their immoral attitude with such considerations as historical fatality, the lesser evil, national or social advantage or even the good of religion. Machiavelli tears away such hypocritical and often transparent veils and theorises the triumph of the useful in political life as he saw it in the XV century.

By suppressing any transcendent idea to which to orient individual and social life as duty, indeed subordinating individual life to a collective advantage represented by the prince, by depriving the head of the State of a basis in moral and juridical legitimacy and giving him instead the sole basis of power, success and personal advantage, Machiavelli in the political field drew the ultimate consequences of the naturalistic pessimism that had filtered into the Renaissance through the Averroist school. Naturalistic pessimism generates individual hedonism, which always passes into a hedonism of an *élite* with the sacrifice of all the rest, and this in politics leads to the dominance of the one or of the few and to the oppression of the many.

Machiavelli's advocacy of politics remote from any moral criterion and from all religious finalism was not only the result of the disgust inspired in him by the politics of papal Rome and ecclesiastical meddling in affairs of State. He did not believe that, in the concrete, men could ever become better and outgrow the inferior stage of evils and vices in which they fulfil their life in common. Hence the need for a head, legislator or tyrant, consul or dictator or prince, who should establish an order, using all means, including violence and cunning, and with the indiscriminate use of good or evil, so long as he succeeded. And since man is moved only by selfish impulses, in the dualism between the head and his subjects, it is the strong and effective head who succeeds in imposing himself, in dominating, in identifying the common advantage with his own.

On this pessimistic background Machiavelli sketches, as though experimentally, a kind of historical dialectic. The founder of a people or legislator is the man who through his own powers couples the will for dominion with the sense of the value of law and the capacity of forming a collective mind: thus the people and the State are born. He is followed by the prince, the man who either to reach power or to maintain it uses force and cunning at home and abroad: he becomes a tyrant or a conqueror. Tyranny often prepares the way for a republic but in the republic the people cannot govern themselves without a strong power, which may become a temporary dictatorship or turn into the tyranny of a prince.

'Fortune', according to Machiavelli, plays her part, together with the will for dominion and the use of force and cunning by the heads, in order that in the unstable co-existence of States one may gain what the other loses. In order to gain it is needful to be strong, and such strength is created by the homogeneity and power of a State, to be acquired by any and every means. But in the conflict between the strong and the cunning it is Fortune that decides.

The Renaissance was never so ultra-pagan (for paganism never suppressed the voice of morality) as to silence every noble sentiment and every human and religious ideal. Machiavelli, although the theorist of the 'political man' of the XV century, knew truth and felt the impulse of lofty feelings as for family, fatherland, freedom, and even for religion itself, to which he turned on his death-bed, like so many of his age. But the concrete was then the term of reaction against abstractionism, and this concrete presented itself with the prevailing colours of a naturalism that absorbed even vice and evil into its reality, so as to induce an appraisement of evil as not evil and vice as no vice, in an effort to resolve all spiritual motives into the so-called 'effectual truth.'

The dualistic debate between the conception of the real and the ideal goes on through the whole period of the Renaissance and gives birth to two extreme currents, the first that of the double truth (a theory that had already arisen in the Middle Ages, but under other aspects), a natural truth, humanistic, experimental, effectual, and a transcendent truth, spiritual, religious, dogmatic. The second is that of the resolution of all objective truth into the subject, whose judgment is free of any

external authority, in personal relationship with God. In this relationship the permanent and ineradicable dualism in man between belief
and practice is synthesised: faith justifies without works. The representatives of these two streams are the humanist Pomponazzi in Italy and
Luther in Germany.

The intermediate philosophical and religious current, in a struggle
that had begun when Machiavelli was still alive between Catholicism
and the two extreme currents, remains that of Savonarola, without the
prophetic and political character with which he had endowed it. It is
the current that seeks to assimilate what in the other two is not in
contradiction to Christian tradition, and answers the needs and aspirations of the thought, culture and art of the Renaissance.

§ 24.—The reflection of the monarchising and even dictatorial attitude
of mind that prevailed after the collapse of the parliamentarism of
Bâle, made Aeneus Silvius Piccolomini first an exponent of imperial
absolutism in his *De ortu et auctoritate imperii romani*; then, as Pius II, the
champion of papal monarchy in his *Bulla Retractationum*. Through his
genius, his vast culture and his three-fold position as conciliary at Bâle,
imperialist at Vienna, curialist in Rome, his influence on his age was
immense. At a moment when all schism and acute dissension within the
Church had ceased, he traced the lines for the monarchic régime of
the Papacy of modern times.

As yet the constitutionalism of the Middle Ages had not wholly
disappeared, either in the Church or in States, and pure theorists
continued to refer to the Community as the fount of political and
juridical authority and to introduce a contractual element into the
formation of society. Yet all this was a survival from the Schoolmen,
preserved to guarantee the rights of immunitary bodies and of aristocratic electoral systems. The monarchic idea, on the other hand, was
upheld by the legists of the Empire and of the various kingdoms,
and by the Roman curialists, both supported by their following in the
universities. On both sides there was the endeavour to draw a veil over
the conciliar period, to reduce to a minimum such electoral forms as
still persisted, and to rebuild on a basis of absolutism the society that
was developing under the aegis of Renaissance classicism.

Side by side with this centralising conception, both secular and ecclesiastical particularism became the more extensive the more the States gained in consistency with the growing strength of their rulers. Thus a political Gallicanism had its ecclesiastical counterpart, that is, the establishment of a special system of canon law for the national clergies, as a bulwark against the claims of Rome, and, in so far as was possible, against the excessive interference of the secular princes. In England, Spain, Germany, the same thing was happening, as indeed throughout Europe, though not everywhere were theories so pronounced or conflicts so resounding as in France.

Gallicanism has had different meanings in different periods. In the strict and political sense, indeed, it is of later date. At the end of the XV century men spoke of the franchises or liberties of the Gallican clergy, calling to witness the Statutes of St. Louis IX, and debating the Pragmatic Sanction of Charles VII. The long quarrel on this point between the Roman Curia and France could find no feasible solution, for neither the clergy nor the Sorbonne nor the King would retreat from their positions. The same disputes arose, with varying degrees of practical compromise, between all the European princes and their clergy.

The substance of these conflicts, which indeed prevented a general reform of the Church, was mainly economic and political. The fiscal system organised by the Avignon popes on a rigid economic basis had withdrawn considerable sources of wealth and a large circulation of money from royal control and from national affairs. This was a serious obstacle to the more rigorous autonomy of the States and to the national interests in process of development. A clash was inevitable. The pressure of the States was too strong, forcing the popes to defence and evasion if they would not lose at least a part of the revenues necessary for the maintenance of the Holy See, the increasing splendour of the papal court, and the encouragement of building and of the arts generally in Rome; above all, if they would not allow the local churches to escape the control of the central authority. The efforts of the Roman Curia to this end and the need for particular understandings led to an extension of the system of concordats, from Constance onwards. It is after Constance that we may speak of real concordats in the modern sense, between the Pope and the rulers of States.

There are canonists who indicate as the first concordat that between
St. Anselm of Canterbury and Henry I of England (1107); others
instead consider it to be that between Paschal II and the Emperor
Henry V at Sutri (1111), or the more celebrated one between Calixtus
II and the same Henry V at Worms (1122), which ended the investiture
conflict and was indeed known as the Concordat of Worms, as indicating the end of a dispute by a compromise accepted by both parties,
the supreme ecclesiastical power and the sovereign secular power.
Alexander III drew up a concordat with the Henry II of England in
1171 and Nicholas IV in 1282 ratified that between King Denis of
Portugal and the bishops of his kingdom. These concordats had a
feudal-ecclesiastical character, or else were confined to particular
matters.

The new type of concordat makes its first appearance at Constance,
when Martin V, in 1418, published his seven decrees of reform and
drew up three concordats with the 'Nations', the first with Germany,
Poland, Hungary and Scandinavia, the second with the Latin countries,
France, Italy and Spain, the third with England. Such concordats, as
we have seen, tended to limit papal intervention, respected the electoral
principle, subject to higher ratification, divided the rights of nomination between the Pope and the local clergy; and restricted appeals to
Rome on judicial questions. The three concordats were intended to
enforce the decisions of the Council for a given period, till revision by
the succeeding Council. But such concordats had an ephemeral existence and insufficient authority. The three-party disputes, between pope,
kings and clergy, soon began again. The pragmatic sanctions of the
kings, the intervention of the Councils and the decisions of the Roman
Curia came one upon the other, leaving uncertainty of rights and a
turmoil of struggles. The dispute with Germany was settled by Pope
Nicholas V and the Emperor Frederick III in the Concordat of Vienna
of 1448. This did not give ecclesiastical unity to Germany, for its
political structure and acute particularism rendered this impossible;
hence the disputes broke out anew and dragged on with a varying
degree of tolerance on the part of Rome.

With France a Concordat was reached only much later and under
the pressure of events and of political interests such as to induce Francis

I to set himself against the Sorbonne and a part of the clergy and to come to an agreement with Leo X in 1516. The Concordat of Bologna was surrounded, by both parties, with many cautious formulas, which contained the marrow of the two theories, that of the legists, or, we might already say, of the State, and that of the Curia or Pope. Leo X promulgated the Bull on August 18, 1516, as a unilateral act, and the following year caused it to be approved by the V Lateran Council. Francis I in his turn published an ordinance, it too unilateral, in May, 1517, by which he promulgated the bull of Leo X as a law of the State. The Pope, in declaring the Pragmatic Sanction of 1438 null and void, was exercising the supreme power by which he was able to annul any laws contrary to Canon Law, and in defining the faculties of the royal power and lay patrons in regard to ecclesiastical appointments, he was exercising his pontifical right to grant privileges or to delegate power, as the case might be. On the other hand the King, in promulgating the bull as a law of the realm, was exercising a twofold right, that of legislating as a sovereign without the intervention of any other power and that of royal control over pontifical bulls. These juridical distinctions were in no wise new. Even in the disputes between Papacy and Empire, both curialists and legists sought by subtle formulas to save the substance of the conflicting legal doctrines. At Worms the Investiture Conflict had been ended by two unilateral and distinct acts, one by the Pope, the other by the Emperor. The practice of giving to concordats the legal aspect of international conventions is wholly recent; the outstanding example is that between Pius VII and Napoleon Bonaparte. In any case, even the contractual theory of concordats is recent, while there are still canonists who maintain that they consist simply in a papal indult or privilege conceded to the heads of States, just as on the other hand certain jurists maintain even to-day the regalist theory of the complete sovereignty and autonomy of the State in approving a concordat.

This 'double truth' in the legal domain, which was so clearly mirrored in the cautious acts of the Concordat between Leo X and Francis I, had a long tradition behind it—ever since curialists and legists had fought over the nature and limits of the ecclesiastical power and the secular power. But whereas in the Middle Ages and in the conflicts between Papacy and Empire, the starting-point was the economico-feudal system, the basis of the claim to right of investiture, by the XV century the process of six hundred years had created two juridical systems, interworking in every sphere of public activity. The organisational diarchy of the Latin Church had succeeded (in spite of fierce struggles) in creating a genuine and single organism, international Christendom, in making the Emperor the secular representative of this organism and in giving to kings a real share in ecclesiastical life; and then after Avignon and after the Schism of the West it had resulted in such a confusion of powers that the only way out seemed to lie in agreements, which, while preserving the form of the traditional rights, centralised everything in the hands of king and pope and thus, in an authoritarian system, was able to ensure something of order and peace.

The concessions to Francis I at bottom were merely formal. Leo X recognised more or less the *status quo* as it had resulted from royal usurpations, many of them carried out with the consent or acquiescence of the Gallican clergy themselves. The right of appointment to bishoprics, abbacies and other benefices was confirmed to the King, to be exercised within six months of vacancy, subject to confirmation by the Pope if he had not exercised his right of refusal. In the latter case, the King was to present a second candidate within three months. For abbots and regular prelates the candidate had to be chosen from among religious of the same Order. For minor benefices, special rights of patronage were to be preserved. 'Expectancies', that is the promises made by the Pope for future successions, were abolished, and the number of 'apostolic mandates' was restricted; by these the collator of a benefice was ordered by the Pope to present a given ecclesiastic, thus suppressing in the particular instance the free choice of a candidate. The Parlement of Paris would not register the decree of Francis I which gave the concordat force of law, so that after ten years of dispute the King caused all questions concerning concordats to be transferred to the Grand Council. While he thus strengthened his absolute power, he was able to hold a constant threat over the Roman Curia: to withdraw his decree and restore the Pragmatic Sanction of Charles VII, if ever the liberties of the Gallican Church were violated.

More or less the same system as that adopted in the French concordat began to be followed all over Europe, meeting with less resistence from the local clergies and tolerated by Rome which, unable to regain the substance, preserved the form and sought to ensure, in so far as was possible, besides a share in revenues, a control over Church appointments and a direct intervention in the cases where the right of apostolic mandate could be applied. Thus the various clergies came more and more to be national clergies and the bishops, through the origin of their appointment and through social position, were increasingly bound to the different monarchies. The bond with Rome was ceasing to be direct, and came through the intermediary of the court and prince.

For keeping in touch with the populations of the various States, for influencing the local clergies or keeping a check on them, for intellectual formation in the Universities, for preaching in the mission countries, and for the protection of the Catholic faith (through the Inquisition Courts), the popes had always relied much on the religious Orders, especially on the Dominicans, the most faithful and the best organised. The Franciscans, after the crisis of the Spirituals, while continuing to argue over poverty, had organised themselves in various families, all loyal to the Church of Rome. But between the Augustinian Franciscans and the Thomist Dominicans a battle raged in the universities, in the schools, in local religious or political factions, and this weakened them, while the wealth of the convents led to a relaxation of morals.

The convents had everywhere become centres of culture and of art; the purest artist-friar of the Renaissance is the Blessed Angelico. Savonarola is the wrathful prophet of God, but Fra Angelico interprets the breath of divinity in purest human beauty. For the most part, the convents did not escape the influence of the time, and their social efficacy, though still great among the people, was small in regard either to the reform of the Church or a strengthening of the Papacy. During the Bohemian wars and those against the Turks, it was the friars who, in the Pope's name, incited soldiers and peoples to resist and fight. St. John Capistrano, Franciscan, is the most combative and popular friar of the age.

When the sea-roads were opened to the East and the New World had been discovered, it was the friars who would go to plant the Missions. They are the first to take up the defence of the natives, despoiled, oppressed and enslaved by the conquerors. Even in the Missions the friars carried with them the fierce and profound dissensions, theoretical and practical, that had weakened them in Europe. Even on the theme of slavery, when it was condemned by the Dominicans we find a Franciscan who sought to justify it.

The discovery of new lands gave occasion to the Papacy to exercise its international authority as this was conceived in the Middle Ages, and which for a long time had found no favourable opportunity for its exercise, save the attempts to unite Europe against the Turk. On the request of the King of Portugal, Calixtus III had granted him the exclusive right of trade and colonisation in the lands between Cape Bajador and Guinea. The King of Castille, by the Treaty of Alcocevos in 1479, accepted this decision. But after Christopher Columbus's discovery the King of Portugal, Emmanuel, wanted to interpret the Calixtine grant to his advantage, and against Ferdinand of Castille, and the latter addressed himself to Rome to obtain recognition of his right. Alexander VI then signed three Bulls. The first and second gave to the King of Leon and Castille the exclusive possession of the islands and territories discovered by Columbus and any future discoveries, on condition of propagating the Christian faith there, and so long as they had not been previously occupied by another Christian prince. With the third Bull he defined the limits of what to-day we should call the spheres of influence of the two kingdoms, Castille and Portugal. The two kingdoms agreed to accept the symbolic line traced by Alexander VI, and thus avoided rivalry and wars.

The concessions of Calixtus III and Alexander VI are a consequence of the curialists' theory in the Middle Ages on the pontifical rights, *naturaliter et potentialiter* over the whole world, in order that the Gospel should be preached and the kingdom of Christ extended. These rights, according to the medieval conception, which Innocent IV did more than others to define, extended (if necessary) to the occupation of the lands of infidels, the dethronement of infidel kings and leaders, and even to war in defence of the rights of Christians. Although, during the Great Schism and after, an attempt was made to attenuate and limit the pontifical right, the traditions of the Curia had held fast to the widest interpretation of such powers. On the other hand, the kings could not with any surety obtain the recognition and respect of their international rights from rival claimants and adversaries otherwise than through a papal Bull; this constituted a legal and religious title of the first order.

It is from this angle that we must read the formulas used by Calixtus III and Alexander VI in their privileged grants to Portugal and Spain. In the Bull of 3 May 1497 we read: ' . . . *omnes insulas et terras firmas inventas et inveniendas detectas et detegendas, auctoritate omnipotentis Dei nobis in beato Petro concessa ac vicariatus Jesu Christi qua fungimur in terris, cum omnibus illarum dominiis, civitatibus, castris, locis et villis, juribusque et jurisdictionibus ac pertinentiis universis, vobis . . . donamus, concedimus, assignamus, vosque . . . potestate auctoritate et jurisdictione facimus.*'[1] In the Bull promulgated later by the same Pope, Alexander VI, in favour of the King of Portugal we read: ' . . . *districtius inhibentes quibusque regibus principibus et dominis temporalibus, quibus jus quaesitum non foret, ne se contra sic se tibi subiicere volentes, quovis modo opponere praesumant.*'[2]

The terms employed are those of medieval usage, but in the Renaissance they had another sound to what they would have had in the days of Innocent III or IV. The infidel against whom Christians had fought from the VII century onwards was the Mussulman, a warlike invader, an enemy who came into Europe with the fanaticism of a faith, the need for expansion and the thirst for dominion. If not under this aspect, certainly from this consideration, the theory of the papal dominion over Christian princes, *ratione peccati*, had been extended to cover the infidel; it was the justification of preventive war, indeed

---

[1]' . . . all islands and lands found and to be found, discovered and to be discovered, with all the dominions, towns, fortresses, territories and villages, and all the rights and jurisdictions appertaining thereto, by the authority of Almighty God granted to Us in Blessed Peter as the Vicar of Jesus Christ on earth, we give . . . concede and assign to you, and make yours by power, authority and jurisdiction. (Raynaldi, 1493, n. 19.)

[2]' . . . strictly forbidding any kings, princes or temporal lords, who have no right to vindicate, to presume in any way to set themselves against those who wish to become subject to you.' (*Id.* a. 1493, n. 33.)

of any war, according to the formula of Ostiensis who termed a war against the infidel a *Roman War* and considered it *always* a just war.

Calixtus and Alexander, in yielding to the insistence of the kings of Portugal and Spain, had three clear aims: the first, the propagation of the Faith; the second, peace between Christian princes; the third, the concession of a right of trade and colonisation in lands reputed as *nullius*, belonging to no-one. Thus a new right makes its appearance, that of colonisation, which is linked up with the old right of conquest of the Roman people over the whole earth. This right in the Middle Ages had become the right of the Empire, which the regalists extended to the whole world. The dictum of Bartolo in the XIV century is celebrated: '*Si quis diceret imperatorem non esse dominum et monarcham totius orbis forte esset hereticus.*'[1] But in the particularism of the Renaissance, the rights of the separate States had rendered the Emperor's right ineffective and almost incomprehensible. The Church alone still possessed a virtue of her own through which earthly rights rested on a basic religious right. Ecclesiastical mediation of civil power returns to life, for a little while longer, in the international field and creates a new right, that of colonisation, sanctioning, in the name of religion, a fact that was coming about through the discovery of new lands and the subjection of the native peoples.

Kings, explorers and conquistadores would abuse this new right with which they were invested, and would make the Faith and the Church serve their particular ends, which would translate themselves into political dominion, economic exploitation and traffic in slaves. Missionary friars like the Dominican Las Casas and later the Jesuits would seek to impede the conquistadores and to safeguard the moral, economic and political rights of the natives. But their generous efforts would be nearly always overruled by the reasons of the Courts, to which the Church did not offer sufficient opposition. Therefore later, during the Protestant controversies, the Bulls of Calixtus and Alexander would be rediscussed, and the question raised whether the popes could give kings such far-reaching powers over lands that lawfully belonged to the native peoples.

[1]'If anyone says that the Emperor is not lord and Monarch of the whole world maybe he is heretical.' (Hostes,I.)

Bellarmin would then declare that the purport of the papal concessions was not that Spain and Portugal should make war on the infidel chiefs of the newly discovered lands and occupy their kingdoms, but only that they should carry the Faith there and protect the missionaries. Suarez and in general all the theologians of the age would say the same. But they, for one thing, gave too little weight to the phrasing of the Bulls, which speak explicitly of a grant of lands, towns, places, villages, rights, etc., of which, the Pope declared, he had made the King of Castille '*Dominus cum plena libera et omnimoda potestate et jurisdictione*—Lord with full, free and complete power and jurisdiction.' In actual fact it was in this sense that the kings proclaimed and enforced their right of conquest and of colonisation of the discovered lands, giving it its widest interpretation, to the point of deposing chiefs, the *debellatio* of peoples and the enslavement of the vanquished. One of the formulas of a proclamation to the natives, in the name 'of the Most High and Mighty King of Castille and Leon', made by Alphonso of Oieda, asserts the full and absolute right granted by the Pope ; hence if the natives did not willingly accept the new dominion, he declared: 'I Alphonso, etc. will enter by force into your country and will make war *à l'outrance* and I will force you to obey the Church and the King, and I will take your women and your children to serve as slaves.'

It is plain that this interpretation of the papal Bulls was illegitimate in spirit and was contested by the missionaries (in so far as they were able); it goes without saying that bishops and religious Orders intervened with the kings, seeking to temper the ardour of the conquistadores. But the fact was that the pagan spirit of the Renaissance had united with the Christian spirit of the Middle Ages, and the spread of the Gospel was a means of legitimising political and economic interests and of justifying new and wider slavery.

# CHAPTER VII

## REFORMATION AND COUNTER-REFORMATION

### FIRST PERIOD (1517–63)

§ 25.—The atmosphere of the beginning of the XVI century was well adapted to a widespread movement of spiritual and political revolt. So great a crop of outstanding individualities, and the intellectual and moral liberty—indeed licence—assured by the Renaissance, with the support of kings and popes, lay rulers and ecclesiastical princes, could hardly fail to produce the man who would lead the way to open revolt and subvert the whole of the West.

The famous Cardinal Cesarini, nearly half a century before Luther started the Protestant reform, wrote to Pope Eugene IV: " When the heresy of Bohemia is quenched, another still more dangerous will arise. . . . Who can fail to see that there is danger of a total subversion? Woe to the ecclesiastics, wherever they may be found. . . . They will be declared incorrigible, decided as they are to live in shameful deformity, cost what it may. . . . The minds of men are full of what they are preparing against us. . . . They will believe they are offering to God a pleasing sacrifice in despoiling and killing priests. . . . They will cast the fault and the shame on the Court of Rome, for in that court they will see the cause of all the ills of Christendom. . . . The princes of Germany will rise up against us. . . . I see it, the axe is at the root, the tree is leaning, and instead of supporting it so long as we can, we cause it to fall to the ground.'[1]

Luther's protest was the sign for a general movement against the established order. But neither the case of Luther nor his personal efforts would have had so wide and lasting a success if the ideas and tendencies he represented had not been ripening for no short period, and if political circumstances had not favoured their course.

[1] *Mon. Gen. Conc.*, Sec. XV, f. II.

From the doctrinal point of view, Luther is connected with John Wyclif and John Hus, whose theories had never been extinguished, in spite of persecutions and crusades. Although in Germany an anti-Bohemian position corresponded to national interests, yet the anti-ecclesiastical spirit of princes, bourgeoisie, towns, universities and the lower clergy drew nourishment, consciously or otherwise, from the Wyclifite and Hussite theories, inasmuch as these sought to break down all barriers between hierarchy and laity and to do away with a power, the papal power, that had become economically burdensome and in many respects morally corrupt.

The occasion was provided in Germany by the preaching of the Indulgences, which Julius II in February, 1507, and Leo X in October, 1513, had granted to those who contributed to the expenses of re-building the Basilica of St. Peter in Rome. When in 1517 Leo X gave permission to the Archbishop of Mainz, Albert of Brandenburg, to keep back a half of the sums brought in by such preaching in order to pay the Fugger bankers, this gave the impression of a financial trans-action. The Archbishop by means of able preachers attracted the faith-ful from neighbouring regions into his domain, among them those of Saxony. This irritated the other princes, especially the Elector John Frederick, if only because of the drain of money which went partly to Rome, partly to Mainz.

It was then that the Augustinian monk Luther was moved to present his ninety-five theses against the Indulgences, causing them to be nailed to the church doors of the fortress of Wittenberg. Apart from doctrinal and religious motives, there were also smaller, human motives for Luther's action. In that moment he was not thinking of a real rebellion against the Papacy. Certainly he was spiritually ready for it, but events would drag him thither when the historical factors were ripe. Luther's attack on the Indulgences found a favourable echo both in the intellec-tual, humanistic camp and among the princes. The defence of Indulgences by the Dominicans and the attacks of the Augustinians, with the contro-versy between the Universities of Erfurt and Wittenberg, would have had the character of a mere friars' quarrel and a question of academic punctilio, if the conflict had not had resounding echoes through the anti-ecclesiastic and anti-Roman spirit circulating throughout Germany.

To this current of rebellion against a social order that had become unsatisfying, combined with the need for a moral reform of the Church, Luther gave theoretical and practical issue, experimenting little by little and adapting it to the vicissitudes of his struggle. The derivation from Wyclifism and Hussitism is plain, precisely in the practice of Communion under both kinds, but, while he made use of heretical elements that had already come into being, Luther's originality declared itself in his theory of Grace and Scripture. Starting from the conviction that we have no true free will, he founds his doctrinal construction and his religious practice on the concept of Justification by Faith, which works in us by application of the merits of Christ, without our free and active co-operation by good works. This Justification by Faith is given, conserved and quickened by the Word of God, which is permanent in the Holy Scriptures and operative in each one of us.

On the basis of the two principles of Justification by Faith and the Scripture as the Word of God, Luther does away with the sacramental mediation of the Church and her authoritative magistracy, after having separated religion (*pietas*) from ethics (*moralitas*) through the denial both of free will and of the necessity of good works. The logical consequence of such doctrines, taken in their absolute sense, would have been the suppression of all associated and visible religious life (the Church) and the reduction of the Christian religion to an individual fact of conscience in the single and invisible relationship of the soul with God. But principles do not always work out the whole of their inner logic; in real life they are amended and rectified by the practical positions into which even the most doctrinaire and strong-willed of men are forced by events.

Luther and the reformers in Germany were induced by the very positions of their fight against the Roman Church to construct a Church for themselves to set against her; this was the 'Church of the Gospel'. Placed at the head of a great movement they could not fail to give it practical and visible organisation. Their 'Justification by Faith' had to pass from the subjective and individualistic stage to an objective and associated one. Individual interpretation of Scripture had to give place to an increasingly rigid orthodoxy, (based on the text of Scripture as translated, on the early Creeds and on the first four Oecumenical

Councils), with no possibility of evading the bounds assigned by the leaders, its inspired champions and fierce defenders. The sacraments, no longer administered by a privileged hierarchy and voided of the significance of instrumental means of grace, remained for the community of the faithful as non-liturgical channels of a grace not bound up with such means—baptism, as signifying Christian initiation, penitence, as outward surety of forgiveness, the Eucharist as a fraternal banquet. These elements of Christian association, combined with liturgical assemblies and preaching, formed the visible structure of the Lutheran Church.

In seeking to overcome the first obstacles placed in the way of the Reformation by the Roman Church, the Empire and the Catholic princes, Luther could not avoid facing the two-fold problem of social ethics and temporal authority. The theory of the Servile Will eradicated any possibility of reconciling individual morality, a man's responsibility for his own actions, with any form of social morality. Obliged by his theory of Justification by Faith to maintain the separation of religion from ethics, Luther could not resolve the problem of associated life save through the conception of a double morality. On the one hand spiritual morality, entirely inward, the morality given by faith in the passive and quietistic application of the merits of Christ—a pure faith that inwardly and without our aid must work the regeneration and elevation of our every faculty and our every act ; on the other, external morality, that of human life in common, based on natural law, written in the Decalogue and enforced by the secular authority.

It was in the spirit of Lutheran thought to attribute a totality of value to inward morality and to leave out of account external morality (the moral issues involved in the necessity of power, force, property, war, and slavery). He echoes St. Augustine's antinomy between the City of God and the Earthly City. But Augustine reconciled this antinomy precisely through the fundamental unity of Christian ethics, as realised by the members of the City of God within the bosom of the Church, whence virtue might flow back into the organism of temporal society. Whereas for Luther unification comes about only in a subsequent phase and in a wholly external form, seeking in the secular power both the moral order of society and an effective and authoritarian organisation of the Reformed Church.

In his treatise on 'Temporal Authority' (1523) Luther divides the Christian from the citizen, the kingdom of Christ from the kingdom of the world. The one is on the plane of faith and grace, the other on that of reason and the law. The kingdom of Christ is purely an inner kingdom; works belong to the kingdom of the world, and have merely an external or civil value, to be regulated by the temporal authority. The kingdom of the world, he holds, comes from the irremediable corruption of our nature, from the 'beastliness' of our inclinations. Society is not a community but a power. The task of the temporal authority, as power, is to give an organisation to corrupt nature and to mortify and correct human beastliness. The political society is a necessary institution. In spite of this it is intrinsically evil. Luther's pessimism goes beyond that of Machiavelli. To govern according to the Gospel, he declares, would be the same as letting loose savage beasts. It is necessary to separate the two kingdoms, 'that where there is pardon from that where there is punishment, that where a man gives up his own right from that where he claims it'. According to Luther 'conscience has nothing to do with the laws, works and justice of the earth'. He reaches the point of writing that a prince may be a Christian but must govern not as a Christian but as a prince. Luther's type of prince, if we consider him carefully, has little cause to envy Machiavelli's; indeed he has something more characteristic, for he absorbs into himself the whole of the power up till then possessed by the Church in temporal matters.

This absolute separatism might seem attractive as an attempt to spiritualise the Church, leaving to the State all the outward activities that had brought so much corruption into the ecclesiastical world. Actually it was an abdication of all moral and organising activity into the hands of the State. To avoid the consequences of this, which in practice would have voided the reform of any features of a Church, Luther in a second phase leaned on the authority of the princes to the point of making them the religious authority unifying the Church itself. This led him to abandon the idea, which he had carried over from Catholicism, of a 'Church one and universal, visibly organised and self-governing'. He now envisaged the unity and universality of the Church only in the inward and invisible Mystical Body, whereas the visible Church would be organised by nationalities, countries and states, according to the territorial divisions of the political power.

The ideas follow events, how closely the various phases of the Reformation show. The first phase, in regard to the social life of the Church and its relations with the State—in Germany it was still possible to speak of Papacy and Empire—was the destruction of the established order—detachment of clergy and bishoprics from Rome, abolition of celibacy as monks and nuns forsook their convents and became secularised, confiscation of church property by princes supporting the Reform, abolition of benefit of clergy, immunities and other recognised rights, and so on. All this was a form of rebellion in which the princes supplanted the local church and Rome in all their rights.

From this destructive process sprang the necessity for a reformed social order. The Peasants' Revolt and the extremist movements of the Reformation itself drove Luther to lean still more on the rich and powerful. The necessity for defence against Rome and against the Emperor strengthened the ties between Lutheranism and the princes who favoured it. These in adopting the Confession of Augsburg made an act of rebellion against the Catholic Church and the Empire. The defence, which meant also armed defence, of the new politico-religious position obliged them to drag with them the populations that followed Protestantism, and to win 'for the Gospel' (as the term went) as many cities and provinces as they could. The political issue dominated the religious problem, but the religious problem forced itself upon the political situation. From the close combination of these two elements arose the Protestant State that was one with the Territorial Church; here the religious element of protest against Rome and faith in Holy Scripture and the tendency to make Christian practice purely inward fused with an absolutistic and intransigent affirmation of political power.

Thirty-seven years after Luther's rebellion the Diet of Augsburg (1555) was able to lay down the celebrated principle that subjects must adopt the religion of their prince—*cuius regio illius et religio*. This actually was a political compromise to end the struggles, persecutions and wars between the various Christian confessions, each supported by princes and cities, but for the Lutherans it was the logical consequence

of their premises in their conception of Church and State. They had
asserted that the visible Church must be territorial, and had proclaimed
the prince as the sole external authority (1523); as their theory and
practice matured they had come to recognise the prince (the type of
prince to which we have referred) as judge and absolute head of the
temporal administration, custodian of the 'two tables of the law' (1528)
and absolute judge of Christian doctrine (1530). The confusion of
reformed Church and State was wholly to the advantage of the secular
power.

The early Lutheran conception of the spiritual order as sustained by
the temporal order of law and power gave place to a complete super-
position of the State, which was invested, *de facto* and *de jure*, with all
powers. These powers extended even to the internal life of the reformed
Church—uniformity of doctrine, administration of property, rules of
appointment of ecclesiastical ministers, punishment of dissidents, all fell
within their sphere. The prince was held to be the supreme member,
indeed the patriarch of the Church, and became its head. Thus while
a new type, which we may call *individualist* (inasmuch as based on free
enquiry), makes its appearance in the diarchy of Church and State, at
the same time the cesaro-papist form of political power returned to life,
with a coincidence, closer than before, of the territory of the State
with that of the Church.

The territorial character of the Church was conceived and wished
for by Luther under the aspect of German nationality, with which he
hoped the Reformation would be co-extensive. He had translated the
Bible into German, not only to make it understandable to all as the
Word of God, but also that it should serve to create and reweld a
German soul. 'If I had to translate Moses', he wrote, 'I should want to
make him a German, I would take away all Hebrewisms so that no one
reading my translation would be able to say that Moses was a Hebrew.'
This idea of Germanism was all the more alive in that it served as a
banner in the struggle against the Italian Papacy and the Latin and Slav
countries. But not all the States and Free cities of Germany followed
the Reformation. The princes faithful to Rome and to the Empire
fought the Reformers, and Luther, who incited the Lutheran princes
to destroy every residue of papism, called upon the Catholic Duke of

Saxony for toleration for the Reformers and recognition of the autonomy of their Church. He lacked logic, for he admitted neither the principle of toleration nor that of autonomy.

As a whole, Luther contributed potently to the affirmation and development of the absolute State of the XVI century and to the collapse of many factors of the communitary or corporative State of the Middle Ages; he installed a new cesaro-papism of the secular power, after disintegrating the community of the Church through religious individualism. He thus went a step further than Machiavelli. The latter subordinated religion to the State and religious and moral ends to political ends. Luther disengaged religion and religious ends from the State and took away from social ethics their inward basis. Machiavelli, while admitting the organism of the Church as autonomous, wanted it to be extraneous to the activity of the State; Luther deprived the Church of any influence over the State and bound the Church itself to the statal power. Machiavelli sought the humanisation of all power, and placed it above all morality and all religion. Luther theocratised power (in a kind of non-priestly theocracy), but by detaching it from inward morality he placed it outside the relations between man and God.

The weakness of this conception lay in the impossibility of a dialectic between the functions of political power and those of moral and religious unification assigned to the prince, who personified the State. This was in substance an *Ubrigkeitstadt*, a State of coercion, wholly power. In order to become at the same time a *Kulturstadt*, a State founded upon education, morality, religion, and to fulfil the function of head of the Church of the Gospel, it would have had to make these values interior to itself, that is, become a principle of conscience. But since this was repugnant to the Lutheran conception, nothing remained but to sterilise the function of *Kultur* into formalism, and resolve it into power, all power, in the hands of the absolute prince.

§ 26.—The movement of the Reformation spread beyond the frontiers of Germany, and found wide consent in both the intellectual and mystical camps. The Baltic countries are influenced by Lutheranism and the princes head the revolt—in Norway and Denmark the two

successors of Christian II, Frederick I and Christian III, and in Sweden
Gustavus Vasa. Holland, too, accepts the Reformation, under William
of Orange. German Switzerland is guided to Protestantism by Zwingli,
who gives it a character of its own, distinct from that of Luther. But
another movement starts from France. It is Calvin who gives a new
imprint to the Reformation, and a stronger, more consistent and more
inward impulse. Driven out of France, he goes to Geneva, whither he
returns after a parenthesis of three years in Strasbourg, and where he
achieves his work as reformer.

Calvinism is important not only through the Geneva experiment
but through its expansion in broad zones, from the Rhine to the Low
Countries, to Scotland, and on the Danube and later in the Americas.
Its influence on the development of Reformed Christianity was far
deeper than that of Lutheranism. Although Calvinism derived the
principles of Protestantism from Luther, it took so different a path,
both in its theories and its practical realisations, as to make an understanding impossible.

The central point of difference is to be found in the theory of predestination, which informs the whole of the religious thought and
outward activity of Calvinism. According to Calvin, Grace is not only
a wholly gratuitous gift of God, but is the absolute means through
which, by the inscrutable Will of Divine Judgment, He destines a
part of men to share in His glory, and makes another part worthy of
His wrath. Calvin derives from Luther the idea of grace disjoined
from human co-operation as good works, and in consequence from
the idea of divine chastisement for our voluntary offences. But the
conception of God as Absolute Will, and, in human parlance, loosed
from all reason, however profound and mysterious, a God who does
not communicate with us in His intellectual light and the fire of His
love, but only through His immutable Will, is all Calvin's. Maybe
he derived it more or less unconsciously from the last of the Nomin-
alists, especially from Ockham, who (as we have already noted) based
all value and order, superhuman and human, religious and social, on
the pure Will of God, voiding the whole of the created world of any
intrinsic reasonableness and intelligibility of its own. However this may
have been (and doctrines have often a secret and subterranean course,

like underground waters), Calvin too fell into the extremes of voluntaristic and activist nominalism, which corresponded better than the
quietism and passivity of Lutheranism to the needs of the active spirit
of Western Europe.

While the Lutheranism of Germany and the Baltic was pursuing its
religious evolution on a semi-mystical plane, leaving all activity in the
civil and religious spheres to the political power, Calvinism, among
more highly evolved peoples dedicated to the active life of thought,
art and commerce, bore the stamp of an external and conquering
activity. According to Calvin's conception men are not placed on this
earth to try them (for this his idea of predestination excludes), nor for
the maintenance and increase of a grace that is a pure gift, but in order
that the elect may manifest in the world the divine activity and
creative nature of the Divine Will. From this came an intense activity
in every sphere, including the political and economic, through a lofty
sense of conformity to the creative Will of God, rendered manifest
by the elect in all the relationships of worldly life, private and public,
individual and collective.

This voluntaristic orientation on the one hand liberated Calvinism
from many theological and biblical questions, with which the Lutherans
were much concerned; on the other it gave to each member of the
religious community a more pronounced personal value. Humanism
had done much to give human personality a significance and value of
its own in the universe. The naturalistic current prevailing in the
Renaissance tended to detach man from the supernatural and to concentrate all the values of personality in earthly life. Luther (for all his
self-contradictions) aroused a religious and mystical reaction against the
naturalism of the Renaissance, but at the expense of personality, which
melted away with the denial of free will, the separation of ethics from
religion, and the complete subjection to the secular power, which was
rendered absolute. Calvin, on the contrary, in giving to each individual
a religious task to fulfil in the world, brought human personality
nearer to earth, after seeking to immunise it against evil by plunging
it in the mystery of the absolute Will of God and of the destiny of
predestination.

From this conception sprang, as from a fertile soil, the kind of oligarchic theocracy represented by Calvinism in Geneva. Calvin's State is a Christian-religious State, based on the Decalogue, not as an external law as Luther would have it, but as an inward moral law and the basis of the activity of each individual. Thus the State is not dualistic, in the sense of representing the outer world or evil, a conditioning of life with which the Christian was not concerned; it was unitary, and for Calvin was a representation and execution of the authority and will of God. He conceived the State as moral and autonomous, and in this he might be deemed, as he often is to-day, the first to have a clear idea of the modern State. But Calvin when he spoke of a moral State meant a Christian State, in which morals, religion and Christianity form a synthesis. And when he proclaimed the autonomy of the State, that is, rid it of any dependence on the Church, he not only did not break off relations between the two but set State and Church on a common ground, the fulfilment of the will of God through Jesus Christ.

His formula might be theoretically expressed in the following terms: the Church is not Christian because the State constrains it to be so, nor is the State Christian because the Church constrains it, but because both are obliged to observe the law of God and to carry out His will. Calvin insists on the biblical parallel of Saul and Samuel—Saul the King, Samuel the Prophet. Both are in agreement because they must serve God; Saul must listen to the voice of the prophet, Samuel must not interfere with the laws of the king. Geneva is not a true theocracy in the sense of priestly dominion over the civil order, but it is an endeavour to impregnate the civil order with religious elements, so that it may become a suitable means for the development of the Calvinist Church. It might be considered as an experiment in a Christocracy on a Protestant basis and under an oligarchic régime, whereas Savonarola's attempt in Florence half a century earlier had been an attempt at a Christocracy on a Catholic basis under a democratic régime.

This system carried with it a wholly religious conception of author-ity, of the duty of active co-operation with it and of obedience to it by conscience. Thus there is a period in which we find the Calvinists in Catholic countries loyal to the established powers, subject to the king who persecutes them, prepared to win their liberty and the rights of their community by moral and legal means. But the climate of religious disputes and struggles did not encourage such a spirit; the political field was a plane of conflicts which ripened into rebellions and wars. The tendency of all the movements of reform was to shake off the sovereign or ruler appointed to them, to particularise themselves and form independent groups, even within the State, or else to entrench themselves in what might be homogeneous regions, or to emigrate into neighbouring States. The cities subject to bishops or princes rose up in arms, like Geneva, to win the freedom to join the reform. Many men called for mutual toleration and not a few princes sought to avoid armed conflicts, making concessions to the Reformers and directly or indirectly favouring them.

Under the pressure of such movements the Calvinists became among the most active and combative, ready for seditions, rebellions, religious wars. The theory of the lawfulness of tyrannicide, which for nearly two centuries had been seeking to penetrate the Catholic world, was revived by the followers of Calvin, who made it their own. It was not a case, according to their conviction, of a purely practical attitude forced upon them by events, but of a spiritual attitude for the fulfilment of the kingdom of Christ, for the sake of which it was a duty to resist and oppose those who raised impediments. In any case, Catholics, Lutherans, Calvinists and Protestants of every kind, each from their own special standpoint, too easily turned religious controversies into bloody battles and civil and national wars. The two spheres, the civil and the ecclesiastical, were too interpenetrant and often confused, and the idea of toleration, often invoked by humanists and religious men, was acceptable neither to the Catholics nor to the Protestants. Thus recourse to coercion on the part of the legitimate power, or to rebellion on that of the other, with war as the inevitable outcome, was part of the general psychology of a Europe in ferment.

The English movement towards the Reformation had a character peculiar to itself. At first it might appear merely a schism. Henry VIII --who for his defence of the Sacraments against Luther had won the title of Defender of the Faith—through the refusal of Clement VII to annul his marriage with Catherine of Aragon, rebelled against Rome, and with the consent of Parliament and of a part of the clergy and of the nobility in 1534 proclaimed himself Head of the Church of

England and of the Principality of Wales. He did not seek changes of dogma, at least in any direct and explicit form. The occasional motives for the separation from Rome, besides the personal case of Henry VIII, were of an economic, fiscal and national character—the feeling for independence from continental politics and for a liberation from tributes and appeals to the Pope, the projects for ending the interference of the Roman Curia in nominations to ecclesiastical benefices, the confiscation of the property of the religious Orders, and, on the part of the clergy, a desire for the abolition of celibacy.

The disaffection of the educated classes towards papal Rome was widespread, in England as elsewhere. In 1517 the Dean of St. Paul's, Pace, described Rome as full of all dishonour and infamy—*omni dedecore et infamia plena*. Charles V after the sack of Rome in 1527 had a momentary idea of stripping the Pope of all dominion; the question was then discussed in the courts of France and England whether it were not desirable to create national patriarchs who would declare themselves independent of Rome. England had at the time a kind of ecclesiastical autonomy, for Cardinal Wolsey, who as Archbishop of Canterbury was *legatus natus*, had obtained the appointment of papal legate for life for the whole realm; he acted as if he did not depend on Rome. Clergy and people were accustomed to see Canterbury and the Court united as the supreme authorities, and Rome came into the picture only when ecclesiastical dues had to be paid or when it was a question of privileges or dispensations or judicial appeals, as in the case of Henry's divorce. Wolsey hoped the Pope would grant him the faculty of deciding the case without appeal. But this was not possible and it went to Rome, which decided against the divorce. This decided Henry to pass into schism. Cranmer as Archbishop of Canterbury began to call himself *Metropolitanus*, instead of *Apostolicae Sedis Legatus*. Henry termed himself at the same time 'king, emperor and pope in his dominions', and the Church 'a body politic', to use Cromwell's expression in a draft of the Bill for the Submission of the Clergy. And the clergy, with a few glorious exceptions, submitted, and lost their liberties, their property, and their very personality.

Merely pragmatical motives could not suffice without a theoretical basis on which to rest; otherwise their effect would have been short-lived. Writings and controversies round about Luther had invaded England, where indeed the Wyclif tradition and the anti-Roman spirit had prepared the soil. Yet Lutheranism did not reach the people, nor did it allure the promoters of changes, nor the upper clergy, nor the court. The English monarchy was seeking to unify the whole of the British Isles in itself. Henry VIII obtained from the Irish Parliament the title of King of Ireland instead of that of Lord; he was able to introduce English laws and customs, and the chiefs of the Irish clans received the title of peers. Over Scotland the English Kings claimed feudal rights, and the continuous wars between the two countries were turning to the advantage of the arms of Henry VIII. With the Continent a policy now of detachment now of understandings or conflicts corresponded to the impulse of maritime and colonial expansion, towards which Great Britain was constrained to tend. The movement of liberation from Rome coincided with the national and absolutistic policy of the age and with the ambitions and whims of the Tudors.

Thus, without raising the problems of grace and predestination as living problems felt by reformers and re-echoing among the people, England was led towards them step by step in the course of the struggle, as a means of finding justification for her separation from Rome. But the ecclesiastical physiognomy of the country remained intact, with the episcopacy grafted into the organisation of the State, with a Parliament that controlled synodal assemblies and their acts, and intervened authoritatively even in the doctrinal and liturgical provisions of the Church; and above all with a king who was at once political and religious head. Thus a peculiar and original type of national hierarchic Church gained consistency, unified by the King and controlled and sustained by Parliament—in substance it was a royal cesaro-papism, tempered by parliament and the synods, and shaped by the intrigues and violence of the court.

The Reformation in England was not the work of the people, nor of men of popular and mystical appeal, able to rouse the enthusiasm of the masses, nor of great figures of the stamp of Luther and Calvin, but of the King, his councillors and ministers, laymen and ecclesiastics. From Henry's schism in 1534 to its final establishment, the reformation was the King's matter, carried out by means of parliamentary legislation, and particularly an intrigue of bishops and courtiers. The opposition of those faithful to the Catholic Church and tradition was not wanting, and they were persecuted and put to death. Of these the greatest and among the first (in 1533) were the Chancellor Thomas More and Cardinal John Fisher, to-day among the saints. The people were divided between those who followed the innovators and those who resisted them. There was no blast of great collective passion.

Henry VIII wanted to remain equidistant from Catholicism and from Lutheranism. After the Ten Articles against the Pope, Purgatory, relics, images and pilgrimages, he promulgated the Six Articles, with penalty of death for those who denied Transubstantiation or who asked for Communion under both kinds and cast doubt upon the Mass and confession. Indeed, in 1540 three Lutheran ministers were burned and three Catholics beheaded. The King's direct action in favour of the Reformation was intensified, with a protestantising tendency, under Edward VI (1547-53), when the First and Second Acts of Uniformity were passed and the Book of Common Prayer issued. And while Mary (1553-8) sought reconciliation with Rome and the re-establishment of Catholicism, Elizabeth returned to the reforming policy of Edward VI; it was then that the final separation from Rome and establishment of the episcopal Church took place, while laws of persecution alternated with mitigating measures of toleration.

It was with the protection of Elizabeth that Protestantism took root in Scotland, propagated by John Knox who, on his return from exile in 1557, spread the spirit and ideas of Calvin with which he was imbued. In 1560 Knox drew up the Protestant Confession. The Scottish Parliament decreed that the Catholic Bishops should no longer have jurisdiction. The understanding between the Scottish Protestants and England led to an anti-French policy, and to the imprisonment and execution of Mary Queen of Scots. The difference between the reform of the Anglican Church and that of Scotland lies in the fact that the first separated from Rome mainly for practical and political reasons, maintaining the episcopal scaffolding and close collaboration with Parliament and Court. In Scotland the reform worked up from below;

the people and the lower clergy adopted Calvinism and fomented an anti-monarchic and anti-French policy. The Bishops were eliminated and the breath of Puritanism petrified minds and customs, preserving the personality of Scotland as distinct from England, in spite of the political union of the two countries under a single monarchy.

§ 27.—In the period that stretches from 1517 to 1545 (the date of the opening of the Council of Trent) the Catholic Church found herself in a crucial position from three standpoints: the internal one of moral, disciplinary and administrative reform; that of resistance to the movements of schism and of Protestant reform, and that of her relations with the Catholic princes and their States. The three standpoints are so interconnected as to be inseparable if, apart from analysis of facts, we wish to maintain their historical and sociological structure. They leap into light with the clash of events and the significance that these reveal.

At the time of Luther's first attempts at rebellion, Germany, divided into so many principalities, was moving towards a unitary administration through the efforts of Maximilian of Hapsburg—a customs union, a single coinage and a single court of Justice. On the death of Maximilian, in January, 1519, the only serious claimant of the House of Hapsburg was Charles, Duke of Ghent, who had become King of Aragon and Castille. Francis I of France was his rival to the Empire, and became his most constant and powerful enemy. Pope Leo X opposed Charles, just as Clement VII would oppose him; both were of the House of Medici.

On becoming Emperor, Charles, as Charles V, found he had to face simultaneously Luther's revolt, the French, the Turks, the Pope, and domestic revolts in his States. It is a great mistake to think of Charles V as a medieval Emperor. He was above all the sovereign of many States that had no common interests to bind them together other than their relationship to the House of Hapsburg. In Germany he was the most powerful of the princes and also Emperor: the Lutheran revolt struck a mortal blow at the imperial unity.

Luther at the time was caressing the idea of a mission for the general reform of the Church, starting from Germany and spreading to all

Christendom, and, in the exalted state of mind of the early reformers, this was believed a possibility. But the resistance of Rome and of the Emperor and of large zones of the German population, such as Bavaria, Austria and the Rhineland, showed at once the vanity of such a dream. Therefore, as we have seen, Luther turned to fixing the boundaries of the reformed Church according to the boundaries of the various States, resting it entirely on the political authority. In any case, the contempt of the Lutherans for the Latin peoples and for humanistic and Mediterranean culture and civilisation, especially that of Italy, ruled out the possibility of a spiritual convergence covering the whole of the West.

Leo X, after sending to Germany the famous Cardinal Cajetan (1518), after summoning Luther himself to Rome to retract (1519), and finding that the path of persuasion led nowhere, in June, 1520, condemned him as heretic and demanded either a retractation or that he should be captured and handed over within sixty days. In agreement with the Pope, the new Emperor summoned the Diet of Worms, over which he presided with the aid of the papal representatives, Caracciolo the Nunzio, and the Envoy Extraordinary, Girolamo Aleandro; it was hoped that Germany would be brought back to religious unity. But Luther did not retract, and, put under the ban of the Empire, took refuge in Thuringia, where no one dared molest him. Charles V in the meantime had achieved his purpose, that of gaining the alliance of the Pope against Francis I. He did not wish to carry his action against Luther and the princes who defended him to too great lengths, in order not to disturb the delicate situation in Germany by turning the dissident princes towards France.

Leo X dies. The Dutchman, Adrien Dedel, the tutor of Charles V, who succeeds him under the name of Adrian VI, with excellent projects of church reform, holds the Papacy for only twenty months, and is unable to check the Lutheran reform by a single step. Clement VII, elected Pope after Adrian, continues the policy of oscillation between France and the Empire, thus rendering the policy of Charles still more complicated. The latter is still a hesitant young man, under the control and guidance of ministers. The trend of his policy is mainly Spanish. The wars against Francis I are hegemonic wars between France and Spain. The stakes are Italy, the Mediterranean, European influence, the rule of the Ocean. HenryVIII of England also oscillates between France and Spain. Francis I, so long as he can fight victoriously against Charles, has no scruples about favouring the Protestant princes and allying himself with the Turk. Charles for his part, and his ministers and generals, subordinating religious interests to those of the House of Hapsburg and the demands of the wars in various parts of the Empire, continue to pursue a policy of compromises, swinging now towards this side, now towards that; this would render the general situation more and more difficult.

In that tangle of hegemonic interests, of unbridled passions, of culpable weakness, of fear of the growing Ottoman power which menaced Europe, the problem of Luther, though it touched both Pope and Emperor nearly, took second place. What is more, it seemed a useful weapon for the enemies of the Emperor and of the Pope, by which to hold in check one or the other or even both at once, in the decisive moments of conflicting policies.

This notwithstanding, the Roman Curia strove to find some possible solution to the German religious crisis. The Second Diet of Nuremberg in 1524 called for the convocation of a universal Council at Spires. Campeggio, the papal Legate, favours the proposal and Rome consents, but the Emperor opposes it, alleging rights and privileges. Francis I is beaten at Pavia (1525); a prisoner in Madrid, he is forced to sign peace (1526). It is the moment for Charles, now secure where France is concerned, to repress the rebellion of the German princes. But Francis, breaking the treaty, forms the anti-imperial League of Cambrai, and Clement VII is of the League. At the same time, the German princes favourable to Luther assemble at Torgau and sign a covenant of alliance to defend 'the Gospel'. Charles V, realising that he is in a tight corner, agrees to the decision of the Diet of Spires (August, 1526) that the ban pronounced against Luther at Worms shall not be enforced, that his life shall be respected and that his propaganda in Germany shall be permitted till the Council or a National Assembly has been called. At the same time he sends the Constable of Bourbon into Italy with a strong army; though the Constable is killed at the gates of Rome the city is sacked and the Pope made prisoner (May, 1527).

To the popular mind, excited by the Lutheran revolt and by the anti-

Roman spirit that was breathing everywhere, the sack of Rome (new Babylon) appeared the chastisement of God upon the Harlot who had prevaricated in the avarice and lechery of popes and Curia. Clement VII, too, in his address to the Cardinals in April, 1528, spoke of the sack of Rome as a punishment for his sins, and urged the need for reforms. In spite of all his efforts, these remained at the stage of projects. The College of Cardinals was more political than religious. The interests of the States of the Church and of the other Italian States that were bound to her by feudal or historical rights or for reasons of family policy, besides the States opposed to her, were a net in which popes and cardinals with their kinships and alliances were all held fast. The conflict of such interests widened to France, Spain and the Empire, for ever since the expedition of Charles VIII of France in 1498, Italy had become a constant battle-field and the prey of the foreigner. No Emperor succeeded as Charles V succeeded in dominating, directly or indirectly, the greater part of the peninsula.

Clement VII wished to claim as part of the Papal State not only Ravenna and Cervia, which were occupied by the Venetians, but Parma and Modena, in the possession of the Duke of Ferrara, Alphonso d'Este, and at the same time he would restore the Medici to the lordship of Florence. It was for these reasons that he had oscillated between the Emperor and Francis I, and, indeed, had favoured the Frenchman till, after the Sack of Rome, he decided to make peace with Charles. The Treaty of Barcelona of June, 1529, recognised these and other papal claims. The Emperor obtained the right to nominate the bishops of the kingdom of Naples, and consented to recognition of the Holy See's feudal right over that kingdom, in token of which he undertook that the Pope should yearly receive the famous *chinea*, the white mule.

This peace was followed by the Treaty of Cambrai between Charles V and Francis I (August, 1529); then comes Charles's meeting with the Pope, his coronation at Bologna in February, 1530, and the signing of peace between the Pope and Alphonso of Ferrara. At the same time there is the imperial expedition against Perugia and its capitulation, the restitution to the Pope of Civitavecchia and Orte, and the siege of Florence. In Florence the spirit of Savonarola revives; the city defends the republic and resists the Pope. But the imperial troops are victorious, the Medici are reinstated, with atrocious reprisals. The Pope causes Alexander dci Medici to be appointed Duke of Florence, President of the Republic for life, with right of succession, and makes Florence subject to the Empire (1530-1).

A contributory motive for the understanding between Pope and Emperor was the threatening pressure of the Turks. After the Treaty of Barcelona, Clement thinks the moment has come to call a Crusade, but the result is negligible and the Crescent advances as far as Buda. The situation in Germany is no better. Luther is still in hiding in Coburg; there seems a possibility that an understanding will be reached at the Diet of Augsburg, which is summoned for June, 1530. But it was precisely then that the *Confession* of Augsburg was formulated, forming the basis of Protestantism. The Catholics replied by the *Confutation*, and no agreement could be reached. The dissident princes, thinking that they could preserve their autonomy only by resisting the Emperor, gathered together at Schmalkalden, where they formed the Schmalkaldic League. In the meantime, Clement was once more drawing towards France. There were certain matters in dispute between him and Charles V, and, what was more, the marriage of his niece, Catherine de' Medici, with the Duke of Orleans, was already in view. The Emperor, faced with fresh hostilities on the part of France and the Pope, and with the advance of the Turks, temporised with the Schmalkaldic League and came to terms in the Diet of Nuremberg, in the course of which the German Consistorial Church was established.

The situation was becoming more and more embroiled and uncertain. Anxieties were increasing. Many bishops and religious-minded men, religious Orders old and new, Clement himself and not a few of the Cardinals felt the urgent need for a reform of the Church in a Catholic sense and for a clarification of dogma in the face of the many affirmations that were held to be heretical (and were so, for the most part, according to traditional theology). They therefore called for the summoning of a General Council. The Germans demanded that it should meet in a German city; the Pope wanted it to be in Italy, at Verona, Mantua or Padua; Charles V was for Trent. In the midst of these disputes, which were largely premature, for nothing serious had been done to prepare the Council, Clement VII died, in the same year that England went into schism. He was succeeded by Cardinal Alexander Farnese, who took the name of Paul III.

With Paul III the will for reform becomes firmer and more decided, but practical difficulties seem stronger than his will and unhappily his nepotism diminished the value of his efforts and the good results of his labours. Before calling the Council he would see a reform of the Curia; to this end he appoints two commissions and prepares the draft of a Bull, but the Cardinals are against it. Paul seeks to over-rule them by nominating new Cardinals, among them Bellay, the Archbishop of Paris, Fisher, Bishop of Rochester, and the famous Contarini of Venice, who was then a layman but already in high fame. There are fresh commissions, fresh difficulties. The Pope delays no longer and in June, 1535, summons the Council for May, 1537, at Mantua, while in order to strengthen the conciliar and reforming parties he appoints yet other Cardinals, among them Caraffa (later, Paul IV), De Monte (later Julius III) and the celebrated Sadoleto and Pole.

The Council of Mantua was postponed at the last moment, because the prince, Gonzaga, declared he could not guarantee public order and the safety of the Cardinals, and asked for police reinforcements from the Pope. The latter refused to send them, in order not to appear to intimidate the Council, This was again postponed and was summoned to meet in the following November, in Vicenza. But opposition to the Council came from every side. Francis I, Henry VIII, the Schmalkaldic League were against it, for one reason or another. Charles V showed himself hesitant and undecided. The Pope continued to fix new dates for the Council and to appoint new Cardinals till, as though vanquished by the difficulties, in May, 1539, he postponed it *sine die*.

The Council plan having failed, Charles V accepted the proposal of a new Diet, which, after various delays, was held at Ratisbon, with the intervention of Cardinal Contarini as Papal Legate. He was a man of open mind and inflexible character, and a firm supporter of the Catholic reform. He was on the lines of Cardinal Pole, of Morone and of the many Italians (among them Vittoria Colonna) who sought to escape from a rigidity in the traditional Catholicism, and to approach— in so far as this was possible on the plane of interpretation—the thought of the reformers. At Ratisbon, Contarini put forward the theory of a two-fold justification, the one through the faith that invests, purifies and supernaturalises nature, and the other, the justice of Christ, a divine gift given to the soul but not inherent in it. Neither Catholics nor Protestants felt enthusiastic over this theory, which would be rejected by the Council of Trent. A commission of three Catholics and three Protestants appointed by the Diet drew up six articles, but on the theme of Transubstantiation their agreement broke down. Then Charles V issued an edict, known as the *Ratisbon Interim*, in which he took note of the agreement on the first five points and referred the sixth to the General Council. He was hard-pressed by the advance of the Turks on Buda. After an encounter with Paul III, he went on his unlucky expedition against Algiers, when the whole of his fleet was destroyed.

Francis I seized the opportunity to renew his offensive against his eternal enemy. This made the Pope hesitate, both because of the general situation and because of the political interests of his son Pier Luigi and his grandson Ottavio. The Council was summoned to meet at Trent on November 1, 1542, and Charles, with the threat of bringing the Council to nothing, insisted that the Pope should abandon his neutrality and declare himself against Francis. Paul III would suffer no intimidation, and appointed the Cardinals Pole, Parisi and Morone to be his legates at Trent. Hardly anyone appeared at the Council. Indifference on the one hand, suspicions and political interests on the other, with the opposition of various princes and the wars raging all over Europe, forced the Pope to yet another postponement. In the meantime, with the commissions of Cardinals, he had begun the reform of the Curia, and by direct acts of his authority he created the central office of the Roman Inquisition in 1542 and the following year started the Index of forbidden books.

Charles for his part, having to propitiate the Protestant princes of Germany in view of the other wars in various parts of the Empire, made fresh concessions in favour of the Lutheran reform, to the intense resentment of the Pope. Finally, in September, 1544, the Peace of Crépy was signed between Charles and Francis, and an *entente* was established for the appeasement and unification of Christendom. Paul III could now call the Council, which, convoked to assemble in March, 1545, opened at Trent in the following November. Unfortunately the Council was too late. The Protestants were not represented. Melancthon had written the year before that it was impossible to go back upon the past: 'already ten thousand married monks and friars form, with their biblical propaganda, the firm and unshakable fulcrum of the reformed community.'

All this anti-ecclesiastical, anti-Roman and anti-Catholic movement had awakened among Catholics an intellectual and moral revival, both as resistance and as counter-offensive; this had brought a fervour of study, an activity of work that served to rouse the sluggish and to stimulate the zeal of the others, quickening a faith that had seemed almost extinct. If the political domain was a turmoil of interests and passions that assumed gigantic form in the axial clash between Charles V and Francis I, if the Roman Curia, though holding fast to dogma and tradition, wavered over means of reform and in its political attitudes, the mystical currents with their new enterprises, the intellectuals by their studies, the artists by their works, brought into the Church the leaven of a new spirit that was like a rebirth.

In the sphere of church reform and pastoral zeal, in 1524 came the Order of the Theatines or Clerks Regular, founded by St. Gaetano Tiene, who had been at the court of Julius II. In 1528 the Capucines were founded by Mathew Bassi. In 1532 St. Anthony Mary Zaccary founds the Barnabites. St. Ignatius of Loyola founds the Company of Jesus in 1534, St. Angela Merici, in 1535, the Ursulines, and in 1540 the Somascians are founded by St. Jerome Emiliani.

These new troops and others that would be formed in the second half of the XVI century—among the most noted being the Oratorians of St. Philip Neri (1564), the Brothers Hospitallers of St. John of God (1564), the Camillines of St. Camillo de Lellis (1586) and the Piarists of St. Joseph Calasanzio (1597)—came from below, from the multitude of the faithful, and inserted themselves among the Catholic clergy with the characteristics of the spiritual and mystical currents which, contained within the bounds of orthodoxy, have always been fruitful of good in the Church. These differed from those of the past in their main task of apostolic activity and practical works among the faithful. They would no longer have an office in common, nor cloistered life;

in their religious Orders they realise the individualistic spirit of humanism together with the corporative spirit of the Middle Ages. Hence a
discipline at once rigorous and mild, a personal and collective responsibility, a training suited to the qualities of the individuals and to the
manifold ends of the community. And whereas the old Orders
abounded in wealth and had become lax in discipline, the new cham-
pioned a poverty without exaggerations but also without fictions or
privileges. And at a time when many friars and monks failed in their
subjection to Rome, the new ones rose up as an aid to the Papacy,
which was seeking to regain its moral position and its religious
influence in the Catholic world.

Among the new foundations that of the Company of Jesus soon
towered above the rest, through its discipline, numbers and activity
and through a group of religious of the highest order in culture, apostolic zeal and eminent sanctity. Besides the founder, whose organising
genius and whose sanctity, at once active and contemplative, were
so outstanding, the names of Francis Xavier, the Apostle of India,
Francis Borgia, Peter Canisius, Robert Bellarmin, are universally
known; all were saints and great men. The Jesuit theologians soon
rival the Dominicans, Franciscans and Augustinians. The activity that
placed them at once in the midst of the people was one of spiritual and
temporal assistance, particularly in Rome, where luxury mingled with
wretchedness, virtue with vice, wisdom with ignorance. In a period
when the rapid and virulent spread of venereal disease showed visible
effects, Ignatius began his work by a home for fallen women and a
radical fight against public prostitution.

Forsaken children, unemployed workers, beggars without resources,
fallen women, the sick in the hospitals, the neglected dying found
help and succour from the pioneers of the various new Orders that
were arising, while the churches, all but abandoned or ill-kept, awoke
to new life. The rites of worship regained their splendour, and souls
thirsting for a living and substantial word found in the new Orders
confessors, preachers, masters, directors and friends. Their poverty,
simplicity, purity made them everywhere an example to clergy and
faithful, while their devotion to the Catholic Church and their defence
of her dogmas repaired the spread of heresy and formed lines of resist-

ance and defence. The new institutions, starting from Rome and Italy, spread everywhere, bringing a new breath of spiritual life. The old Orders, too, either in the face of the peril of heresy, or through the desertion of many convents, especially in the Northern countries, or through the example of the new-comers, pressure from the faithful, and a public opinion oriented towards a reform of morals, return to life with renewed discipline. They had never failed to produce men of the highest order, in sanctity, sacred sciences and preaching. The great Carmelite and Franciscan reforms of the second half of the century are associated with the names of St. Teresa of Avila, St. John of the Cross and St. Peter of Alcantara.

Before this religious movement of spontaneous reform a wide intellectual movement had taken shape in the domain of sacred studies, such as to renovate decadent scholasticism and the inadequate textual criticism of the Scriptures and patristic writings. This movement is linked up with the humanism and theology and philosophy of the previous century, and thus with the great names of Cardinal da Cusa, St. Antoninus of Florence, Cardinal Cesarini, Marsilio Ficino, Savonarola. With the invention of printing, a revision of the sacred texts became urgent. At a moment when the heretical current was basing itself on the Scriptures, the need for a revision of the Vulgate and of the Greek texts was felt by all.

To this task Erasmus of Rotterdam dedicated himself, the most celebrated of the humanists and the most temperate of the reformers. He wanted a return to the Bible and to a wider diffusion of the text of the Gospel. 'The surest means of restoring and consolidating religion is that the faithful should hold fully to the wisdom of Christ, and that before all else they should learn to know the Master's thought in the books where the celestial word still lives and breathes.' Thus his preface to his *Annotationes in Novum Testamentum*, published in 1519. Erasmus's comments on the scriptural text seek to place the figure of Christ in the historical environment in which He lived, laying greater emphasis on the Incarnation and on love for His humanity. Erasmus was responsible for the edition of the Greek and Latin Fathers which Frober of Basel now started to publish, amid the applause of the learned and of the churchmen of the period.

He was the object of recriminations, criticism and attacks; he was too great for it to have been otherwise; he himself had used a biting criticism and satire. In the *Praise of Folly* (written in the house of his friend Thomas More, to whom it was dedicated) and in other writings he had bitterly attacked bigoted piety, verbal scholasticism and the temporal Papacy. He had not spared the friars and monks, he himself an Augustinian monk who had won permission from the Pope to remain outside the cloister and wear no habit. His criticisms were not wholly free from exaggeration, and some of his theses might seem hazardous, even before the Council of Trent. At the  beginning of Luther's reform, he had been believed favourable to that movement; although adverse to verbal violence and acts of rebellion, he thought that some good might come of it. This did not lead him away from Catholicism. Through his exceptional position in European culture and through his friendship with Pope Leo X, he sought to induce the Church and Catholic writers and preachers to be less bitter in their polemics and more disposed for great reforms.

His correspondence with Leo X, Adrian VI and Clement VII on resistance to heresy, on the reform of the Church, and on peace is interesting as indicating his theoretical and practical outlook on religious and moral questions. His letter addressed to Clement VII closed with the following period, which might seem a warning: 'Believe me, you will outstrip the glory of all your predecessors, if Your Holiness will appease the tumult of wars and of discord. You will be able to succeed if, on the one hand, you show yourself just to all princes, and on the other, disposed to change certain things that ought to be changed for the good of religion.' Seeing how Clement was supporting Charles V against Francis, Erasmus wrote: 'It is not for the Pope, who is the father of all, to conclude alliances with this man or that, but to maintain an equable concord among all.'

This spirit of equilibrium, moderation and good sense, which to the one side inclined towards rationalism and a humanistic reform, and on the other, holding fast to the fundamental dogmas, blamed the excesses of the reformers, could please neither the Lutherans nor the Catholics, involved as they were in a fight to the death. Both wanted him to pronounce himself clearly for one side or the other. His enemies said that he was a Protestant at heart and that he cherished the advantages of remaining a Catholic. But he never wished to overstep his role of humanist and man of letters and culture, till, angered by Luther's book *De Servo Arbitrio*, he decided in 1524 to publish his reply, *De Libero Arbitrio*. He thus broke off his relations with the reformers, but he never abandoned his spirit of moderation and his character as a scholar.

He continued his critical and humanistic works, which had so great an influence on the culture of the time. His last publication was the *Liber pius de preparatione ad mortem*, in 1534. By then he had seen the collapse of everything from which he had hoped a religious rebirth, an appeasement of nations, and a new orientation of the Papacy. In that climate of struggles, revolts, wars, an ebullition of all the collective passions, it was impossible for the voice of moderation and good sense to be heard and acted upon, unless men's minds were prepared by an inward reform of morals and an intimate spirituality had grown up, beginning from below. To this Erasmus certainly contributed, and not only he but the whole pleiad of religious writers, Catholic humanists, intelligent and modern theologians, who had no fear of either textual criticism or history. These prepared the new currents of thought in the bosom of the Church. When all the political and practical difficulties had been overcome, and the Council of Trent could begin at last, we find a phalanx of theologians, philosophers and learned men who were able to contribute much to the formulation and solution of the arduous problems it treated. We find too in nearly every country and in the various strata of European culture a greater preparation, traditional indeed, but rejuvenated and invigorated by controversy with the reformers and by the necessity of going forth to meet the spiritual revival represented by the new religious Orders and their affiliations.

With this revival is connected the religious movement in art, which from Savonarola onwards had found a new expression, suited to the two-fold spiritual and humanistic movement of ascetic reform and of human exigencies interpreted in a Catholic sense. The religious art of the XVI century was not an exterior art, concerned with the pure quest for beauty in the expression of a humanised religion and a mythicized humanity. Here is one of those ready-made ideas that historical criticism and art criticism are now demolishing. The Lutheran reformation put a brutal stop to all religious art, destroyed paintings and statues, and froze the artistic conception of faith in the same way as it separated the political world and all human works from faith, reducing it to a solitary inner flame. The spiritual revival of Catholicism had on the contrary a decisive influence on religious art. It is true that the pagan myth continued to adorn the walls and ceilings of palaces and its allegories reached the threshold of the churches and even penetrated within, yet its general trend was to reveal human sentiments, the value of beauty and a sound and noble nature. In the endeavour to associate that part of nature that can be raised to a higher order with the religious mystery of sin and redemption, in a harmony of the two lives, natural and supernatural, lies the profound significance of cinque cento art. Its protagonist is Michelangelo, like Dante in genius, who, like Dante could bring out human grandeur and divine revelation. The Last Judgment of the Sistine chapel is the greatest poem ever written with colour and paint-brush.

The spiritual revival of Catholicism, at once mystical and active, theological and critical, humanistic and artistic, marks the beginning of recovery from the profound crisis into which the Church had fallen. But while spiritual life once again flows and circulates in the Catholic body, the structural situation of the Church, politically and economically, and her relations with the princes that had remained Catholic showed the greatest disorder and were complicated by the gravest difficulties. Local hierarchies were disorganised. Concordats no longer held good or were no longer observed. The kings and princes appointed their favourites as bishops, abbots or abbesses, and gave benefices *in commendum* even to soldiers or to ladies anything but fitted to be the representatives of nuns. The discipline of many ancient monasteries was such that, in the first years of the pontificate of Paul III, a Cardinal suggested forbidding any novice to be received in them till that generation of monks and nuns had died out and the intrigues and interference of the princes could be abolished.

But the popes were involved in the wars of Europe and made wide concessions in matters of Canon Law, now to one side, now to the other, according to political happenings and the prevailing interests of war or peace (as with Charles V over the clergy of Spain and Naples), so that the question became more and more complicated. It was almost impossible for the popes to resist the kings, and the attitude of Clement VII towards the divorce of Henry VIII of England was the beginning of the schism and subsequently of the Protestantism of Great Britain. We do not say this to blame Clement—even though his conduct in the matter was overshadowed by political considerations—but in order to show in what a tragic tangle the Church of Rome found herself, and how in such conditions only a Council could restore to the Pope himself all his authority and liberty and re-establish on clearer lines the troubled and intricate relations between the Church and the States.

§ 28.—In November, 1545, the Council of Trent opened. The first sessions were sparsely attended; distrust was widespread in the Catholic camp and even among ecclesiastics; suspicion and opposition reigned in the courts of the various States and about the Emperor. The Protestants, knowing the spirit of resistance in the Catholic episcopate to their profound innovations in dogma and discipline, not only took no part but began to attack the Council fiercely. There was a middle stream, of those who sought for a line of convergence between Catholics and Protestants, especially after Luther's death (1546). To this end at Trent a party had formed itself which wished the council to postpone dogmatic decision to a later period and to begin only with the disciplinary questions. Charles V was of these ideas. He indeed maintained the thesis that in the Germanic countries that had remained Catholic the widest toleration should be granted to Protestants, in order that the rupture should not be rendered final. But this policy was blamed by Paul III, who accused the Emperor of breaking his engagements. There was then much resentment in Rome against Charles V and a continuous oscillation between the various political currents, especially after Henry II of France renewed the struggle of his father, Francis, against the Hapsburg. Paul III complained that the Emperor wanted to have all Italy at his free disposal, to secularise Spain, to give his orders at Trent, and to judge the great German religious controversy at his own tribunal.

While Charles would have wished the Council to suspend its dogmatic decisions, the Roman Curia was pressing for it to suspend disciplinary measures. Not that Paul III was against the reform of the Church, indeed it was he who had been the first to make serious reforms in the administration of the Holy See and to create the Roman Inquisition and the Index. He feared the various Courts that had remained Catholic and the opposition of the clergy themselves of the different States, and would have wished for a prudent and wary procedure. But the Council Fathers assembled at Trent, and even the papal Legates, saw the danger of separating the dogmatic part from the disciplinary, and decided to discuss the two alternately —especially since, with the failure of the conversations of Ratisbon, as the Emperor's last endeavour to reconcile Catholics and Protestants (February, 1546), there could be no reason for further delays.

The Council little by little came to life. Bishops and advisers came from France and England and from other parts of Europe; the religious Orders asserted themselves, with men of eminent culture and piety. With the alternation of dogmatic and disciplinary decisions a really constructive work began. This helped to give confidence to the reforming and mystical streams which were gaining ground more and more in the Catholic Church; they brought the influence of their culture and zeal to bear, to dissipate the political, worldly and time-serving tendencies that were developing both within the Council and on its margins, through the intrigues of the Courts and of the court bishops. None the less, after a few months of work, opposition to the Council revived, stronger than ever. Charles V himself questioned its authority. Many refused to consider it as oecumenical. A section of the clergy followed the policies of their own States, now favourable, now adverse. There arose a demand for suspension or adjournment. The wars in Germany and Italy were still raging, the former of a religious character, the latter exclusively political. There were also epidemics. It was decided to transfer the Council to Bologna, but the partisans of the Emperor and others, on the side of the Pope, remained in Trent to prepare its further labours. The Council, carried to Bologna, was obliged, after its June session, to adjourn indefinitely. Thus its first period closed.

Charles V, after his victory at Mühlberg over the Schmalkaldic League (1547), needed to reach an understanding with his German adversaries in order to be free for his wars elsewhere. In view, therefore, of the adjournment of the Council and of the impossibility of bringing the Protestants within its compass, he summoned the Diet of Augsburg, where a *modus vivendi* was settled. The Protestants were to be allowed a non-celibate clergy and communion under both kinds, while on the other hand, the Catholic hierarchy and rites were restored where they had ceased to exist, and the fasts and feasts of the Roman Calendar were reinstalled. Paul III condemned the *modus vivendi*. In spite of this it came into force through the authority of the Emperor and lasted till the Protestant princes could once more raise their heads.

The second period of the Council of Trent, summoned anew by Julius III who succeeded Paul III, runs from May, 1551 to April, 1553. The difficulties were enormous. The French delegates failed to appear. Henry II of France was hostile, and went so far as to threaten the Pope through his ambassador to call a national council himself and to see to the reform of his own clergy. The Spanish delegates were on the side of the Emperor. The latter wanted the Protestants to take part in the Council. A few delegations actually came, but they demanded that the decrees already issued by the Council of Paul III should be discussed all over again, and this neither the papal delegates nor the conciliar assembly could allow. Thus Charles's new endeavour ended in failure.

The Council, in the midst of party difficulties and political intrigues, continued to examine the question of the Sacraments and decisions for reform; but the war that had broken out over the duchies of Parma and Piacenza had spread through nearly the whole of Northern Italy and made communications between Rome and Trent extremely difficult. In such a war—which, in substance, was fought between Henry II of France, whom the Duke Ottavio Farnese had called in to help him, and the Emperor Charles V—the Pope was involved through his temporal rights over Parma and his investiture of Ottavio Farnese with the duchy and with the office of Gonfaloniere of the Roman Church. At this moment, reversing the situation completely, came the treachery and revolt of Maurice of Saxony against Charles; thus war broke out in Germany. The Council was suspended and Julius III could not revive it. He thought to bring the Council Fathers to Rome, to collaborate with him in the reform of the Church, but they distrusted the Roman environment and replied in the negative. Thus two years passed, till the death of Julius. His successor, Marcel II, would have been a great pope, but he held the pontificate only for twenty-two days, and was succeeded by Paul IV (Carafa), who gave no further thought to the Council.

Paul IV came into the Papacy when Charles V, after accepting the (for him) humiliating Convention of Passau, in which he granted the Protestants full and entire freedom of worship till the next Diet, was about to sign the Peace of Augsburg (August–September, 1555), which established the principle of compulsory State religions—*cuius regio illius et religio*. The religious and political severance of the Protestants from the Empire was now complete. Paul IV was by temperament contrary to all long discussions; filled with zeal for reform he thought that he could bring it about by piling decrees on decrees, by strong measures and by a reign of terror. Unfortunately he fell into the hands of his relatives and nephews, who not only frustrated all his efforts at reform, but created about him an atmosphere of scandal, simony, financial corruption and armed intimidation; of all this the holy old man remained unaware. The 'Cardinal-Nephew,' Carlo Caraffa, Secretary of State, was one of the gang; to obtain dominion over Siena he provoked the disastrous war between the Holy See and Charles V. When the Pope learned what was happening, from the Florentine Agent, Gianfigliazzi, he made a clean sweep of his nephews and their followers, and showed himself inexorable to all. His temperament led him to an exaggerated rigour, which indeed he practised first of all upon himself. He went so far as to suspect Cardinal Pole (who died just in time to escape imprisonment) and Morone, who had already been Legate at Trent, and who was isolated in the Castle of Sant' Angelo and subjected to a harsh inquisitorial examination till, on the death of Paul IV, he was set free with his innocence fully recognised.

The four years of the pontificate of Paul IV were a continual tempest, so that at his death all sought a peace-making pope, who would reopen the Council and restore confidence to the hierarchy of all countries in a Rome inspired by prudence, conciliation and reform. The new Pope was Pius IV. The victory of the Emperor's arms at Saint Quentin in 1557, the abdication and death of Charles V, the subsequent Peace of Cateau-Cambrésis (1559) and the death of Henry II of France had allowed a certain respite in the turbulent affairs of European politics. The first difficulty that Pius IV had to overcome regarded Ferdinand, who had succeeded Charles V as Emperor. Paul IV had not wished to recognise him as Emperor because he had signed the Passau Convention and the Peace of Augsburg. The new Pope showed himself ready to give his assent if Ferdinand would give adequate assurances of a Catholic attitude in regard to the Protestant conflict and to the education in the Catholic faith of his son and heir Maximilian. Ferdinand declared that the conventions signed had been merely 'interims' pending the decisions of the Council, and gave the requisite assurances on the religious upbringing of Maximilian. This eased the way for a *rapprochement* between Pope and Emperor, but the Council was still a very long way off.

Ferdinand wanted a fresh Council, that would not meet at Trent. Philip II of Spain (who had here succeeded his father, Charles V) demanded instead an assurance that the new Council would be merely a continuation of the Council of Paul III and Julius III. But while the Protestant part of Germany and of the Baltic countries could now be looked upon as lost, and England, under Elizabeth, was taking the decisive step of severance, France had become the neuralgic point of the situation. The Huguenots had advanced prodigiously; in various provinces they dominated completely, and the quarrels between Catholics and Protestants were acute. Francis II wanted to settle them amicably, in a national council. There was, however, the party that wished to avoid a national council (which would have been very dangerous) by the convocation of the General Council, and therefore it urged Rome to make a speedy decision.

The three years that preceded the opening of the Council were full of grave vicissitudes, and it needed all the moderation and diplomacy of Pius IV and his able collaborators, and his firmness in willing the Council, and, in substance, of willing its continuation, to make it possible, in the midst of conflicts, mistrust and also of questions of punctilio, for it to reopen at Trent on January 18, 1562. The Protestants, who were invited, did not intervene, taking their stand on the negative decision of the princes who supported them, who had met at Namburg. In any case, no one could delude himself into believing that an understanding was now possible. Neither direct nor indirect endeavours, with the Calvinists, Anglicans and the various Swiss confessions and with those of Bohemia and Hungary, had any result. The Council of Trent from the beginning was always confined to Catholics, and the dissidents took no part in it. The Catholic princes sent their representatives with various reservations, concerning not only their rights but their attitude, towards Protestantism. The French clergy arrived in Trent very late; little by little all countries had their representatives there. The debates were not easy; their course from time to time grew tempestuous. Discussion bore on the themes of the Mass, Ordination, Matrimony, Purgatory, the cult of Saints, interspersed with decisions on reform of discipline, till, by speeding up its business, the Council could be declared closed on December 4, 1563.

In this final phase three men of outstanding character played their part. Cardinal Morone, after the death of the two chief Legates, Gonzaga and Seripante, took their place and was able to steer the Council to harbour, at a time when it seemed in danger of sinking through the intrigues of Philip II, the oscillations of the Emperor Ferdinand, the opposition of the Court of France, and the inevitable dissensions among the bishops. Morone had been one of the most authoritative papal legates of the first and second periods of the Council. Though tried by Paul IV on suspicion of heresy, he came back more respected than before, as the most authorised defender of Catholicism, the Pope's confidential agent, highly esteemed by the Emperor and respected by the other reigning houses and by the whole Council. None the less he represented an age that was already of the past, that of the men of learning and wisdom, moderates, reformers, enlightened Catholics. Trent saw the flower of them, among the greatest being Contarini, who died too soon. All were true Catholic humanists, whose labours were not in vain, but whose idea, that of an understanding with the Protestants, could not be realised. The gulf was too wide to be spanned, and, moreover, the policy of the Courts and the conditions of the Papacy presented too grave an obstacle.

Those who represented the future were, among others, two interesting figures, to whom in large measure the Council of Pius IV owed its success. The first was Cardinal Charles Borromeo, the second Father

Laynez, General of the Jesuits. Cardinal Borromeo, appointed Secretary of State at the age of twenty-three by his uncle Pius IV, was not like the usual Cardinal-nephews, men of the world and intriguers who subordinated the interests of the Holy See to those of their own fortune or that of their families. No man more disinterested, hard-working and scrupulous in the fulfilment of his charge had ever occupied the post. Intelligent, cultured, zealous, his collaboration eased the relations between the Pope and the Council, between the Pope and the various Courts; he helped to give an impetus to the reform of the Curia by his advice and his example. Contemporaries perceived the importance of this young Cardinal only when, leaving Rome, he gave himself up to the care of his Archbishopric of Milan, leaving an indelible imprint as shepherd of souls, father of the people, defender of the faith and one who aroused heroic virtues. He was the type of pastor that had arisen in the spiritual renaissance of Rome with Gaetano Thiene, Ignatius of Loyola, Philip Neri and all that pleiad of saints who lived in the midst of the Roman people, reawakening them to virtue. He incarnated the spirit of the Council of Trent for the reform of the episcopate and of the Cardinals, and he became its most signal and revered figure, soon to be counted among the saints.

Father Laynez took part in the Council of Trent first as theologian and then also as General of the Jesuits, signing its decisions in this quality. He was one of the orators who were most readily heard. His speeches, on the long side, were always clear, interesting, theologically sound and often effective. Not all that he said pleased or mirrored the mind of the assembly, divided as it was in its practical trends and even in its theological premises, but to all he said he brought an enlightened knowledge and a profound conviction. Laynez may be considered the strongest representative of papal monarchism, the defender of the principle of authority; he was hostile to the electoral bodies and went so far as to say that in regard to bishops he preferred appointment by the king to appointment by cathedral chapters and assemblies. Behind him he had the Company, which was then beginning its ascendancy and its wide influence in society, among both aristocracy and people, and which already awakened jealousy, mistrust and opposition. This would grow in Rome with the first attempts to apply the reform to the Curia, for the Jesuits, who were called in to co-operate, applied so much zeal to the recalcitrant as to give the impression rather of police work than of religious discipline. At Trent not a few Gallican bishops and even Roman ones already felt that the Company was a reinforcement of the Papacy.

Outward events and the agitated course of discussions, between the various tendencies of the episcopate, the political anxieties of Rome, the intervention of the Emperor and of the courts of France and Spain, did not prevent the Council from achieving a good part of its work, or from accomplishing it in so effective and permanent a form as to leave its mark on the Catholicism of the succeeding period and make its effects felt up to our own times. In the whole of Church history there is no council that by its acts excercised so prolonged and permanent an influence on the Church, except, perhaps, the first oecumenical councils, and these had not to deal with all the intricate web of legislative, dogmatic and disciplinary matters that formed the object of the Council of Trent. For those who still hoped that a General Council would restore peace between Catholics and Protestants by theoretical and practical compromise, Trent was a disappointment. Perhaps a Council held twenty years earlier, with the aim of a clarification of dogma and a real reform of morals, would have been in time to prevent the heretical currents from creating dissident churches. The Council of Trent was not a platform for an understanding with adversaries but a reinforcement of the Catholic party, which on a clearly defined plane was beginning to fight against the infiltration of errors into the countries that had remained faithful to Rome, setting up a barrier to Protestantism and schism. It was thus a starting-point for a reform of the clergy and for a better discipline in morals.

To this end, from the beginning the theory of grace and predestination were defined at Trent, as opposed to the Lutheran and Calvinist theories which had not only undermined the dogmas in question but had given society a different ethical basis. According to the Council, grace cancels original sin, creates in us supernatural life, and only by grace can we freely perform good works. Grace itself, either preserved after baptism or regained by penitence and fecundated by good works, gives us a title to the eternal reward. Divine predestination is not in contradiction to personal merits. Grace cannot be acquired save by the application of the merits of Jesus Christ, by means of baptism either actually received or its desire, and subsequently by means of the Sacraments, administered by the Church. Faith alone without good works cannot operate our salvation.

At Trent three principles denied by Protestantism were reaffirmed: (a) The intermediation of the Church in the relations of man with God, a doctrinal and sacramental mediation, which not only does not destroy but perfects our direct contacts with God ; (b) the affirmation of free will and the necessity of good works as the practical outcome of faith, as an inward conformity to the divine precepts, and as a means of acquiring merits for the reward ; (c) the value of tradition, equal to that of Holy Scripture and interpreting Holy Scripture itself, both being authoritatively taught and defined by the magistracy of the teaching Church.

The consequences of these principles (apart from the other manifold decisions and measures of the Council), through the logic of their application, extended to social life and the relations between the power of the Church and that of the State. The doctrinal and sacramental mediation of the Church, between man and God, cut away the base of the individualistic principle of free inquiry and of the laicist principle that there was no hierarchic difference between the faithful and the priest and bishop. The hierarchic order of the Church led towards its autonomous organisation, independent of the secular power, while the affirmation of free will and the necessity of good works (as well as faith) for eternal salvation, resoldered the nexus between individual and inward morality and public or social morality, making the two one. By this very fact, the field of activity of the Church's teaching, doctrinal and practical, dogmatic and moral, extended to social and political activity, and hence the Church maintained implicitly her right to intervene over the secular power.

Although the problem of relations between Church and State was not directly faced, the principles contained in the capital decisions of the Council implied a re-assertion of their respective positions—the spiritual supremacy of the Church and a close collaboration with th

Catholic sovereigns, who as princes were held to be defenders of the faith, collaborators, supporters and protectors of the Church. This old conception, in view of the position, had become inconvenient to both Church and sovereigns. The Church had already found how easy it was for the princes in those conditions and with the idea of a national church to lead their peoples into schism and encourage heresy. The princes who wished to remain faithful to the Church had to reckon with vassals and subjects who rebelled, with fanatics who instigated sedition, and with court sympathies for the reformers, among whom were men of authority and genius, fervent for religion and for reform as they understood it, and able to arouse assent and enthusiasm in those about them.

The policy of conciliation, mingled with that of 'reason of State,' or of usefulness to the dynasty, was grafted on to a concern for the Church and for the faith according to the prevailing counsels of the local clergy, of bishops and cardinals who might be men of integrity or intriguing and evil; it was swayed now by the reaction of the Catholics and of the Pope, now by that of the Protestants in a wearisome see-saw, in which war and peace, assemblies and protests, interwove and developed with dizzying rapidity. The situation during the Council of Trent had not changed; indeed it had worsened in England and in Scotland with the advent of Elizabeth, in France with the Huguenot agitation, in Flanders with the government of Philip II, indeed everywhere, through the confusion of questions of religion and faith with purely political and dynastic ones, and questions of reform with economic and fiscal ones.

The Council of Trent had accomplished its labours with a vision of the supreme interests of the faith and of the Catholic reform, always in contact with the three Popes who summoned it and caused it to be guided by their legates, with a good number of bishops who were faithful, indeed attached, to the Holy See. None the less preoccupations in regard to the various courts, great and small, troubled bishops and delegates, and certain ambassadors, like the Count of Luna, ambassador of Philip II, held the episcopate of their countries in a real subjection. Yet the Council dropped the proposals that concerned the rights and duties of the heads of Catholic States, the so-called 'reform of princes,'

though this was an important point in the general plan. Everyone feared
lest local privileges and the rights of the national clergies might be
called in question, lest the authority of the sovereigns be challenged
and respect for them lessened, and lest rights and privileges hallowed by
usage or even acquired by abuse might be prejudiced. The best excuse
was that the reform had to begin with Rome. Indeed from Paul III
onwards the reform of the Curia was constantly sought. Paul IV went
to extremes and therefore was the less effective. The action of Pius IV
was wiser and more organic, yet not only did he fail to achieve a complete reform, but even he fell into certain abuses, such as appointing
two youths aged fourteen and eighteen as court Cardinals. However,
when the Council had ended, he was able to hold his own against the
staff of the Curia and to enforce the execution of the Tridentine canons.

The true reason why the reform of princes was dropped at Trent
was that the Church was not in a position to avert the danger of new
national churches even in the countries that had remained Catholic.
The clergies were too much bound to the sovereigns and too much
concerned with their privileges, while the populations were divided
and disquieting. The Papacy could count neither on clergy nor people
and the orthodox mystical stream inclined towards a strengthening of
the power of the Catholic sovereign in order to make a strong front
against invading Protestantism. Although many had other views and
wished to see the reform imposed on all, the princes included, they were
forced to give way and to leave the question for Rome to deal with
when the right time came. Cardinal Morone, in burying the proposals
of reform, summed up the situation in these significant words: 'They
(the princes) are men, not angels. We must deal with the princes as
with the heretics, lead them to good by good examples and not by
threats, proceeding in all things with wisdom, piety and Christian
prudence.'

# CHAPTER VIII

## REFORMATION AND COUNTER-REFORMATION

### SECOND PERIOD (1563-1648)

§ 29.—The second period of Reformation and Counter-Reformation may be bounded by the close of the Council of Trent (1563) and the Peace of Westphalia which put an end to the Thirty Years' War (1648). It is true that there is always something arbitrary and conventional in determining a period; history continues its process, a continuous inter-weaving of human wills and natural forces even when we believe there is a pause, and, as we say, a period has closed. But this practical manner of establishing the data of the historical process is not without foundation; certain series of events have characteristic elements, which give us the key to the enigma of their reality.

The first and natural duty of the post-Tridentine popes was to carry out the Counter-Reformation as decided at Trent, both through decisions of canon law and by safeguarding, spreading, and defending the doctrine formulated by the Council in the name of the Catholic Church. The popes were, therefore, bound to defend the Council itself as legiti-mate and oecumenical. Pius IV proceeded to give immediate approval to the Council, in spite of reservations and opposition on the part of Cardinals (which bore especially on certain faculties recognised to the bishops). He therefore issued the Bull of January, 1564, published the following June, with the usual request to Catholic sovereigns to 'receive the Council' in their States. This request corresponded to the legal usages of the period, and meant that the decisions of the Council had to be promulgated in each State as its own law, which, as such, obliged the secular jurisdiction to observe and enforce it and to respect the canonical rulings resulting from the Council.

Given the juridical system of the time, there is nothing to wonder at in either the acceptance or the resistance of the Catholic States. In either case their attitude was determined mainly by practical considerations—how best to safeguard, in so far as was possible, the rights and customs of the secular power in the face of the ecclesiastical power, the legal, political and fiscal independence of the States from interference by the Papacy, the traditions of the local clergies, not to speak of papal privileges obtained (or extorted) by monarchs or clergy, against Roman centralisation.

The Catholic princes had kept a very watchful eye on Trent lest the decisions for reform should prejudice the rights of the secular power, and in great measure they were successful. All the same there was no lack of pretexts for reservations or even for sheer opposition to acceptance of the Council. Among its decrees was that excommunicating any secular authority (even a king or emperor) that authorised duelling in its dominions. There was the suppression of appeals *ab abusu*, that is, recourse to the secular authority against an alleged abuse on the part of the ecclesiastical authority. There was the abolition of the right to give benefices *in commendam*, and other minor measures that conflicted with the habits of the lay power of intruding in religious matters. Moreover, the new matrimonial regulations were inacceptable to many, and still more so the right of exemption of the regular clergy from the authority of the bishops. Even the dogmatic decrees gave rise to discussions, fed by sympathy for Lutherans and Calvinists, for these still had influence and ascendancy at certain Catholic courts and in certain strata of the clergy.

The most tangible and preoccupying question was the German one, raised by the Emperor Ferdinand I both during the Council and after, on the celibacy of the clergy and the use of the chalice. On the other hand, in spite of the fact that his ambassadors had given their signatures at Trent, Ferdinand, finding there was opposition in Lower Austria and in Germany, was in no hurry to publish the Council. Meanwhile discussions between Rome and Vienna continued. The Pope wavered and under certain conditions (and not everywhere) granted the use of the chalice. This concession brought confusion to the one side, enthusiasm to the other. On the death of Ferdinand (1569) the Emperor Maximilian who succeeded him pressed for a dispensation from celibacy; in certain regions there was no longer a single priest who wa not married. Philip II, who considered it his mission to oversee and control the Pope, strenuously opposed any papal concession in the matter, which could never have remained confined to Germany. On the other hand the Jesuits, above all Peter Canisius, strove to restore confidence and vigour in Catholic observance and in the Tridentine discipline among the Catholic clergy and populations. The Holy See protested against Maximilian when he released the University of Vienna from the obligation of the Catholic oath. Finally, in 1566, the Diet of Augsburg met, and the Catholic princes of the Empire ended by accepting the Council.

The Catholic cantons of Switzerland declared that they accepted the Council, but they would not promulgate it for reasons of practical policy, in view of their very weak position in the face of the neighbouring Protestant cantons and of the clergy themselves and the different currents even in Catholic regions. In Poland the Council was accepted by royal edict in August, 1564, and the Parliament sanctioned it the following year.

Philip II, who had made the Council the object of so much opposition and so many intrigues, promulgated it in Spain, Naples and Sicily in July, 1564, reserving the rights of the Monarchy, and of local traditions, usages and privileges in so far-reaching a form as to render not a few of the conciliar measures unworkable. In respect of Sicily, faced with the observations of the Governor on the existence of the Tribunal of the Sacred Sicilian Monarchy, Philip hastened to withdraw his decree. In the Low Countries there was considerable resistance to Trent and acceptance was made with the express reservation of local privileges, uses and traditions. The Holy See in 1565 declared all privileges contrary to Trent to be null and void, but these survived and were vigorously defended by monarchs and clergy.

The Monarchy of France never accepted the Council of Trent and the dispute that began in 1564 was never definitely settled; it was complicated by the whole politico-religious position of the kingdom and dragged on from epoch to epoch down to our own times. The beginning of French hostility to the Council of Trent dates from its close, when the French ambassadors refused to set their signatures to its acts (1563). The next year the Pope's request was examined by the

Royal Council at Fontainebleau, but no decision was taken both in order not to irritate the reformers and because of an unwillingness to apply certain provisions such as those on benefices *in commendam*. Catharine de' Medici, who was then regent, promised the Pope to see that the particular decisions of the Council were carried out without their publication. The Pope put a good face on the matter, but the upper clergy and the Sorbonne were then in favour of integral publication and treated those who opposed it as schismatics; the lower clergy drew a distinction between the parts relating to faith, where no reservation or discussion was admissible, and the disciplinary parts where, they held, reservation should be made of the privileges of the Gallican Church. The Parlement of Paris and the lawyers were against publication altogether. At the States-General of Blois (1579) certain Tridentine decisions were inserted in the royal ordinance, but over the Council as a whole the battle went on for some time. At the beginning of the League the bishops believed they had won. Henry III undertook (in accordance with the Edict of Union of July 21, 1587) to accept the Council '*sans préjudice toutefois des droits et autorité de Sa Majesté et des libertés de l'Eglise gallicane*'. But in spite of this, at the second States-General of Blois in the following year, Henry III went back on his steps, returning to the position of the Royal Council at Fontainebleau. When the League found itself momentarily victorious Mayenne, as Lieutenant-General in the States of 1593, published the decrees by which the Council was to be held as law of the realm, but, through the accession of Henry IV, this promulgation remained without effect. Henry IV, at the time of his reconciliation with the Church, promised Pope Clement VIII to settle the question of the Council, excepting those measures that might disturb the tranquillity of the realm, but the negotiations he started with Rome had no decisive outcome.

At the States-General of Paris in 1614 the bishops brought up the question anew, but the Third Estate opposed them. Its President, François Miron, in order to ensure the non-reception of the Council, maintained for the first time in France the thesis of the non-competence of the secular power in religious matters. In regard to the dogmatic canons, he said, their publication by the king was totally useless; in regard to discipline, let the clergy begin by observing the decisions of the Council that concerned them, such as that against pluralism. The Peace of Loudun (May, 1615) between the princes of France included an article that the decisions of Trent would not be promulgated. The clergy, for their part, held an assembly (July, 1615) in which they made a unilateral but important declaration that they unanimously recognised the Council, holding themselves bound in conscience to 'receive' it, and promising to do their utmost to observe it, through their pastoral and spiritual functions.[1]

This decision was communicated to the King and thenceforth was considered ecclesiastically and morally valid, so that Bossuet could write: 'It is indeed perfectly true that the discipline of the Council of Trent, authorised for the most part by what is known as the Ordinance of Blois (1579) . . . is becoming more and more established in the Kingdom, and, save for a few articles, is universal.'[2] Actually various of the conciliar decisions were embodied in royal ordinances, but the Council of Trent, according to the public law of the time, was never juridically received in France, only by the bishops, and always with reservation of the Gallican liberties. The same may be said of the Protestant countries separated from Rome, where Catholics could not receive the Council of Trent otherwise than as faithful, but even they reserved their local rights and traditions as recognised by the secular power of each State.

While all this may appear merely the juridical aspect of the problem, it implied something more important, the trend of behaviour of the Catholic States in their relations with Rome, and the conception of Church and State in Catholic countries and in Protestant ones. The events enable us to trace the evolution of post-Tridentine thought in this respect, so as to ascertain its accidental causes and to perceive the deeper and real causes.

All the countries that had remained Catholic were troubled from

[1]'Ont unaniment reconnu, reconnaissent et déclarent être obligés, par leur devoir et conscience, de recevoir, comme de fait ils ont reçu et reçoivent aujourd'hui, le dit Concile, promettant de l'observer, autant qu'ils le peuvent, par leurs fonctions et autorité pastorale et spirituelle.'

[2]'Il est meme très véritable que la discipline du Concile de Trente, autorisée dans la plus grande partie par l'ordonnance appelée de Blois (1579) . . . s'affermit de plus en plus dans le royaume, et qu'à peu d'articles près elle est universelle.'

the religious and political standpoint by three currents: that of orthodoxy of faith which combined and under certain aspects coincided
with loyalty to the reigning House, with the national personality or
with the political party defending it; that of the defence of local rights,
liberties and privileges against the Papacy and the defenders of the
Papacy, the Jesuits first of all; thirdly, that of reform, which could not
but suffer a Protestant influence and which embraced at once spiritual,
ethical and philosophic motives and mundane, political, and emotional
ones.

The outstanding figure of this post-Tridentine period is Philip II.
He incarnates all three currents and seals them with his sombre and
enigmatic personality. The division of the Germanic Empire from his
Spanish possessions by Charles V, who assigned the first to his brother
Ferdinand, the second to his son Philip, led to a dualism of forces
which for a century was wholly to the advantage of Spain. Spain
became the hegemonic centre of Europe and the most powerful colonial
nation. This political position gave Philip II the advantage that the
greater part of Catholic interests centred in Spain, apart from the frag-
ments of the Empire which Ferdinand I and Maximilian II sought to
keep united to Vienna. Philip felt he had a kind of mandate to act as
guardian to the Papacy, which, to his mind, was too weak in dealing
with heresy and with the princes. His pretensions were such that he
believed it his right to interpret the Council of Trent through an
ecclesiastical Council of State peculiar to Spain and the countries subject
to his crown.

Philip's conception was strictly cesaro-papist. He did not, like the
Protestant princes, declare himself head of the national church, and
he recognised popes and councils, but he felt himself truly the head
of the bishops of his State, the authorised counsellor of the Pope and
the mainstay of the interests of the Church (which he tended to
identify with those of his States and of his crown) in the face of the
deficiencies of papacy and council. To augment the influence of Spain
in the world was for him the same as to augment the influence of
Catholicism; the opponents of his policy, were they kings or popes,
were at the same time opponents of Catholic faith and interests.
With this idea, his cesaro-papism, though framed in the most rigor-

ously orthodox Catholicism, became prevailing and all-absorbing, and under certain aspects resembled the cesaro-papism of the Protestant princes. Philip II was not the only Catholic sovereign to stress this conception; they were all, some more, some less, of his way of thinking, but in his case there was added a personal and mystical conception, the idea of a kind of divine mandate extending even to countries outside Spain and his States.

The conditions of the Spanish clergy favoured this exaggerated idea. All the bishops and archbishops of Spain, Naples and the Spanish colonies were under royal patronage; he disposed of them at his will. The riches that were flowing into the Church subsequently returned to the royal Treasury, under various pretexts and with the Pope's consent, (which might or might not be voluntary), for the wars against the Turks or against England and France, or to repress the risings in the Low Countries. In the royal Councils, bishops, friars, theologians predominated. Everything tended to bring about a kind of fusion, Catholic, ecclesiastic, monarchic.

The Spanish Inquisition, founded by Ferdinand the Catholic and Isabella and approved by Sixtus IV, was aimed principally against the Jews, Moors and Maranos, who were converted by force and then considered as heretics. Reinforced by Philip II it was directed against Protestantism and the heresies of the day. He wanted to extend the authority of the Spanish Inquisition to the other States and dominions under his crown, but he met with resistance and opposition; this was one of the motives of the insurrection of the Low Countries. By papal privilege the King of Spain had been granted the title of Papal Legate and hence took a share in the papal jurisdiction; the tribunal of the Spanish Inquisition was his emanation and placed under his authority. It had thus become an instrument of political domination, and as such was removed from the influence of Rome.

The dispute between Pius IV and Philip II over the trial for heresy of the Archbishop of Toledo, Mgr. Carranza, became notorious. The Council of Trent seeks in vain to have the case referred to its jurisdiction; Spain refuses. The Archbishop appeals to Rome, and the Pope asks in vain that the accused should be consigned to him with the documents of the case in order to pass final sentence. Philip does not admit that an accused person can be withdrawn from the tribunal of the Spanish Inquisition. He agrees to the sending of papal delegates, who, chosen among the best men of the Curia, arrive at Toledo. By coincidence, three of these delegates would become pope, Boncompagni as Gregory XIII, Fra Felice of Montalto as Sixtus V, Aldobrandini as Clement VIII. But Philip claims that the final verdict must rest with the Spanish Inquisition assisted by the papal delegates, and not with the delegates alone. To this they will not consent. In the meantime, Pius IV dies and the delegates return to Rome. Pius V, the new pope, succeeds in getting Mgr. Carranza handed over to him, but when the rumour spreads that the papal verdict will be an acquittal, contrary, therefore, to the Spanish verdict, diplomatic machinery is set to work to retard the conclusion of the trial, and at the same time an interesting controversy breaks out on the powers of the King of Spain and of the Pope. Pius V was not able to settle the case of the unfortunate Archbishop, and when in 1576 Gregory XIII, after over fifteen years of proceedings, recognised that Carranza was not heretical but had merely been imprudent, and sentenced him to five years' banishment at Orvieto and suspension from his faculties as archbishop (and this, maybe, in order to propitiate Philip II and his Inquisition), poor Carranza died.

A position juridically similar to that of Spain existed in Sicily. There, under Roger II in the days of the Normans, the Sacred Tribunal of the Sicilian Monarchy had been set up. It was a kind of central and final ecclesiastical authority in the hands of the King, in his quality of papal legate. This state of affairs was contrary to the Tridentine spirit and the popes wanted to put an end to it. But they were faced with the resistance of Philip II, who, on advice from the Governor, withdrew the order to promulgate the acts of the Council in Sicily. The dispute between Rome and the various monarchs of Sicily was never settled till Pius IX, by a bold stroke, issued a Bull of abolition in 1858. The time was then ripe, and royal and clerical opposition to the papal act had no practical consequences. In the XVI century matters were otherwise. The position of Philip II in the face of Catholicism was politically so strong that the popes had to take it into account. The problem of the Turks was still a pressing one, even after Lepanto (when Philip behaved extremely badly) and the popes wished to maintain the Holy

League against the Turks in an efficient and harmonious condition; the strongest (if not the most valiant) champion of the League was Philip. The other States too counted for much, and the popes gave way over Church revenues in order that the sovereigns concerned should be enabled to meet expenses—though those of the League were actually the least part of them. In the same way the popes yielded over ecclesiastical privileges, protracted their disputes with the various courts over the Council, mitigated those of its measures that were most criticised, and tolerated the vindication of certain rights. In spite of this, the League fell to pieces. Venice, disillusioned by Spain, made a separate agreement with the Turks, Maximilian took no part, France was mistrustful and Genoa aggrieved, while Philip was engaged in the conquest of Portugal and turned a deaf ear to the voice of the Pope. In the meantime the Turks were able to consolidate their forces after the defeat of Lepanto and the capture of Tunis.

The war against the Turks was a European necessity, to which all should have contributed, yet the main resistance continued to be confined to Venice, Vienna, Hungary and Poland. Philip was pursuing his Catholic-Spanish policy in the West and expanding his vast power on the seas. At this time he hoped to gain the hand of Elizabeth and dominate England, and therefore insisted and intrigued in Rome that no final measure should be taken to effect a rupture. Elizabeth, for her part, during Alba's repression in the Low Countries, was in favour of Philip and congratulated him on the Duke's victory, just as Pius V congratulated him—deceived, says Pastor, by the official reports. When the Pope launched his excommunication against Elizabeth, Philip put forward objections. But he too would be obliged to break with her; his interests in the Low Countries and his dominion on the seas, rendered decisive by the capture of Portugal, conflicted with the trend of English policy. The various revolts in Scotland, Ireland and England gave Philip the opportunity of intervention, while the treaty between Elizabeth and France in 1572 provided the motive for a more decided struggle.

From 1562 Philip supported the Catholic party in France. It was the beginning of the Wars of Religion (civil and international) which left a bloody trail through France and would extend all over Europe, to form the long chain of wars that stretches to the Peace of Westphalia.

The Edict of Saint-Germain (January 17, 1562) allowed the Huguenots to meet outside the towns. The Parlement of Paris rejects it; the partisans of Guise and Condé confront each other in the streets, Catharine de' Medici is held a prisoner by the triumvirs of Paris (Montmorency, Guise, St. André), churches are assaulted, everywhere are horrors and crimes. The Huguenots call in the help of England; the Germans enter France to join Condé at Orleans. The first act of the terrible religious drama of France ends with the Peace of Amboise (1563). The war with England (in which France finally won Calais) goes on till May, 1564, but the struggle between Catholics and Huguenots breaks out again immediately, in acute form. Philip II is perturbed, fearing what would actually come to pass—the revolt of the Low Countries in 1566, which has a sequel in France where the Huguenots again take up arms and at the battle of St. Denis Montmorency is killed (1567). The civil war continues. The South is in the hands of Coligny, who threatens Paris. Catherine offers him the Peace of Saint-Germain (August, 1570). By this peace the Huguenots were granted the right of public worship in the cities where this had existed before the war, freedom of worship in private houses, the restitution of their goods, and four cities, known as the 'cities of surety': La Rochelle, Montauban, Cognac and La Charité.

Coligny, at the height of his power, tries to induce the young King Charles IX, who is now of age, to carry the war into Flanders in support of the revolt against Philip II. Catherine dissuades him. The Duc de Guise thinks that the moment of vengeance has come. Mourevert's murderous attack on Coligny only partially succeeds; the Huguenots are threatened and keep a watch on the Louvre; there is fear of an attempt to seize the King's person if De Guise is not brought to justice. It is then that (on the pretext of preventive action against the Huguenots) the famous Night of St. Bartholomew is planned (1572), a night of horrors and blood, which extended to the rest of France. La Rochelle was besieged. Catherine renewed the alliances with the protestant princes of Germany, with the insurgents of the Low Countries, while France was almost wholly a prey to insurrection and disorder, and the unhappy Charles IX died in 1574.

The wars between Catholics and Huguenots continue under Henry III. The Germans sweep down on France and threaten Paris, with the

King's brother, the Duc d'Alençon, at their head. The peace imposed at Beaulieu (1576) includes freedom of worship for the Protestants (except in Paris), the usual cities of surety and a kind of division of France into zones of dominion, the centre going to d'Alençon, Guienne to Henry of Navarre, Picardy to Condé and Languedoc to Damville, all Calvinists. The Guise brothers, supported by the Catholic party and by the clergy, with encouragement and help from Philip II and the Pope, formed the League, which aimed at exterminating the Huguenots and consolidating the Catholic religion as the sole religion of the State (1576).

But on the death of the Duc d'Alençon, since Henry III had no sons, the problem of succession to the throne came to the fore. The heir-presumptive of the Valois branch was Henry of Navarre, the Calvinist. This prospect aroused great apprehension among Catholics, the League, the Pope and Philip. On the other hand, Henry of Navarre did not wish to lose his rights and held his own against the League, which sought to put forward the Guise family. It was then that the Treaty of Nemours (July, 1585) was signed between Henry III and the League, with the aim of suppressing Protestantism in France. Of the Huguenots a part were converted and a part emigrated, while Sixtus V excommunicated Henry of Navarre and Condé. These are the gloomy years of the execution of Mary Stuart in England, of the expulsion from London of Mendoza, the Spanish Ambassador, and of the war between Elizabeth and Philip (1586), of the Great Armada (1588), of the assassination of the Duc de Guise and his brother the Cardinal (1588), and of the assassination of Henry III himself by Jacques Clément (1589).

The position was now clear. Henry of Navarre proclaims himself King of France as Henry IV. He is once more excommunicated by Innocent IX. After two more years of war, in 1593, Paris surrenders, Henry abjures his Protestantism, and, in the following year (1594) Clement VIII lifts the excommunication. Wars and struggles go on till the Treaty of Vervins; Henry publishes the famous Edict of Nantes, and Philip II dies (1598). Thus the first period of the wars of religion ended with the XVI century.

§ 30.—If it had not been for the great revival of the mystical currents, the new religious orders, the radical reforms of the older orders, it would have seemed as if the Tridentine Counter-Reformation had ended in the wars of religion, in conspiracies and bloodshed, with the Catholic Church leaning entirely on the Inquisition and on the powers of the monarchies. This picture of the Counter-Reformation formed for a long time a polemical motive of superficial histories, while on the other hand Catholic historians and polemists have brought forward all the acts of intolerance and violence, the massacres and wars promoted by Protestants and the Protestant monarchies, which, in their turn, emulated and outstripped the Catholic monarchies. The historico-sociological problem of the period is in reality far more complex, and we must seek in the theoretical systems and doctrinal battles of the time for the explanation of these melancholy events.

It must be remembered that the conception of the State was then inseparable from that of the Christian religion. If the Protestants abandoned Rome, it was to create a State adhering still more closely, to their mind, to Christian life and faith. If the Catholic monarchies and national clergies resisted Rome, it was through the greater solidarity between monarchy and religion as organised and felt in each separate State. The struggle therefore went on on two planes—the first, between Catholic orthodoxy and Protestantism; the second, between the remains of ecclesiastical internationalism, centring in Rome, and the monarchico-ecclesiastical autonomy of each separate nation. One of the outcomes of this struggle was the State religion. We must give careful analysis to this phenomenon in the XVI century, in order not to confuse it with similar facts earlier or later.

We have already touched on the system inaugurated in Germany during the first phase of Lutheranism, with the principle *cuius regio illius et religio*. The principle on the face of it is an offence both to the personal right of every man not to be forced to accept a religion as a legal duty sanctioned by punitive laws, and to that of the Christian religion in its catholicity to expand in every place. An extraneous principle was thus introduced into Christianity, that of political loyalty appraised by religious criteria recognised and imposed by the State. Here is something more than what the Roman Empire did with its subjects. For Rome left each people its own religion, save for the obligation of recognising the divinity of Rome and of the Emperor as a sign of loyalty and conformity. And she dispensed the Jews from the imperial cult and would perhaps have done the same with the Christians (as in fact happened in the periods of comparative peace between one persecution and another) had she not seen in them at once an antagonistic force, the negation of all the other religions of the Empire, and a new, conquering force. The position of the Roman Empire, with another mentality, other aims and values, would be repeated in modern times. But in the period of early Protestantism it was inconceivable that a State should grant liberty of conscience and worship and be able to recognise the loyalty of its subjects on purely political and national grounds.

The positions created in Germany in the first period of the Reformation present themselves under three different aspects. We must note that Germany was divided into so many principalities, kingdoms, free cities, episcopal cities, electorates, as to make wide combinations possible. Certain regions became wholly Protestant, others remained Catholic. In a certain number Catholics and Protestants represented forces which, if not equal, were respectively important. In almost every petty State there were minorities, either Catholic or Protestant. The internal strife between Catholics and Protestants in each town or village, and the wars of the Protestant leagues against the Empire, had brought some thirty years of disturbances, persecution, slaughter. A pacification was desired by all. Since neither toleration on a basis of the civil and political parity of all citizens, nor a loyalty to the reigning house and the State that was not founded on religious unity, was feasible or conceivable, it was decided to give homogeneity to the States on a basis of religious observance. The dissidents, Catholics or Protestants, either emigrated and took refuge in the States where their own church was recognised as the State religion, or submitted to all the vexations of the Government and to the suspicions of the official churches, becoming crypto-Catholics or crypto-Protestants as the case might be, or else they suffered the fate of persecuted minorities.

It is strange to think that State religion thus conceived in those days could become a source of social tranquillity, ensuring a freedom of worship not individual but for the homogeneous group, which as such had been persecuted or had suffered the effects of the religious wars and strife. It is understandable that on the one hand Rome protested against a similar principle, subversive of the whole system of Medieval Christendom and which moreover prevented or seriously impeded the spread of Catholic worship and the defence of Catholics in Protestant countries; and that on the other hand the Germanic Emperor, not wishing to lose his dominion over the Protestant territories, especially the mixed regions that had remained faithful to the House of Hapsburg, sought systems of compromise for the Protestants, of safeguards for the Catholics, facilitating the concessions that Council or Pope opposed or tolerated, as the case might be.

The spread of Protestantism outside Germany and the resulting wars or revolts in England, France and elsewhere, set the problem in other terms. Although these States were still divided into distinct zones and sovereignties, yet compared with Germany they revealed a homogeneity of forces tending to consolidate itself in national unity. The religious question could here lead to the division of the State into various sovereignties determined by religious confession, or else to a loss of autonomy; in either case it was an impediment to the monarchic unification already in process.

England after the brief reign of Mary Tudor relapsed into Anglicised Protestantism; the Catholic minority, those who refused to yield, were subjected to legal disabilities and periodical persecutions. The same was the case with the nonconformists, the dissenters, for the State religion was bound up with the national character which the monarchy was more and more assuming.

When Pius V excommunicated Elizabeth and declared her deposed, this had no political effect in international relations, but it made the Protestants more decided than ever to permit no papist infiltrations into the kingdom, and rendered the conditions of Catholics more difficult. By the Bull of Pius V the latter were released from their oath of loyalty to the Queen. This medieval formula, which held good when a vassal was bound to his sovereign by a kind of free proffer, a contract *sui generis* which formed the feudal bond of sovereignty, had not the same sense in the period of the formation of the modern State, which was growing up round the idea of the nation. Catholics were obliged to take the oath of allegiance, which created a fresh and prolonged strife between the Papacy and the English monarchy, and divided Catholics themselves between those who wanted to resist at any cost, even that of life, and those who sought a compromise, with or without the tolerance of Rome.

But the religious problem was overshadowed by the political problem. The persecutions under Elizabeth (which were no less than those under Mary) followed the oscillations of domestic and foreign policy. One of the noblest victims was the Jesuit Campion, guilty of having administered the Sacraments to Catholics secretly in their own houses. He had brought from Rome a copy of a profession of Catholic faith and national loyalty, which had been recommended to the Jesuits by St. Charles Borromeo. The declaration in the will of Shakespeare's father is simply a translation of this formula.

The question of the security of the throne in the Elizabethan period was not merely a question of the religious formula of an oath, but involved political realities. The monarchy then had neither its own treasure nor its own army; it was maintained only by the loyalty, sympathies or interests of the various political and ecclesiastical *élites* of the kingdom. Adversaries could question the legitimacy of the succession, since Elizabeth could be considered as the bastard of Henry VIII. Plots against her life, either real or invented, were not wanting. She had, moreover, a rival who attracted the attention of popes, foreign courts, and rebel subjects in Mary Stuart—Catholic, rightful Queen of Scots, widow of the Dauphin of France, daughter of a Tudor, at any moment she could imperil the throne of England. History tells us of the fascination and misfortunes and failings of the romantic type of Queen that was Mary Stuart, of the intrigues woven about her to make her fall into the hands of her butchers, and to remove for ever the danger that she, a prisoner for nineteen years, could claim the throne of England on the death of Elizabeth; and finally, at what a price her son James VI of Scotland became James I uniting the two crowns. Round this question of succession (as round that of the throne of France) the hopes and intrigues of Catholics and Protestants were centred.

France had never lost her character of a Catholic State. Paris during half a century of strife was the citadel of Catholicism. But France had to face three perils—that of the advance of Protestantism, which was becoming serious in the South and in provinces of the Centre and North; that of the factions that might divide and weaken her in the face of the two enemy States, England on the North, whose power was waxing, Spain on the South whose power was at its height; finally, that of the succession to the throne after the death of Henry III, when the crown fell to a Huguenot, Henry of Navarre. Moreover, France had a particular mistrust (which reached the pitch of aversion) towards Rome, in the name of the liberties of the Gallican Church, which made clergy and State hold jealously to their own personality. Not every ill comes to do harm: the Gallicanism of the XVI century (which differed in certain respects from that of the century following) saved France from Protestantism, for it served to maintain her personality as conceived by the ecclesiastics, by the friars and the laymen of the Sorbonne.

From the point of view of State religion, it was never questioned that the religion of France was Catholic, in union with Rome as the See of St. Peter. The problem for France was identical with that of Charles V and his successor Ferdinand I—how to reconcile this Catholicism with the existence of the reformed church. But there was this difference, that Charles V was faced with a multitude of States and Statelets, which evaded his influence or rebelled against it, whereas in France there were instead noble houses or military leaders, like Condé and Coligny or even Navarre (though Navarre was a kingdom by itself), or cities like Orleans or Montauban where the majority turned Calvinist.

Hence the series of edicts, assemblies, peace treaties that we have already noted, under Henry II, the Regency of Catharine de' Medici, Charles IX and Henry III, and continuing under Henry IV, to culminate in the famous Edict of Nantes of 1598—half a century of ebb and flow and strife, civil wars and foreign wars. What might seem a question of safeguarding the rights of conscience of a Protestant minority involved in substance both the safeguarding of the Catholic religion against Protestant assaults—assaults that in certain respects were completely successful, or showed a growing and preoccupying strength—as well as the security of the tottering throne in the hands of the last of the Valois, whose power was so contested that they must have recourse to domestic and foreign backers, to stratagems, massacres and wars. Hence a see-saw policy on the part of the monarchs, between Catholic Paris, the Sorbonne, the clergy, the parlement, or Rome on the one hand, and the powerful families of the Huguenot leaders on the other; with now concessions like those of the Peace of Saint Germain (1570), now massacres like St. Bartholomew's Eve (1572).

The various endeavours to enable a Catholic majority and a Calvinist minority to co-exist might be said to have failed, for they speedily degenerated into strife, revolts and wars. One of the means attempted was that of giving the Huguenots special cities. This created centres of resistance, fortified for struggles and wars, a State within the State, which lasted till Richelieu abolished the remains of an immunity that was still effective.

Every attempt at toleration of worship during these fifty years ended in faction, on one side or the other, for the Huguenots readily engaged in proselytism and reached the point of outrages against Catholic worship such as to arouse an irrepressible reaction. And transition from the sphere of religious quarrels and controversy to the political sphere and the formation of armed factions was too easy, in so incandescent an atmosphere and under so feeble a monarchic authority, in a country torn between the powerful forces of the nobles, the clergy, the rich bourgeoisie, the Sorbonne and the Parlement. Religious toleration could be achieved only as a truce of factions, as something imposed by the victorious party on the vanquished, as a concordat sanctioned by the King but such as to be rescinded or allowed to drop at the first moment that factions were again in the ascendant. And since it was the monarchy that, in its own interests and in order not to alienate the heads and following of the two parties, tended towards compromise, the monarchic and State problem became the most pressing problem, the real problem of the day.

The growth of anti-monarchic theories makes a clear beginning after the Eve of St. Bartholomew, and naturally it is the Huguenots and philo-Calvinists who support them. To this period belong François Hotman's *Francogallia* (1573), the *Discours de la servitude volontaire* of E. de La Boétie (1574), *Du droit des magistrats sur leurs sujets*, by Théodore de Bèze (1574), and later the celebrated *Vindiciæ contra tyrannos* (1579) attributed to Du Plessis Mornay. It is at this date that the anti-monarchic movement passes from the Huguenot to the Catholic camp when, after the concessions of the monarchy to the heretics, the *Sainte Union* (the League) is formed, led by Guise and Mayenne and supported by Philip II and Gregory XIII.

The political aim of the League after the death of the Duc d'Anjou is to put forward a Catholic claimant to the throne (a Guise) instead of the Huguenot Henry of Navarre. In 1586 the lawyer Louis Dorléans published a pamphlet entitled: *Avertissement des catholiques anglais aux François catholiques*, which had extraordinary success. In substance he borrowed from the *Francogallia* by the Protestant Hotman the arguments against the hereditary monarchy and in favour of a monarch chosen by the people, in order to vindicate the right to set aside Navarre for Guise. Certain Catholics did not wish to abandon the principle of hereditary legitimacy and would not follow the Guises, but after the assassination of the Duke and his brother and the excommunication of Navarre and Condé by Sixtus V, the democratic theory takes root and becomes general among French Catholics. The Monarcomachs are in the ascendant. These are of all types. Petit-Feuillant is a religious, known as a saint; one of the most fervent monarcomachs, Feuardent, a famous Sorbonnist; Guincestre, one of the most respected parish priests of Paris; Guillaume Rose, who wrote *De justa reipublicæ christianæ in reges impios auctoritate*, Bishop of Senlis; above all, Jean Boucher, who at the age of thirty was Rector of the University of Paris, and who wrote the pamphlet: *De justa Henrici Tertii abdicatione* (1589).

The ideas maintained by Catholic monarcomachists were in substance the following : a people is obliged by natural and divine law to obey a head chosen by itself, but just as the people has bound itself to a head, it can also release itself. The people remains 'eternally guardian of sovereignty, judge of sceptres and kingdoms, being their origin and source,'[1] for the people 'is the base on which the King rests and without which he has neither arm nor foot nor leg, and would fall like a colossus did its pedestal collapse'.[2] De La Boétie had written:

[1] '. . . éternellement garde de la souveraineté, juge des sceptres et des royaumes pour en être l'origine et la source.' (Jean Boucher, *Sermon 3ème sur la simulée conversion*.)

[2] '. . . est la base sur laquelle le roy pose, et sans laquelle il n'a ny bras, ny pied, ny jambe, et tomberoit comme un colosse dont le soubassement est fondu.' (loc. cit.)

'Be resolved (poor wretched people) to serve no longer, and you are free. I do not want you to shove or shake him, only cease to sustain him and you will see him, like a great colossus from which the pedestal has been taken, crash down by his own weight and break'.[1] It is the revival of the medieval theory of the social contract, which the Calvinist, Theodore de Bèze, had refurbished and the Catholic Leaguers put forward against the succession of Henry of Navarre and in favour of a free choice of monarch.

It was not only in France that the pressure of events encouraged the growth of this anti-absolutist and democratising current. Post-Tridentine Catholicism had found itself in a position of conflict not only with the Protestant princes, who based their dominion on the re-union in a single hand of the temporal and spiritual powers, but also against the Catholic princes, who invaded the ecclesiastical domain and assumed they could direct Church affairs in their States, now intensifying reaction to excess, like Philip II and the Spanish Inquisition, now giving way to the Protestants or the broader trends as in France, Venice, and even in Vienna. A Catholic democratic movement thus enters the lists, historically to be identified with the political movement of the Jesuits at the end of the XVI and beginning of the XVII century, and which is known by the great names of Suarez and Bellarmin. By these the problem was given a wider range than the monarcomachs could have expected, for they brought back under discussion two acute problems that had never found solution either in the minds of jurists or in popular consciousness—that of the international unity of Christendom and that of the supremacy of the Pope over the civil power.

Suarez and Bellarmin sought the most balanced theoretico-practical solution possible, in view of the times and current controversies, and both anticipated the evolution of theories and events. The first in the international sphere recognises that the medieval empire has fulfilled its function and is no longer tenable, especially since Christendom has

[1] 'Soyez résolus (pauvres gens misérables) de ne servir plus, et vous voilà libres. Je ne veux pas que vous le poussiez ny le bransliez, mais seulement ne le soustenez plus et vous le verrez, comme un grand colosse à qui on a dérobé la base, de son poid mesme fondre en bas et se rompre.'

been broken up and every kingdom claims autonomy. He, therefore, maintains the empire of an international law, regulating the relations between sovereign States, and providing moral and legal sanctions based on Natural Law. But for Suarez, as for the whole Catholic current guided by the Jesuits, the function of the Pope did not fall outside the international organism, but within it, both for the moral interpretation of the law and the guardianship of the religious interests of Catholicism. The other pillar of the juridical edifice of society is the People, whose consent (tacit or expressed) is essential for the formation of the political order and supreme authority. The people is the most natural channel of concretisation of power; it must not be deprived of its right. The King thus found himself in a vice, between the Pope above and the people below.

But the post-Tridentine atmosphere was not propitious for a restoration of the medieval Papacy. Although popes like Pius V, Sixtus V and Paul V were strong enough to put into practice the theory of *direct power* over kings and princes, and to find bold supporters not only in the Curia and among the religious Orders, but also among independent laymen and ecclesiastics, the political and religious currents of Europe were hostile and found it more convenient to lean on the people, to instigate revolts and challenge each other in wars, than to recognise full and effectual direct power to the Pope in temporal matters.

Among the solemn papal acts in this connection was the excommunication and Bull of deposition against Elizabeth. As we have seen, Philip II disapproved, while the other Catholic sovereigns ignored the excommunication and continued to have relations with England. The net result was the final separation of England from Rome. Another solemn act was the excommunication of Henry of Navarre by Sixtus V. The legitimist French Catholics deplored it and continued to support Henry, who was proclaimed King of France. In order to pacify the country he was converted to Catholicism, and soon after issued the Edict of Nantes, which favoured the Huguenots. Finally, Paul V decreed an interdict against the Republic of Venice for the jurisdictionalist laws passed by the Senate in 1605. But the interdict was not observed by the clergy, who all (except the Jesuits and a few rare friars) sided with the Republic. The dispute ended in 1607 through the mediation of France, though the decrees of the Senate were not noticeably modified in the sense desired by the Roman Curia.

In all three cases what the Papacy lacked was popular consent, without which it was impossible to gain the better of the sovereigns. This was lacking because actually the clergy was in the service either of the court or of a faction, while the universities and centres of culture were in general still more or less imbued with the conciliar spirit of the XV century (Pisa, Constance, Bâle) and with the liberties of the national churches and the growing nationalism of the State.

The Jesuits, a picked body, intellectual and strong-willed, thought to heal the breach between the Papacy, the people, the world of culture, and the courts by a drive of conquest in every camp, while reasserting simultaneously the right of the Papacy and that of the people. Between the extreme wing of those who brought back into circulation the *Unam Sanctum* of Boniface VIII, and those who denied the Pope any right of intervention in temporal matters, Bellarmin introduced the theory of *indirect power*. The Pope has no power in temporal things but only in spiritual things, yet if through a decision on spiritual matters the secular power is affected, this must suffer the consequent limitation. If a king turns heretic and the Pope excommunicates him as a member of the faithful who has deserted the Catholic faith, the Pope is fully within his spiritual right. If thereupon, through the effects of the excommunication, the subjects, unable to communicate with the King, depose him and choose another, this will be a legitimate consequence entailed by a spiritual act on the Pope's part and never a direct act of papal power in temporal matters.

Bellarmin's theory on its first appearance created such scandal in Rome that Sixtus V had prepared the decree placing the audacious tract on the Index. On the other hand it was attacked in France and elsewhere not only by the legists or *Politiques*, who ruled out all papal intervention, but also by the greater part of the upper and lower clergy, by the Sorbonne and by the moderate Gallican current. These last maintained a thesis somewhat different from Bellarmin's: that the Pope could certainly excommunicate a king for spiritual reasons, but that the right to depose him or not remained with the people. If it deposed him the excommunication would have a temporal effect, if it did not depose him, the excommunication would affect the King in the use of the Sacraments and in his other relations with the Church, but it could not prevent his exercising his regal magistracy, which was a natural right that no ecclesiastical right could take away. This was not the thesis of the *Politiques*, who while they did not yet go so far as to deny a certain intervention of the popular will in the constitution of a State, denied any right of intervention to the pope and any right of final pronouncement to the people; on the contrary, they were working out the theory that would prevail, that of the Absolute State.

The clash between these three currents came about over the most vital theme of all, that of the State religion. The failure of toleration had been due to the necessity in which the monarchies were placed of basing civil conformity on religious uniformity. The Pope and the Catholic clergies would have wished for religious uniformity in the Catholic countries and toleration of Catholicism in the Protestant ones. But since they did not admit the principle of freedom of worship, they could only base themselves pragmatistically on either the courts or the court parties, or on popular reaction and open or secret propaganda, or on the outcome of revolts and wars and the successive and very variable peace treaties, concordats and edicts.

Thus the clash of ideas did not clarify the theoretical position of any of the conflicting parties, and their practical outcome was never satisfactory, being inspired by criteria of court or party interests, or by the none too far-seeing aims of papacy and clergies. It is not surprising that the majority looked to violence and wars for what juridical criteria or theological discussions could not then give.

§ 31.—The last refuge of the popular or democratic trend of the end of the XVI century was the theory of tyrannicide. This, condemned at the Council of Constance with the ambiguous phrase we have already noted, was revived in France by the Calvinists and then, in rebound, upheld by the League. The Protestants saw a martyr in Poltrot, the assassin of the Duc de Guise, just as those of the League saw a martyr in Jacques Clément who assassinated Henry III. All th literature of the League is imbued with this idea, and priests and friars were found to declare that they could absolve the murderer of a king. This factious state of mind, born of political passions and religious fanaticism, did not find issue in a representative theory of the popular rights nor in an abolition of the monarchy (as would come later through the French Revolution), but exaggerated the popular title to correct the monarchy by methods of force. And since this could not be done by revolt, it turned to assassination of the king as the right of tyrannicide.

When the League was nearing its collapse and the star of Henry IV was rising, Jean Chastel was inspired by religious aberration to make an unsuccessful attempt on his life. By that time the general opinion was hostile and the ardent advocates of tyrannicide ten years before either kept silence or had turned into champions of the theory of the King's absolute power. One of the reasons for the change in French public spirit came from the growing prestige of the new king and his orientation towards Catholicism, with the need for order and tranquillity after the stormy years of the League and the wars that had so weakened France. The theory of the right of the people had thus lost its charm and that of the divine right of kings was emerging under a new aspect. The Theological Faculty of Paris, which had once supported the League, turned towards the monarchy and took its stand side by side with the Parlement, with its political Gallicanism. Since the greater number of bishops and ecclesiastical writers came from the Faculty, their influence too became more and more decidedly anti-popular.

Another reaction, which grafted itself on to the first, was determined by the clash between the Jesuits and the University, the latter supported by the Theological Faculty and the Parlement of Paris. The Jesuits during this period represented the rivals of the University and the supporters of the papal power, and hence the last defenders of the right of the people. The quarrel was very significant, and spread from Paris to have notable repercussions in nearly all Catholic and Protestant States. The Jesuits had been banished from France and their goods confiscated in 1594, as a sequel to Jean Chastel's attempt on the King's life. Chastel had been in relations with the superior of the Jesuit College at Clermont. When a search was ordered manuscript notes on the League, extolling Jacques Clément (the murderer of Henry III) and maintaining the legitimacy of tyrannicide were found in the room of Father Guignard. Father Guignard was hanged and the Jesuits were expelled within fifteen days. At once their French and Roman friends began to press for their return. Pope Clement VIII several times let it be known to Henry IV that the readmission of the Jesuits would be the best proof of his sincerity in his conversion to Catholicism. Negotiations went on for a long time; the University remained hostile.

One of the most famous writings of the time, which put the anti-Jesuit struggle in clear terms as concerning the relations between the spiritual-papal power and the secular-monarchic power, and struck a mortal blow at the right of the people, was the *Franc et véritable discours au roi sur le rétablissement qui lui est demandé pour les Jésuites.* The author was Antoine Arnauld, but it was published anonymously. He attacked the thesis of the Jesuits, on the indirect power of the popes in temporal matters. Arnauld finds it easy to maintain that the *indirect power*—by which the popes may intervene in temporal questions if they are connected with spiritual and moral interests—does not differ in its effects from the *direct power*, which was still maintained by many Roman canonists and by the Curia itself. If the Pope, through a religious conflict with the King of France, (there had been heated controversy over whether Henry IV was really converted or had remained a Calvinist, and the Edict of Nantes had made the situation still more difficult), decided to excommunicate and depose him and invited the people to choose another king, the political result would be the same, whether he justified his action by the theory of direct power or by that of indirect power.

In either theory the Gallicans saw a limitation to the absolute power of the King and therefore a subjection of the State to another power which, entering the political sphere, became political—a power which, in the practical case in question, either because it had fallen into error or because it had been circumvented and influenced by the policy of another State, Spain for example, would even involuntarily injure the French monarchy, leaving it defenceless and at the mercy of hostile parties.

In the meantime Antoine Arnauld, by dwelling on the absolute power of the kings, by denying the Pope even the right to excommunicate the King of France, and presenting all this as the traditional Gallican theory of the Theological Faculty, prejudiced the position of the clergy, which had never denied the Pope's right to excommunicate the King, but merely, as we have seen, declared that in such case it was the people's right to judge if the excommunication should carry temporal consequences or no. The people did not set itself up as judge of the Pope, but as judge of the King and of the temporal interests of the country. Thus it was that neither the excommunication of Louis XII by Julius II, nor that of Henry of Navarre by Sixtus V, had temporal effects, but only spiritual ones, and this through the will of the people and of the clergy combined.

This was the true Gallican tradition through the whole of the XVI century, (it would later be revived by the Fronde, but only for a brief space), and it received a mortal blow in the Jesuit controversy. Of the anti-Jesuits nearly all (including the clergy) became absolutists, denying the right of the Pope and the right of the people together. While the Jesuits and their champions, by maintaining that the indirect power of the Pope was binding in all its effects even on the people, made of the people the executive instrument of the Papacy, and no longer the final judge of the interests of the country as between the temporal demands of the Pope (in consequence of spiritual causes) and the politico-religious position of the Sovereign.

To-day all this discussion may seem idle through the fact that the popes, while accepting the Jesuit theory of indirect power, hardly ever applied it against the kings, with whom instead they always sought concordatory compromises. It has, however, an historical and sociological interest from the fact of the elimination of the people from participation in the sovereign power of the State and the decisive introduction of the divine right of monarchs. The Jesuits, though maintaining the theory of the popular origin of power, compromised it on two heads, by making it an instrument of papal policy and by maintaining, *ultima ratio*, tyrannicide for religious motives.

It was at this time (in 1599) that the Spanish Jesuit Juan Mariana, who had taught in France at the College of Clermont from 1569 to

1574, published his famous book, *De Rege et Regis Institutione*, dedicated to Philip III of Spain. The censor, the Mercedarian Pedro de Oña, not only approved it, but gave it high praise. In the first edition, speaking of Clément who murdered Henry III, Mariana wrote: *Sic Clemens periit, aeternum Galliae decus ut plerisque visum est.*[1] This sentence was omitted in the later editions. Mariana passed into history as the supporter of regicide; he was one of the last exponents of the democratic principle of sovereignty and was certainly bold in his various hypotheses favourable to tyrannicide. But up to 1610 neither in Spain nor in France did the book arouse the outcry it did after May, 1610, when Ravaillac killed Henry IV. It was this event that struck the fatal blow at the Jesuits' popular theory and silenced every other voice in favour of the rights of the people over the monarch, opening the way for a royal absolutism no longer controlled either by people or by pope.

The Jesuits who, in spite of the Parlement's protests and the opposition of the Sorbonne, had been allowed back to France, save to Paris and Clermont, in 1602, and in 1604 to the whole of the kingdom, were blamed for the assassination. The struggle against them and their theory became sharper. Mariana's book was condemned by the Parlement. The Père Coton, who had been confessor to Henry IV, and who wanted to defend it, had to sustain a bitter controversy. Jealousy between the University and the Jesuits played its part, for the latter's teaching was free and gratuitous, and their colleges were centres of culture which competed with the Sorbonne. But at the bottom the politico-religious question was the prevailing one. There was a wish to impose on all France as official theory that of the monarchy by divine right; to this the consent of the theologians was necessary. On the other hand, the true Gallicans deemed the theory prevailing at the Roman Curia almost heretical; the Jesuits who were its exponents in almost every social strata, aristocracy, bourgeoisie and people, had to be reduced to silence since it was thought impossible to obtain from them a sincere repudiation.

The quarrel had a pause at the beginning of 1612, with the end of the prolonged proceedings promoted by the Parlement against the decree authorising the return of the Jesuits to France. The decision of

[1]So Clement perished, an eternal glory to France, as he seems to many.

the Council of State laid on them the obligation to undertake to teach the doctrine of the Faculty of Theology, which the King's Advocate, Servin, summed up in three provisions, and to these the superiors of the Jesuits had to subscribe: (1) that the life of kings was so sacred that no one might ever attempt it, 'in the name of any authority, spiritual or temporal, for any matter or cause whatsoever, even because of their morals or religion.' [1] (2) that the King of the French recognised no superior in temporal things save God alone, through whose grace he had entire dominion over his subjects, and that it was not permitted to the spiritual authorities, under pretext of piety and religion, to invade the King's power, just as it was not permitted to the King, in the name of the royal authority, to invade the spiritual domain. Therefore the Jesuits could no longer teach similar doctrines, 'indeed recognise that the subtleties of the School change only the terms and not the thing, in order to establish an absolute power in the Church, for the destruction of all secular states, and to transform the spiritual power into temporal by attributing to the sacerdotal dignity a temporal dominion like the right and government of a king.' [2] (3) That every subject, whether cleric or layman, had the duty to obey the King, emperor and magistrates, according to the example of Jesus Christ and the teaching of the apostles, and therefore the Jesuits must teach 'que nulle puissance, quelle qu'elle soit, non pas mesmement l'Eglise, assemblée en concile ou autrement, n'a droit de dispenser ni d'absoudre les sujets du roi du serment de fidélité et obéissance qu'ils lui doivent par toute sorte de droit, divin, naturel et humain'.

The Jesuits at first vacillated and replied evasively, but they ended by signing the declaration imposed by the Parlement, as 'immediate assent without reservations' to the doctrines of the Theological Faculty. On February 22, 1612, the Provincial of France, Father Balthazard, and the Fathers Jacquinot, Fronton, Simond and Tacconius, in obedience to the decision of the Court, declared themselves 'in conformity

[1] 'Sous le titre d'autorité quelconque, spirituelle ou temporelle, pour quelque sujet et cause que ce soit, mesme pour cause de leurs mœurs ou religion.'

[2] 'Ainsi reconoistront que les subtilités d'eschole changent seulement les termes et non la chose, afin d'establir en l'Eglise un pouvoir absolu, à la destruction de tous les Etats séculiers, et transformer le pouvoir spirituel en temporel, en attribuant à la dignité sacerdotale une domination temporelle, à la façon d'un droit et gouvernement d'un roi . . .'

with the doctrine of the school of the Sorbonne, even in what concerned the conservation of the sacred person of Kings, maintenance of their royal authority, liberties of the Gallican Church, always and from ancient times kept and observed in this kingdom'.[1] The historians favourable to the Jesuits have sought to attenuate the scope of this submission, saying that the declaration was in vague and general terms. Actually it was precise, with clear reference to the conclusions and decisions of the Council of State. Only there was an important datum in favour of the Jesuits, that it was not possible to speak of one official doctrine of the Theological Faculty of Paris, for even then there were still two currents, which in certain periods balanced each other, and which, either by the influence of the Court on the theologians, or by that of the various theologians on the Court, might alternate and create movements in public opinion. This was growing more and more divided for or against the Jesuits, their theories, their methods, and their power.

In that turbulent year of 1612, and after the formal submission of the Jesuits, the Bishop of Geneva, St. Francis de Sales, on June 2 wrote to the nephew of Paul V, Cardinal Scipione Caffarelli Borghese, a characteristic letter.[2] The saint saw that the polemics on the papal power were doing harm to the Church, agitating the kingdom, creating dissension among the clergy, and increasing the strength of heresy. He feared that when in a few years' time Louis XIII came of age, he would incline towards the anti-papal party (whereas his mother Maria de' Medici tended to lean rather towards Rome); he therefore advised that the Pope should turn towards the King, showing him confidence and kindness, to induce him to silence the controversies, and, by means of prudent prelates should obtain a reconciliation between the Jesuits and the Sorbonne (a matter for perspicacious approach to the Queen). In any case, the saint advised that the Pope's partisans should not reply to the attacks against the papal power, and that an authoritative word should be spoken to invite all to obedience and submission to the Crown.

[1]'Qu'ils sont conformes à la doctrine de l'école de la Sorbonne, même en ce qui concerne la conservation de la personne sacrée des Rois, manutention de leur autorité royale, libertez de l'Eglise gallicane, de tout temps et ancienneté gardées et observées en ce royaume.'
[2]Published in 1935 in *Aevum*, Milan, Jan.–May.

The voice of Francis de Sales fell on deaf ears. He was concerned only with the kingdom of France, and with method, without touching the substance. But the onslaught on the papal prerogatives was general all over Europe, the Protestant countries included. The Roman Curia wanted to hold its own, both by means of its diplomacy and by means of publications and polemics, so that the substance of the rights of the Papacy should not be allowed to drop into oblivion in public opinion. Therefore, while blaming or restraining the Jesuits in their polemical fervour, Rome supported them and sometimes identified her cause with theirs.

The controversy had reached England, where James I was king. He prided himself on his theology and political philosophy and would give addresses and write pamphlets and books. The occasion for a recrudescence of anti-papism was provided by the Gunpowder Plot (1605), which was associated with the missionary and political activity of the Jesuits; the Provincial, Father Garnet, was hanged with the conspirators for having failed to reveal the plot. New measures of persecution against Catholics followed and the obligation of the oath was enforced with the utmost rigour; it denied the Pope any authority that might touch the power of kings. The theme interested England as much as France. Discussion on the oath was opened immediately by Cardinal Bellarmin and by George Blackwell. James I entered the lists in 1607 with his anonymous pamphlet: *Apologia for the Oath of Allegiance.* Bellarmin replied under the pseudonym of *Matthaeus Tortus,* attacking the King root and branch. Then James ordered his agents and ambassadors to publish all over Europe his reply, entitled *Triplici nodo triplex cuneus sive apologia pro juramento fidelitatis adversus duo brevia pp. Pauli quinti et epistolam cardinalis Bellarmini ad G. Blakvellum, etc.* It was translated into French and secretly circulated by the English ambassador in Paris. Henry IV wanted a reply to be written. This was entrusted to Father Nicolas Caffeteau, and Rome was not pleased, for it was feared that the Dominican would not wholly uphold the theory of the Curia. Bérulle joined in also, from the dogmatic standpoint, and other replies were made by Jesuits and by an ex-Calvinist, Hilarius, who was then esteemed as a fervent Catholic neophyte. The anti-English argument formed the theme for the

Lenten preachers in France, and the celebrated Père Coton was one of the most valid and successful controversialists.

The same year saw the publication of William Barclay's *De potestate papae aut et quatenus in reges et principes seculares jus et imperium habeat*, (London, 1609). It had a vast success in France and elsewhere, and many in the Sorbonne began to comment on it. Cardinal Bellarmin confuted it with his *Tractatus de potestati Summi Pontificis*, published in Rome in 1610. The Republic of Venice, which had prohibited the book of James I and then had hastened to send its ambassador Contarini to give satisfaction to the English sovereign, practically prohibited Bellarmin's book also. The Parlement of Paris by a special decision forbade anyone to 'print it, sell it or read it, under pain of proceedings for *lèse majesté*'. Suarez wrote, in 1613, a *Defensio Catholicae Fidei contra anglicanae sectae errores*, which James I ordered to be publicly burned. He protested to Philip III of Spain against harbouring in his dominions such a declared enemy of kings.

The controversy continued with varying degrees of heat throughout Europe, even when a certain calm had been re-established through the agreement between Rome and Venice, a less rigorous enforcement in England of the laws against the recusants, and the attitude of the French clergy in the States-General of 1614, even though they there defended the Council of Trent. Undoubtedly in France there were unfortunate incidents between Gallicans and Jesuits, but what brought renewed agitation, with still profounder consequences, was above all the anonymous writings or 'libels', among them the *Mysteria politica* and the *Admonitio ad Regem Christianissimum*, attributed, rightly enough, to two Jesuits. Richelieu, who was then at the helm of French policy, was clearly and sharply criticised, from the point of view of Catholic interests, sacrificed to aims of domestic and foreign policy. But Richelieu did not remain passive. The Parlement condemned the libels and forbade their circulation *under pain of death*. The assembly of the Bishops of France, in censuring the libels, through their official spokesman made such professions of regalism that they could hardly have gone further. Among other things, we read that it is matter of universal consent among peoples and nations, foretold by prophets and confirmed by apostles and martyrs, 'that kings are ordained of

God; and not only this, but they themselves are Gods . . . Yet it follows that those who are called Gods are Gods not by essence, but by participation; not by nature, but by grace; not for ever, but for a certain time, as being the true lieutenants of God Almighty who, by imitation of His Divine Majesty, represent His image here below'[1].

The bishops, on perceiving that their spokesman had overstepped all measure, drew back and modified this exaggerated attitude. There was a sequel, for Sorbonne, Parlement, Council of State intervened, and Richelieu pursued a policy of balance which it would be wearisome to follow, till a new and graver incident occurred, the '*affaire* Santarelli'.

Santarelli was an Italian Jesuit, who had written and in 1625 published in Rome a *Tractatus de haeresi, schismate apostasia, sollicitatione in sacramento paenitentiae et de potestate romani pontificis in his delictis puniendis*. Santarelli's thesis favoured the widest possible papal powers, with the customary declaration that the Pope could deprive heretical and schismatic kings of their kingdoms and release their subjects from the oath of allegiance. The whole book was in sheer opposition to Gallican theories. The Sorbonne therefore found an easy pretext for intensifying the struggle against the Jesuits, who, for their part, strove in vain to hide the copies of Santarelli's book in order not to pour fresh oil on the flames. The book was condemned and was burned in the house of the Jesuits itself, in the presence of all the Fathers. The superiors were obliged to subscribe to another declaration, graver and more precise than that of 1613, in which they declared that they repudiated and detested the evil doctrine contained in Santarelli's book with the rather comical addition that 'we are ready to shed our blood and risk our lives on every occasion in confirmation of this truth'[2], and so on. Not only the superiors but other fathers were forced to sign, and they did so reluctantly in order to avoid worse.

The affair had yet a graver sequel. The Theological Faculty of Paris

---

[1]'Que les rois sont ordonnées de Dieu; et non cela seulement, mais qu'eux-memes sont Dieux . . . Pourtant il s'ensuit que ceux qui sont appelés Dieux le soient non par essence, mais par participation; non par nature, mais par grace; non pour toujours, mais pour certain temps, comme étant les vrais lieutenants de Dieu tout puissant et qui, par l'imitation de sa Divine Majesté, représentent ici bas son image.'

[2]'Nous sommes prets d'épandre notre sang et exposer notre vie en toutes occasions pour la confirmation de cette vérité.'

assembled on April 4, 1626, and in censuring Santarelli's work proclaimed that the doctrine therein contained (which was the current doctrine on papal power in the Roman Curia) was condemned 'as new, false, erroneous and contrary to the word of God, rendering the dignity of the Supreme Pontiff hateful and opening the way to schism; derogatory to the sovereign authority of kings, which depends on God alone ...'[1] The University of Paris, approving and praising the act of the Theological Faculty, made it binding upon all in a rigorous form, under pain of loss of titles, degrees and faculties, and the brand of infamy for all transgressors. The Parlement wished to register the University's decision in order to give it force of law, but the King (seeing the peril of a bitter conflict with Rome) wrote that the matter should go no further, in view of the fact that the Jesuits had repudiated Santarelli's theories. The Santarelli affair had echoes throughout the realm and the various universities more or less followed the example of Paris.

The attitude of Rome, up till the decision of the Faculty of Theology, had been one of calm and prudence, but seeing that matters were going from bad to worse Rome reacted as best she could, both diplomatically, and by means of faithful friends and servitors—the best known of these being Duval and the Oratorian Bérulle, later Cardinal —and also through Père Joseph, the Capucin who was Richelieu's intimate adviser and collaborator. From the plane of theological controversy and theory, the matter passed to the political plane, with closet-intrigues and compromises. Battle raged as though either the monarchy of France or the Holy See were in peril. Richelieu, who wanted to find a compromise, was placed by the Nunzio, Spada, in the alternative of either giving satisfaction to Rome or an open breach, and this within the year of 1626. At that moment a rupture with the Papacy might have proved dangerous to Richelieu's far-seeing policy, and, after much hesitation and conflicts with Sorbonne and Parlement, he so managed that Louis XIII himself ordered a reconsideration of the censure on Santarelli's book; in the sense that while its antimonarchic and anti-Gallican theories might be condemned, no decision

[1]'Comme étant nouvelle, fausse, erronée et contraire à la parole de Dieu; qui rend la dignité du souverain Pontife odieuse et ouvre le chemin au schisme; qui déroge a l'autorité souveraine des rois, qui ne dépend que de Dieux seul ...' etc.

could be taken on points of faith, this being matter solely for Council, pope and bishops, and not for the University and Parlement. And it was no easy task to persuade the University and Parlement to accept the King's order, which was contested for many months with the ferocious pertinacity peculiar to scholars and men of letters.

The complete change in the orientation of political thought in France was largely due to Cardinal Richelieu's policy of strengthening the Monarchy. He imposed its dominance not only over the struggles between Parlement and University on the one hand and Jesuits and Rome on the other, but also over an undisciplined, turbulent aristocracy, jealous of the sovereign power, and the governors and local administrations, which claimed excessive autonomy at the expense of the royal authority—apart from his activity abroad, by diplomacy and wars, to enhance the prestige of France.

A similar trend is to be noticed in all the other European States, whether Catholic or Protestant. Everywhere there was an effort to subdue the aristocracy, which through the factions and wars of religion had assumed too strong a position in the face of the royal power, and the clergy, whether Protestant or Catholic, who, for different reasons, exercised too strong an influence in the courts and royal councils. The Jesuits formed a category apart. They were either looked upon askance by the upper court clergy, or else protected in every possible manner, according to the turn of events and the interweaving of interests. They had everywhere acquired two solid platforms, one among the people through education, preaching, and their church services (which were often gorgeous, appealing to the imagination), while on the other hand they penetrated into the Catholic courts as confessors to the King or Queen, with a well-defined office that no one any longer challenged. In Protestant countries they penetrated among the people and in the courts under the most varied guises, courageously facing the risks involved and shrewdly utilising their advantages.

They were, therefore, the objects of hatred and admiration, of boundless trust and of preconceived hostility. But their indomitable will, their iron discipline and their incomparable ability carried them to extraordinary potency, so that the struggle was rather against the Jesuits than against the Papacy and Catholicism, which they sought to propagate, defend, and impose throughout the world. In their enterprises they held entirely to the structure of the Catholic Church, as it had taken shape from the Council of Trent onwards—rigid in dogma and in the discipline of the faith, uncompromising in regard to rights, yet deeply involved with the interests and political means of States and Courts and factions, in order to maintain the influence of the Church in the Catholic States and to bring back Catholicism to the Protestant States. To this end we have seen the Church favouring the League in France against Henry of Navarre and helping the rebel nobles with money and arms; favouring Philip II in his war against England, helping in the repression of the revolt of the Low Countries against Spain; moving King Sigismund of Poland to make war on Sweden in order to impose a Catholic restoration, and supporting the Hapsburgs of Vienna and the King of Bavaria in war against the Protestant princes.

But as the popular leagues and the revolts of great nobles give place to the growing ascendancy of the sovereigns—as in France under Richelieu and also under Mazarin during the minority of Louis XIV, in Spain under Philip II and Philip III, in Vienna under Ferdinand III, in Bavaria under William and Maximilian—the doctrine of the divine right of kings, even in religious matters, becomes more and more fundamental. The Jesuits themselves must drop entirely their Suarez, Bellarmin and Mariana, who stressed the democratic aspect of the origin of power; barely (and with repeated repudiations) are they able to maintain the indirect power of the popes, without any longer insisting (and such is the wish of their generals, who send cautious instructions from Rome) on the right of the popes to depose sovereigns and release subjects from their allegiance.

In any case, this theory was valid only in so far as the people had a voice. When all popular right, real or hypothetical, had melted away, when the aristocracy had been reduced to a court ornament, and the clergy had become a court clergy, the papal thesis could no longer be sustained otherwise than as a juridical hypothesis of positive law, that is, as a canonical or Tridentine ruling. This last refuge would henceforth be attacked on jurisdictionalist grounds. The new phase of this drama would still be set in Paris; the actors would be Louis XIV, Bossuet, and Innocent XI.

§ 32.—The Thirty Years' War closes the second period of the Counter-Reformation and opens that which moves from intolerance towards toleration. It would be superfluous to speak of the proximate causes of the Thirty Years' War and of its well-known phases—the Palatine (1618-24), the Danish (1626-28), the Swedish (1630-35) and the French (1635-48). What is interesting to note, for our purposes, are certain characteristic features, which make this war, in which nearly all Europe was engaged at once the last war of religion and the first hegemonic war of modern States.

As war of religion, its remote origin lay in the Treaty of Passau, which settled the position of Protestants in the Germanic Empire. But, whereas the Catholic princes had taken up strong and very intransigent positions in regard to the reformers, the latter, scattering their energies in dogmatic and biblical quarrels, had suffered no little injury. The motive was provided by the election of a King of Bohemia. Protestant princes and Catholic princes formed leagues; war broke out over what seemed a personal question—the choice of Frederick Elector Palatine or the Archduke Ferdinand—but at bottom it gave an opportunity for the Protestant princes to seek to get their own back against the Catholics of the Empire, and for the Empire to impose on the Protestants the rigid rules of the Counter-Reformation.

Little by little, all join in—Denmark and Sweden, England, Spain, France. Fighting goes on in Germany, in Italy, in the Low Countries, in Spain. The war of religion changes into a war for hegemony between France and Spain; the Catholic France of Richelieu allies herself with Gustavus Adolphus of Sweden and the Protestants of Germany, while Spain supports the Hapsburgs. This can truly be called the first hegemonic war of modern States, for though the wars between Charles V and Francis I, or between Elizabeth of England and Philip II, had been hegemonic wars, the conception of kingdoms as the patrimony of the reigning Houses, which was still alive in the XVI century, had now given place to that of States of a public character; at the same time the conception of States bound in an international solidarity, were it that of Church and Empire or that of Catholicism and Protestantism, had given place to the conception of States as completely autonomous and national. The religious phase of the Thirty Years'

War was swallowed up in the political and juridical phase. It is from now that the modern order of Europe begins.

These aspects of the historical evolution of the first half of the XVII century are thrown into light by the theory of 'reason of State', by the formation of international law, and by the growth of theories of religious to leration.

The idea of 'reason of State', in its essential immoralism, is as old as politics. It is nearly two thousand years since Caiaphas's 'It is expedient that one man die for the people', and before Caiaphas the method was all too well known among all governments of all peoples. This notwithstanding, the systematic and theoretical presentation of 'reason of State', that is, of the superiority of politics to ethics, comes from Machiavelli. But in Machiavelli's time neither the term 'reason of State,' had been invented, nor was its anti-Christian and anti-moral content accepted as avowed political praxis, although Machiavelli's books had crossed the Italian frontiers and become known throughout Europe. Indeed an anti-Machiavellian wave followed immediately, to the point that the political ills of various countries were readily laid to the charge of the Florentine Secretary. The publicists of the Reformation and Counter-Reformation wished to be moralistic and affected an anti-Machiavellism that was only skin-deep. Machiavelli in reality was triumphing in all countries in the name of the religious passions, the political interests of thrones and of the people, but the noblest ends were put forward to justify the means that for a century drenched all Europe in blood.

Little by little the idea of the State had come into being, as something different from the realm or principality bound to a reigning house. The State meant a determined territory, no longer as the patrimony of a crown, but as an entity in public law, an entity as distinct from the sovereign as from the classes represented in the states-general and from the Parlements. The idea of public law was so far wanting; the idea of a contract between people and king, the idea of privilege for classes and corporations, the idea of spiritual and temporal power still prevailed. But the idea of an entity that would be in itself the source of power, right and force, summing up in itself all other rights, not through a private relation between the diverse individuals hierarchically organised, but through a value inherent in the collective entity, had not yet emerged. It was being shaped by experience.

The rebirth of Roman Law, the conception of a law higher than contracts and derived from the nature of society, independent of any religious conception, laid the foundations of the conception of the modern State. And although Roman Law in the XVII century was not recognised as the fount of law for the greater part of Europe, which had still a complex legal system, canonical and feudal, yet it was penetrating into the systematic constructions of the philosophers and publicists. The idea of the modern State presented itself as already mature in the theory of *sovereignty*, which, fully worked out, made its appearance with Jean Bodin's *Six Livres de la République* (1577). For Jean Bodin sovereignty is 'the absolute and perpetual power of a republic'. Here republic means State, a very different idea from that of realm or king.

The 'subjective' sovereignty of the King was being transmuted into the 'objective' sovereignty of the State. The King was not above the law, free of the law; it was the State that was the fount of the powers of the sovereign. Bodin and the other publicists of the time still held to the conception of the popular origin of power, but without practical conviction, only as a means of rationally justifying the formation of society. What concerned them, however society might have been formed, was the establishment of an objective sovereignty, standing by itself: that is, the creation of the State-entity, or the State in public law.

The theory of the sovereign State was confused with two elements, which then could only with difficulty be distinguished. The first was the religious power in temporal matters, which in the reformed countries had become one with the secular power and in the Catholic countries presented itself dualistically, giving rise to the great controversy on the papal power (direct or indirect) over sovereigns. The second was the Divine Right of Kings, which excluded the collective factor, the people. The first element transported an extraneous power into the State, and the second transformed the objective power of the State into the subjective power of the sovereign, and made the King's conscience alone responsible before God.

To-day, with the experience of history behind us, we can see how the conception of the modern State expunged from itself both religious power, as extraneous (whether this power resided in the King or in the Pope) and the divine power of the King, as a power of extra-statal origin. But in the phase that we are studying we catch a glimpse of the State only through the idea of sovereignty. Its disengagement from the two elements extraneous to it will slowly come about with the triumph of jusnaturalism, yet a practical disengagement, in the ethical sphere, was beginning to take effect through the theory of 'reason of State'. This mysterious phrase, then, emerges when the idea of the State is identified with objective sovereignty and a public entity; its existence, its enlargement, its utility, its advantage are suffi-cient reason for the autonomy of politics. We do not mean by this that in the governments of the time politics were always and wholly divorced from any religious or moral concern, and that all were cynical and unscrupulous like Machiavelli's Prince. Indeed kings and princes had their ecclesiastical counsellors and even (the Catholic kings) their Jesuit confessors. And yet the conception of 'reason of State' was coming to prevail as a finality containing in itself both the religious exigencies of the population and an inner morality. Richelieu's *Maxi-mes d'Etat* tend towards a separation of morality from politics. 'In State affairs it is not as in others; in the one case we must begin by elucidating where right lies; in the other by execution and possession'.[1] It is true that in Richelieu's writings there are pious affirmations and moral suggestions, but his hints at an autonomy of politics have in him another sonority through his action.

Gabriel Naudé (Mazarin's librarian,) in his *Considérations politiques sur les coups d'état*, speaks of two prudences, the one ordinary and easy, the other difficult and extraordinary, which was that which was then reigning. Without secrecy, St Bartholomew's Eve would have failed in its purpose, as would the murder of the Guises. According to Naudé, from time to time princes are compelled to abandon right in view of the common good, known as 'reason of State'. Naudé expresses the mind of Cardinal Mazarin. Joest Lips (Justus Lipsius) wanted

[1]'En affaires d'Etat, il n'est pas comme des autres: aux unes il faut commencer par l'éclaircissement du droit: aux autres par l'exécution et possession.' (LXXX.)

sovereigns to be moral, but he admitted two moralities—that of private persons, which was more rigorous, and that of the sovereign who must have wider and freer scope because of the great, heavy and dangerous charge that he bears. 'He must sometimes evade and twist, mix prudence with justice, and, as they say, sew to the lion's skin if it is not enough a fox's skin . . .'[1] Yet the same Joest Lips sets three conditions before he will consent to this 'wider scope'—public utility, legitimate defence and a spirit of measure.

The Piedmontese Botero, a pupil of the Jesuits and for a time a Jesuit alumnus, was for many the theorist of the 'reason of State' of the Counter-Reformation, that is, of the use of political means, even of violence and dissimulation, (something more than the 'wider scope' indicated by Joest Lips) for the supremacy of the Catholic States and to crush the Reformation. The spirit in which the Houses of Austria, Bavaria, and Spain fought in the Thirty Years' War, showed this assimilation of the political cause with the religious, and in this they were encouraged by all Catholic forces, which counted on a complete victory of the Empire over the Protestant princes. Botero played no important part and his work does not rise to heights of speculation. He won fame through the title of his book, *Della Ragion di Stato*, published in 1589, which then seemed to suit the purpose of the Counter-Reformation since he set religion as the foundation of kingdoms. Thus Botero passed for the man who rendered Machiavelli's theories moral and placed them at the service of the Church and of the Catholic sovereigns.

Fra' Paolo Sarpi admitted 'reason of State' in the anti-curial and anti-ecclesiastical sense. Involved in the struggle against Rome and against the Jesuits, which was vigorously carried on by the Venetian Republic, he maintained the jurisdictionalist theses of secular intervention in ecclesiastical affairs, and in this he anticipated the spirit and ideas of the Febronianism of the XVIII century. But from the point of view of reinforcing the power of the Republic, he did not disdain that moral 'breadth' that was expressed in theory as 'reason of State.'

This theory in substance was the symbol of the emancipation of

---

[1] 'Il lui faut quelquefois esquiver et gaucher, mêler la prudence avec la justice, etc., comme l'on dit, coudre à la peau du lion, si elle ne suffit, la peau du renard' . . .

the political power from objective morals, represented for Catholics by the Papacy as religious authority, and for Protestants by the Bible as the living voice of God. For the sovereign there remained the bond of subjective morality, in his personal relationship with God, whose authority he reflected (with now no mediation either of Church or people). But the judge of this morality of conscience was the sovereign himself. If he was a Catholic he sought the support of his official confessor, and if a Protestant, of the court chaplain. This support was not always to the point, and often the harshest reprisals against adversaries in religion (Catholics or Protestants) were attributed to these court ecclesiastics, who were assuming a preponderant role—almost as great as that of the King's mistresses, who in those days had a public post and court honours.

Through this fact the theory of 'reason of State' (when it was not openly anti-ecclesiastical or libertine) assumed a moralistic character. Educational books for young and adolescent princes abound, and others teaching the art of government, all books professing the most unctuous morality, and thence arriving little by little at the conception of 'reason of State.' The theory that the end justifies the means is not openly proclaimed as in Machiavelli; indeed anti-Machiavellian tirades are not wanting, but at the same time the idea that the good of subjects, the stability of the kingdom, the glory of the prince, the peace of the Church must be the goals of the sovereign's activity, gives rise to that relaxation of ethical limits that would end by a contempt for right, a violation of human personality, and the promotion of useless and long-drawn-out wars.

As a reaction to this divinisation of the sovereign, there arose the conception of international law, based on natural law, The most interesting manifestations of this new thought are two great books on war, that of the Dominican Francesco da Vitoria, *De Indis et de Jure Belli*, which appeared in 1557 as a section of his *Relationes theologicae* (in a very defective edition, which was later corrected), and that of Hughes de Groot (Hugo Grotius), *De Jure Belli et Pacis*, published in 1625. With these the names of Alberico Gentili, Suarez and Althusius must not be forgotten. We have already mentioned the conception of an international law, above States, regulating the relations between sovereign States no longer bound together either by the religious-Catholic unity of Christendom, nor by the authority of the Holy Roman Empire. This international law could therefore be neither Canon Law nor the imperial-feudal tradition. The Law of Nature was making its reappearance in the juridical conception of the time, no longer as the ethical premise of the positive laws, canonical or traditional and the actualisation of eternal law, but as a rational imperative inherent in human nature. International law was the law of nature itself as applied to relations between peoples. Suarez had seen the danger of a similar theory, when he had maintained that international law was founded on the law of nature (*jus naturae*) but was not to be identified with the law of nature. He thus provided a primary motive of distinction between natural law considered as moral law, and its actuations in positive law, which should find their basis and their *raison d'être* in the moral law, though being themselves only its imperfect realisations, with an historical character.

But at the time this was not the prevailing problem, which lay rather in the quest for a firm platform in international law that would establish in objective form the rules of relations between States, when no tribunal could now be invoked that had authority over kings and princes. The sovereignty attributed to the entity known as the State led to an objective conception of its international limits, limits that could not fail to be fixed by a fundamental natural law that was just and recognised as such. The *jus gentium* or Law of Nations of the ancients, preserved and amplified by canon law, became autonomous international law.

The 'reason of State' invoked by each separate sovereign in the fulness of his powers—since he no longer bowed before the law of the popes, and indeed contested it in the name of sovereignty, nor any longer accepted the very pliable limits of subjective morality, which conflicted with power-morality—found a first barrier in international law. The wars of glory and prestige and the wars of religion had to come to an end as contrary to the criterion of international justice; just wars could not be other than those with a foundation in natural law juridically expressed.

The Treaty of Westphalia marks the end of the Counter-Reformation. The endeavours of a century, on the part of Rome and the Catholic princes, to bring back the Protestant States to obedience to Rome and to reconstitute Christendom, were doomed to failure. The Counter-Reformation succeeded in restoring to the Catholic Church a moral and disciplinary unity, a force of expansion, a dogmatic clarification, that were wanting in the Renaissance, but the politico-ecclesiastical conception of the monarchic Papacy found the Catholic princes and even the clergy mistrustful and hostile. The struggle between Protestants and Catholics for supremacy and to protect the rights of their minorities reconsolidated the principle of the Peace of Augsburg, which was confirmed at Westphalia, that of the State Religion.

In the meantime the elements of the new period were ripening in this century of strife. The absolute sovereignty of the States led to the pseudo-religious theory of the 'Divine Right of Kings' and to the pseudo-morals of 'reason of State.' The separation of the States among themselves and their disengagement from the authority of the Papacy led to the jusnaturalist conception which in relations between peoples created a secular international law, and in relations between the religious confessions would lead to a theory of toleration.

# Date  Due

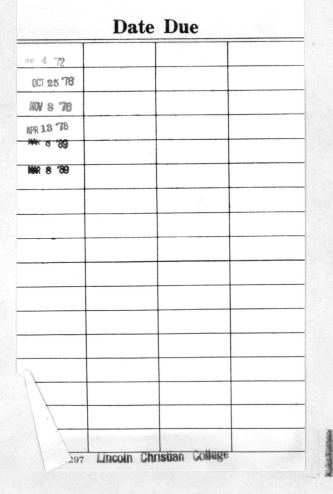

| JAN 4 '72 | | | |
|---|---|---|---|
| OCT 25 '76 | | | |
| NOV 8 '76 | | | |
| APR 13 '78 | | | |
| MAR 8 '89 | | | |
| MAR 8 '89 | | | |
| | | | |
| | | | |
| | | | |
| | | | |
| | | | |
| | | | |
| | | | |
| | | | |
| | | | |
| | | | |
| | | | |